A Curious Life:
The Biography of Princess Peggy Abkhazi

Merry xmas 2002
Ronni
love
Pamand Chris

A Curious Life

The Biography
of Princess Peggy Abkhazi

KATHERINE GORDON

Katherine Gordon

sononis
PRESS
WINLAW, BRITISH COLUMBIA

To my parents, Juliette and Michael Palmer

Copyright © 2002 by Katherine Gordon

National Library of Canada Cataloguing in Publication Data

Gordon, Katherine, 1963-
    A curious life.

      Includes bibliographical references
      ISBN 1-55039-125-9

      1. Abkhazi, Peggy, 1902. 2. International Settlement (Shanghai, China)—Biography. 3. Victoria (B.C.)—Biography. I. Title.
FC3846.26.A24G67 2002   971.1'2804'092   C2001-911745-0
F1089.5.6G67 2002

Sono Nis Press most gratefully acknowledges the support for our publishing program provided by the Government of Canada through the Book Publishing Industry Development Program (BPIDP), The Canada Council for the Arts, and the British Columbia Arts Council.

The quotation on page 123, from Stella Dong, *Shanghai: The Rise and Fall of a Decadent City* (New York: HarperCollins, 2000), is reproduced with the permission of HarperCollins Publishers Inc.

Edited by John Eerkes-Medrano
Cover garden photos © Kmit
Cover and book design by Jim Brennan

Published by
SONO NIS PRESS
PO Box 160
Winlaw, BC V0G 2J0
1-800-370-5228
sononis@islandnet.com
www.islandnet.com/sononis/

Printed in Canada by Houghton Boston.

The Canada Council | Le Conseil des Arts
for the Arts | du Canada

Contents

There are some odd facets to life, and one runs into the oddest characters—knowing all the time that one's own character is just as odd.

— PEGGY ABKHAZI, *A Curious Cage*

Acknowledgments

MANY PEOPLE FROM VICTORIA, AND MUCH FURTHER AFIELD, ASSISTED me with the research required for this book, and I would like to thank each one of them by name. Most people went out of their way to be helpful and to share their treasured mementoes and memories — as well as stirring their own personal stories into the rich mix of history that surrounds this story. They also seemed equally to be on a mission to ensure that I was at all times supremely well nourished. In the course of my research I was welcomed into people's homes, lavished with home-made cookies and, depending on the time of day, plenty of coffee, tea, wine, or sherry! It seems that the spirit of gracious hospitality the Abkhazis held dear is shared in abundance by their friends, acquaintances, and Victorians in general. Thus I learned a great deal about Victoria and its suburb of Fairfield, where much of this story takes place, and about the people who lived in Victoria throughout the period during which the Abkhazis lived in the city. As much as the Abkhazis and their garden in Fairfield are now part of Victoria's contemporary folklore, Victoria, conversely, provided the perfect background for the Abkhazis' life together. The city lent its social structure, its gardening community, and many of its personalities to Peggy Abkhazi's story.

I wish to acknowledge in particular and give special thanks to the descendants of the Mackenzie and Langtry families, who provided me with support and resource material: Rod Breen and Susan Hamersley. Special thanks also go to Philippa Proudfoot (née Davys), Peggy's goddaughter, who shared with me her letters from Peggy, spanning more than twenty years, her stories about Peggy and about her father, Stan Davys, and many of the wonderful photographs from Peggy's childhood and youth that grace the pages of this book.

I am very grateful to Christopher and Pamela Ball and to Maria Serafina Camara, Peggy's closest companions in her later years. They gave me much of their valuable and limited spare time to help me with my inquiries. It was painful and sad at times for them to talk about the woman for whom each of them had had a deep affection; but they all talked freely about her, and the impact, both enormously positive and very difficult, that she had on their respective lives. I appreciate their candour, and their trust, a great deal.

Professor Toby Jackman, who edited Peggy's book, *A Curious Cage*, was also very supportive and helpful. Professor Jackman and his uncle were frequent guests and companions of the Abkhazis for many years.

Then there are Mrs. Joan Alston-Stewart, Malcolm Anderson, Cliff Bate, Lynn Beak, Jeff Bell, Mrs. Black, Mr. Ernest Blaney, Jim Bramley, Gretchen Brewin, Michelle Brus, Barry Campbell, Capital Health Region, Christine Cardinal, Mrs. Olga Chadwick, Brad Chatwin, Darlene Choquette, Mr. Harold Craven, Judge Jacob de Villiers, Ralph de Vries, Caroline Duncan, Mr. and Mrs. J. and E. Fiddess, Joan Fraser, Kerry Frazer, Mrs. Anita Galitzine, Ken Gibson, the Hallmark Society, Mike Hamilton of the Union Club, Margaret Hantiuk, Suzanne Hare, Norm Hardy of Bluebird Cabs, Alan and Sheila Hodgson, Fiona Hyslop, Mrs. E. Javorsky, Mr. Graeme Lee, Miss Enid Lemon, Mark Johnson, Reverend G.A.C. Jones, Gordon Mackay, Mrs. M.F. Marshall, Drs. John and Jean McCaw, Joan MacCormick, Bill McElmoyle, Judge Lloyd and Betty McKenzie, Diane McLaren, John McLoughlin, Sue Miller, Chris Milne, Sylvia Modelski, Rear-Admiral Robert Murdoch, Valerie Murray, Roger and Barbara Napier, Mr. George Nation, Carey Pallister, Mr. Patt, Freeman Patterson, Jane Perry, Bob Phillips, Ian Phillips, Alison Quentin-Baxter, Ken Roueche, Dr. R.H. Roy, Al Smith, Evelyn Smith, Alison Spriggs, Philip Steenkamp, Jill Stewart Bowen, William Thackray, Mr. Jack Todd, Mrs. Rosita Tovell, Bill Turner, Jane Turner, Rebecca Wagner, Ian Waterlow, Terry Williams; the staff at the provincial Land Titles Office and in the planning department of the City of Victoria; and of course, all the volunteers who continue to work to preserve the Abkhazi Garden.

Last but most certainly not least, my thanks to Diane Morriss of Sono Nis Press for deciding that this book should be written; to John Eerkes-Medrano for his superb editorship; to Jim Brennan for his beautiful book design; and to my husband, Quinton, for his patience, love, and unflagging support. Thanks for washing all those dishes.

Quotations

Peggy Abkhazi had a habit of writing favourite quotations inside the covers or back pages of her appointment diaries. Some of them were clearly meant to be inspirational. More often, they seem to form neat summaries of her life or of events that had an impact on her life. She was particularly fond of poetry, favouring T.S. Eliot, Herbert Trench, W.H. Auden, John Donne, and Rupert Brooke, among the eclectic list that she appeared to enjoy. Peggy was also a prolific letter writer. In her correspondence with friends she enjoyed discussing and analyzing at length her favourite authors and poets, as well as recent literary reviews. She would frequently copy out by hand in their entirety reviews that she had enjoyed, to send with her letters. She was also given to starting or ending letters by using quotations that she felt were apt to the discussion. These letters disclose a great deal about their author.

In a similar spirit, many of the quotations found in this book at the beginning of chapters are from her letters to various friends, in particular to her goddaughter Philippa Proudfoot (née Davys) during the period 1966 to 1988. For the most part, the remainder of the quotations are from Peggy's draft memoir that she began to write in 1980 in the form of a lengthy, somewhat disjointed letter to Maureen and Elizabeth Mackenzie. She entitled it *A Dragon Aunt Remembers*. A typed copy of the manuscript is publicly available at the University of Victoria Archives. The original handwritten copy is held by Maria Serafina Camara, of Victoria; the original typed copy is in the possession of Rod Breen, of Parksville, British Columbia.

Introduction:

the princess
and the pea

"The life of every human being is governed by the decisions they make, and there is no escaping the results of one's decisions."

—Peggy Abkhazi, letter to Philippa, January 8, 1970

Princess Peggy Abkhazi, as she became in the second half of her long life, went through several major transformations and upheavals during her ninety-one years, far more than most people ever experience. Most dramatically, having been adopted at the age of four by a retired British "taipan" and his young wife who had both spent all of their adult lives in Shanghai, China, Peggy went from facing a dismal future as a penniless orphan in the working-class industrial town of Lancaster, England, to becoming a wealthy socialite; with, ultimately, an acquired royal title and an elegant property and home in Victoria, British Columbia, the "garden city" of Canada. In the intervening years she lived through two worldwide conflicts, led a disappointingly constrained youth under the iron grip of a possessive and controlling adoptive mother who also held the purse strings, and suffered a disastrous first marriage. On the other hand, she travelled widely, living and studying music in Paris during a time of intense artistic change and activity in the 1920s and residing in Shanghai when it was considered one of the

OPPOSITE: *Princess Peggy Abkhazi at the Lieutenant-Governor's Ball, early 1960s.* FIONA HYSLOP

10

most exciting multicultural cities in the world. And by the time she emigrated to Canada in her forties, in direct contrast to her aimless youth, Peggy was very determined about what she wanted out of life – and no longer hesitated to seize the opportunities that came her way. In particular, she set about creating "The Principality of Abkhazia" – her little realm – as well as her role of being a princess in it. The second part of this book, starting after the end of the Second World War, could quite aptly be entitled "Carpe Diem."

As a result of the global political turmoil that occurred over the decades of her life, many of the places that Peggy lived in and visited now have different names. In most cases, I have simply used the place name applicable at the time that she was there. Peggy also changed her name, or had it changed for her, a number of times. Born Mabel Margery Jane Carter, she initially was called Margery (perhaps to avoid confusion with her mother, who was also called Mabel); became Peggy Pemberton when she was adopted; added "Carter" back to her name to become Peggy Pemberton-Carter in her late thirties; and finally became Princess Nicolas (Peggy) Abkhazi at the age of forty-three. To further complicate matters, despite the spelling of her name as "Margery" on her birth certificate, throughout her life Peggy always spelled it as "Marjorie" – a personal preference, perhaps – or, as sometimes happens, a spelling mistake on the birth certificate. We shall never know. Peggy also reversed the order of her names, for some reason, to Marjorie Mabel. In deference to her obvious preferences, and in a bid to keep things as simple as possible, I refer to her as Marjorie in the first few chapters, until her adoptive name change to Peggy. Occasionally, however, I have also referred to the adult woman in those chapters. In those instances, of course, I have used the name Peggy.

Different spellings also abound for the names of Peggy's second husband, Nicolas Abkhazi, and his family members. Their names were originally bestowed upon them in the Georgian alphabet, which would be illegible to most English readers. When they moved to France, Nicolas and his mother adopted the French spelling of their names, which differs slightly from the English spelling. The versions of their names used in this book are those appearing on official documents, such as passports and marriage certificates, in both France and Canada. Nicolas signed letters as "Nicolas" or "Nico." "Nico" was Peggy's pet name for her beloved husband, but she preferred others not to use it. In deference to that preference, I refer to him as Nicolas, except where quoting Peggy.

One more name is important. Peggy always adored dogs, but it was perhaps her very last dog that she loved the most, a little sheltie that she affectionately called "Come-Come." She initially recorded his name as Seamus in her diaries and letters. However, his registered pedigree name was spelt "Shamus," as Peggy herself noted. Christopher and Pamela Ball, who adopted Shamus once Peggy was no longer able to care for him and looked after the dog for more than ten of his thirteen years of life, preferred that spelling because it was more unusual, and that is the spelling used in this book.

Although I was fortunate to have access to a substantial number of documentary records in the writing of this book, there were naturally some gaps in the material. Anecdotal information has been very revealing, but must of course be relied on with some caution. Such information from the early years was sparse, because many of Peggy's contemporaries are no longer around to tell of those days. Anecdotal information also tends to suffer, not only as a result of age, but with the passage of time, distance, lack of attention, or intimacy.

Since Peggy's death in 1994 a fair amount of mythology has also emerged, especially in the media, around the initial relationship between Peggy and Nicolas Abkhazi, from the time that they first met in Paris in 1922. Much of the mythology arose from the misleading suggestion of a grand mutual passion that is claimed to have existed between Peggy and Nicolas from the moment of that first meeting, and of two star-crossed lovers separated only by the cruel forces of war. Although their individual stories do involve adventure, romance, and heroism – Nicolas Abkhazi was a Georgian prince who escaped the Bolshevik revolution in Russia, and his story alone could also fill a book – the reality of their eventual love story is far more human than the mythology implies, and far more interesting as a result. Young as they were, both Nicolas and Peggy were already survivors when they met. There is no doubt that the two had many common interests and formed a strong friendship on meeting. It is even quite possible that either one or both of them entertained the thought of romance in those heady days in Paris, or later, as they corresponded through the years. But in the end, the facts speak for themselves: Peggy and Nicolas went their separate ways for more than twenty years, even though they maintained a connection strong enough that, when the time was right, the decision was finally made to be together. Their choice to be together after the end of the Second World War was, as Peggy put it herself, a natural one, and the beginning of a marriage based on love, attraction, friendship, familiarity, comfort, and as time went on, deeper and deeper devotion. But it was most definitely a choice they had made — just as the fact that they were not together before then was also their choice.

It is natural that people absorb the mythology as time goes on, come to believe it, and repeat it as fact. However, mythology, like oil spilled into water, tends to rise to the surface when investigated and to stay there. Sufficient information exists to enable reasonable conclusions to be drawn, and in many cases it is information provided by Peggy herself. Peggy, however, also contributed directly to some of the inconsistencies about real events. Certain of her own stories were subtly altered as she got older and as her recollections evolved, or started to fade: in her letters, for example; in her book, *A Curious Cage*; and also in *A Dragon Aunt Remembers*. The latter is the primary source on which the early chapters of this book are based. But all three types of document, as well as her diaries and the interviews that she gave from time to time, sometimes contradict each other. Not only did Peggy recount different events differently to various people, she also enhanced some aspects of her life, as is natural, and conveniently omitted others, or related them in ways that suited her at the time. Some of her friends recalled that she was an excellent storyteller who had the ability to recount a story told to her in such a way that her version was better than the original. She also had a flair for understanding what people expected or wanted to hear, and for making sure that they heard it. In the retelling of her stories over the years, Peggy may also have come to believe her own romanticized version of some events.

The Abkhazi Garden, for which Peggy is now best known — her beautiful if somewhat unintended legacy — became more and more the focus of the latter half of her life. She is famously and frequently quoted for recounting a Chinese proverb: "If you would be happy for a week, take a concubine; If you would be happy for a month, kill your pig; But if you would be happy all your life, plant a garden." But the celebrated garden is really inseparable from the legend of her royal title. After marrying Nicolas Abkhazi, Peggy definitely preferred to be thought of as a princess. As down-to-earth as she was, and as much as she may have downplayed her acquired title to some close friends, she also did nothing to dispel her royal image. More often, she actively promoted it, adding to the mythology. She was, as one friend observed, her own best invention. And after all that she had been through in her life, Peggy was not only pragmatic, but she also had a very clear understanding of human nature. Being a princess bride was more than just a bit of fun or a charming experience – for the new arrival in the tough social enclave of Victoria, Canada, it served her needs and her purposes very well indeed.

But that, in the end, is what makes Peggy's story even more irresistible. She was a very compelling woman, especially in the second half of her life – and still is, well after her death. Late one evening during the writing of this book I was walking past the Abkhazi Garden, where the ashes of Peggy and Nicolas are scattered together. I found myself stopping by the garden gate. It was very quiet, as it usually is in this part of Fairfield at ten o'clock at night. It is a good thing that there was no one around. Without stopping to think about what I was doing, I leaned into the fence, as if I was compelled to, and whispered into the dark, "I promise I'll do a good job, Peggy." Feeling rather absurd, I continued on my way. I was not, however, surprised to have made that commitment to her.

After all, Peggy seems to have had that effect on people.

August 17, 2002

I

From small beginnings

"It does not sound an auspicious beginning."

— PEGGY ABKHAZI, *A Dragon Aunt Remembers*

MARJORIE MABEL JANE CARTER, A RATHER UNDERSIZED INFANT TO HAVE such an imposing name, was born on December 12, 1902, in the International Settlement of Shanghai, China. It was the Year of the Tiger, during the season of the Water Cycle. Chinese astrologists, if they were consulted, might have predicted a volatile and enigmatic future for the child, typical when such an opposing sign and element collide: a lifetime of struggle between the inherent passivity of quiet, steadily flowing Water, willing to take the shape of any vessel into which it is poured, and the magical, mercurial Tiger's equally strong desire to lead and to persuade all others to follow. The mists of the little one's future were far too thick then to provide any glimpse as to which of the two symbols would eventually prevail.

On the surface, little Marjorie's prospects at birth certainly looked promising. Her father, William John Blaylock Carter, was a young British architect of some renown, with a pleasant and apparently well-heeled existence among the large expatriate community living in the International Settlement of Shanghai. Handsome, fair-haired, and blue-eyed, William Carter was an engaging young man. Although he came from a rather dubious background, he had had the good fortune to be sponsored in England by a "rich old gentleman who had taken an interest in him." Carter was very charming, he was good at the traditional English sports — tennis, rowing, riding — and he had ingratiated himself quickly and seamlessly into the right circles. Upon receiving his architectural credentials in the late 1890s and while still a bachelor, he obtained a position with Lester, Johnson & Morriss, an architects' firm in Shanghai, and in 1899 he left England for China to begin his professional career. His attractiveness and charm, and his aptitude for games, stood him in good stead in the fun-loving social circles of the International Settlement. His work thrived, and he was well-regarded in professional circles in those early years. A "modern" designer, one of his popular creations was the Palace Hotel, at the corner of the Bund and Nanking Road. By 1902 money seemed plentiful, a bevy of Chinese servants saw to the Carters' every need, their social life appeared to be active and amusing, and there was little cause for most outsiders to suspect that everything was not as it should be. The birth of their first child should have provided cause for great celebration. However, it did not — and part of the reason why lay in the circumstances of the Carters' marriage one year earlier.

Shortly before leaving for Shanghai, Carter had become engaged to Marjorie's mother, Mabel Blackburn. It is uncertain how they met, for Mabel came from a more traditional middle-class background, the eldest daughter of several offspring of William Blackburn, an entrepreneur and importer of cod from Newfoundland. The Blackburn family — William, his wife, and daughters Mabel, Emily, Agnes, Winifred, and Ida — lived in a large, prosperous-looking house in West Kirby, a small village on the peninsula known as the Wirral, on the mouth of the River Dee in Lancashire. William Blackburn's wife had died while the family was still quite young, and the main burden of child-rearing and house-keeping had fallen to Mabel, as the oldest. Her father later remarried a "handsome, buxom lady" known as "Big Auntie," who

Peggy's biological parents were Mabel Blackburn Carter and William Carter. William is at the back, far left; Mabel at the front, right, with other members of the Carter family. UNIVERSITY OF VICTORIA ARCHIVES

produced the girls' two half-brothers, Gray and Eric, who were both fated to perish in the 1914–18 war.

By the time of her engagement to William Carter, Mabel was nearly thirty years old, a dangerous age for a spinster in those Victorian days. It is unlikely that she was enjoying the domestic arrangements in her father's house, with a new stepmother, no matter how amiable, and two new young brothers, all of whom were usurping her father's affections. Her daughter's later remembrances of Mabel Carter relied mostly on the stories that she had been told about her mother rather than on her own memories, but her recollection was of a slim, very short woman with dark, trim hair, dark eyes, and a fresh complexion — a woman of "great courage and a very strong character." The chance of escaping to a life in the exciting city of Shanghai with the attractive and charming William Carter apparently proved irresistible to this intelligent young woman, and Mabel had agreed to marry him.

William immediately left for Shanghai to start his new job and organize a home for his bride-to-be. The understanding was that when he was ready, Mabel should come out to join him and the two would wed on her arrival. However, for reasons that were not clear to Mabel at the time, this seemed to take longer than had been expected. Peggy, as Marjorie later became known, recalled: "Once in Shanghai, I gather that this personable young man, with his charm and his ability at sports, stepped into a life the like of which he had never dreamed of." For at the turn of the twentieth century, the International Settlement in the city of Shanghai was one of the most exciting places on earth for a young Englishman to be trying to make his fortune.

At the time that Carter moved to the city, its population was already well over two million souls. The expatriate community represented a fraction of that number — somewhere between 35,000 and 100,000 non-Chinese were in Shanghai at any given time between 1880 and 1940. The International Settlement itself consisted of a series of foreign concessions, governed by a conglomerate municipal council representing all of the countries involved. It had been created in the mid-nineteenth century to provide a base for the increasing numbers of traders that were coming to China from Britain, France, Germany, Japan, and other nations, all seeking to make a fortune and retire quickly to their homeland. Many of them did make their fortune — it was possible to become a millionaire in Shanghai very quickly in those heady days — but if they thought they would leave again quickly, they were mistaken. Seduced by the heady excitement of ready money and the exotic magic of China, most stayed far longer than they had ever imagined they would — and many never left at all.

In this conglomerate of small international concessions, each country enjoyed extraterritorial rights in its own settlement, applying its own laws and customs free of any Chinese rule or interference. During the 1860s the Chinese government had granted Britain domain over what looked like a prime piece of land, right at the intersection of Soochow Creek and the Whangpu River. Ships could come right up the river to discharge their goods and take on new cargo, and the residential districts would capture what small sea breeze there was to dispel the enervating summer heat. But the piece of land was in reality simply a swamp, and all of the British buildings had to be built on a series of floating "rafts" that were constructed to accommodate the movement of the tide up the mouth of the Whangpu River. It did not seem to deter the British population one whit. They built extravagant homes and stocked them with the best furnishings and supplies. They hired Chinese servants to manage all of their domestic requirements. They created parks and hotels and exclusive clubs, and began living a heady lifestyle that was a constant round of socializing, riding, partying, and travelling – and would continue to be so for decades.

In this exciting international city, William Carter was earning plenty of money, enjoying his professional success, and living the high life. He was also enjoying a social milieu unlike anything he had ever encountered previously, with plenty of attractive and wealthy young single women, no doubt eager for the attention of the handsome young man. His enthusiasm for having Mabel Blackburn join him seemed to founder, and using one excuse after the other, he found reasons to delay sending for her. Finally, the ongoing Boxer Rebellion provided him with an excellent opportunity to send a cable insisting that it was quite unsafe for any young woman to travel out to Shanghai until such time as the "troubles" might be over, an indefinite period with no prospective end in sight.

Receipt of the cable finally spurred the Blackburn household into action. Suspicious of his future son-in-law's prevarication, and dismayed at the prospect of remaining responsible for his oldest daughter after all, Mabel's father immediately made inquiries of the Foreign Office in London and the British Consulate in Shanghai as to the dangers of travelling to China. The puzzled replies, when they were received, advised William Blackburn that there was no danger at all anywhere near Shanghai. All the fighting was taking place near Peking and Tientsin – three days' travel by steamer from Shanghai. Satisfied that his suspicions seemed to be well-founded, Blackburn promptly made arrangements for his wife to escort Mabel to Shanghai, accompanied by her trousseau, and to stay until she had ensured that her stepdaughter was safely married to Carter. And, ignoring this first disturbing signal of things to come with her fiancé, Mabel Blackburn elected to go ahead with the marriage. It was perhaps to her the lesser of two evils. She was an intelligent and sensitive woman. The prospect of remaining a spinster in her father's house no doubt dismayed her as much as, if not more than, it did her father. She may have also reasoned that once they were reunited, her fiancé's enthusiasm would revive itself and all would be well.

Events were not, unfortunately for Mabel, to unfold in quite this way.

Shortly after she arrived in the International Settlement with her stepmother, William Carter did accept the inevitable, and Mabel and William were duly married. They settled eventually into a large and attractive home on Carter Road, off Bubbling Well Road, and a little over a year later, little Marjorie arrived on the scene. What Mabel Carter could not have known, and discovered far too late to do anything about, was that her husband was an alcoholic and a gambler. His charm and athletic capability masked a weakness of character far beyond his control; and the lifestyle of Shanghai, with its expatriate community hell-bent on spending their wealth, enjoying night-long parties and revelries, came with the dangerous expectation that to succeed one must participate to the fullest extent possible. It was an unstable environment, and one in which William Carter's health and sanity were slowly disintegrating into ruin. By the time Mabel became pregnant in early 1902, William was already suffering from regular bouts of *delirium tremens*. More than once, in the throes of the "DT's," it was claimed that he would chase poor Mabel with a carving knife until she could escape to the nearest police station for protection. Begging forgiveness, and promising to give up drinking, William would persuade Mabel to return, at least until the next episode occurred. Mabel had little choice but to return to her wayward husband. Leaving him to retreat to her father's home in England would have been an unacceptable contravention of social expectations, despite William's behaviour toward her, and she would not have been able to survive in Shanghai on her own, with no money.

And so, with no other alternatives available to her, Mabel bore her only child in unresisting silence. To the extent that she could, she drew a net of protection over Marjorie, keeping her away from her unpredictable father. The infant was lavished with care and given every luxury, and had a complete floor of the house devoted to her. The nursery was a white room with high, airy ceilings, and two French doors opened on to a deep veranda. The room had its own fireplace and gas lighting, and a cot with a mosquito net set up near the doors to capture the breeze. An English nanny, a "chow-chow" amah or wet nurse, a wash amah, and a nursery amah all cared for her. The one thing Marjorie did not have was the attention or visible affection of either parent. Mabel, having ensured that the child's every need was seen to, withdrew into herself. She rarely took Marjorie with her anywhere. Many of the Carters' friends were unaware that the couple even had a child.

But as an infant, Marjorie was happy enough, surrounded by her nannies and amahs and kept company by a black cat she adored. The survival instincts that stood her in good stead throughout her later life were developed early, however. An obedient and well-behaved child, she sensed even then that impeccable behaviour and invisibility were the best strategies for not attracting unwanted attention from her parents. The adult Marjorie, known as Peggy, supposed half-humorously that she should have developed some sort of "rejection disorder" as a result of this parental disinterest. Rather than holding a grudge, however, she apparently maintained not only respect but also sympathy for her mother's insupportable circumstances and remarked that "though I never recall a single caress from either of my parents, I certainly never was unhappy. I must have been a very self-contained, detached child." Nevertheless some sting from the absence of tangible maternal love must never really have vanished. Even eighty years later, she described her birth as a "calamity" for her mother; and in relating a tale about a diphtheria epidemic that occurred when she was a toddler, in which many "loved babies" died, Peggy also remarked with some cynicism: "Guess who survived? Quite right. The calamity." However, the benefit of being an unwanted calamity, she went on, was that her survival was probably due to an in-built immunity from having been breast-fed by her Chinese "chow-chow" amah, rather than her own mother.

Mabel's own health started to suffer from a combination of stress and the tropical climate, and by the spring of 1906 she was diagnosed with "tropical sprue," an incurable gastrointestinal disorder. Finally — although terribly — Mabel had the excuse she needed to go home to England. Refusing to die in the place where she had been so unhappy, she told her friends that the milder English climate might offer some temporary relief, packed up Marjorie, and returned home to West Kirby. Still only in her early thirties, Mabel died almost immediately after her return. Peggy later wrote: "She had such a sad, unfulfilled life. Her 77-year-old daughter wonders whether she felt betrayed by life — for in her will she asked that her ashes be scattered to the winds (an unusual request in those Edwardian days and I would judge that the solid Blackburn family was conventional to the last degree). Perhaps all she wanted was oblivion."

Despite the tension in his marriage, the loss of his wife appeared to be the last blow for William Carter, and every aspect of his life seemed to fall apart completely after Mabel's death. He was suffering from a serious case of galloping tuberculosis; his drinking was out of control, his professional work suffered immeasurably, and his penchant for gambling put him in serious financial difficulty. William must have had no idea what to do about his daughter, but he must also have known enough about himself by then to think her better off where she was — and so, while he sent what money he did have back to England for her upkeep, he also made no attempt to communicate with her or to seek her return to China. Marjorie remained at her grandfather's house, cared for by the Blackburn family.

Her mother was gone, and her amah, seen as quite unnecessary by the Blackburns, returned to China soon after Mabel's death. For the first time in her life, the little girl experienced the feeling that the ground had shifted substantially under her feet. She was not treated unkindly by her Blackburn relatives and her Aunt Emily did her best to provide some motherly affection, but overall the family was at a loss as to how to deal with the small burden that had landed on their doorstep. As a consequence, Marjorie suffered greatly from a benign sort of neglect. The change in routine was also bewildering for the young child. Used to being hand-fed by a retinue of Chinese servants in her own room, suddenly she was required to sit at the long dining-room table, presided over by her grandfather at one end and Big Auntie at the other and filled with adults in between; and not to move from her place until she had eaten everything on her plate. Unable to consume the huge adult-sized portions of English food put in front of her, she recalled sitting quietly for what seemed like hours in the empty dining room, in front of a dish of food that she had no chance of finishing. Not given to tantrums or belligerence, the little girl would instead stay in her chair in the dark, oppressive room crying silently, not knowing how to deal with her upheaval and the sudden, enormous gap in her life, which she could not possibly have understood. With no bedroom of her own, the weeping child had to sleep with a different aunt every night — no one wanted to have to share a room with such a nuisance permanently. Only the "nice, fat" cook showed Marjorie any real affection — her favourite sleeping arrangement was in the cook's warm and cozy bed; and with her, the little girl never wept at all.

As long as the money could be expected to come from her father regularly, this arrangement was acceptable to the Blackburn family — but an even better solution presented itself within a few days, when William Carter's sister Polly offered to take the child. Aunt Polly also had a daughter, Daisy, a few years older than Marjorie. It is not clear whether Polly had been widowed or whether her husband had deserted her, but at the time she offered to take Marjorie in, Polly was certainly a single mother with a number of outstanding debts. Unlike her brother, she had not had the good fortune to find a wealthy benefactor to rescue her from her working-class background. The income from William Carter for Marjorie's upkeep was a significant sum, thirty pounds a month, and would help to solve her financial problems. The Blackburns, apparently much relieved, and no doubt thinking it a more suitable arrangement, readily agreed; and a cheap little cottage was rented for Polly and the girls at Bolton-le-Sands, a small seaside resort not far from Lancaster in Lancashire, on the west coast of England. Aunt Polly, three-year-old Marjorie, and seven-year-old Daisy moved there for the remainder of the summer of 1906. Of those few weeks at the beach, the adult Peggy remembered little, except that her aunt almost immediately removed the pretty silver bracelets that she wore – a gift from her Chinese amah – and placed them on her cousin Daisy's wrists instead. She claimed not to have suffered any angst over it – but she also could recall the incident clearly, more than seventy-five years later.

It was to be only a temporary sojourn in the sun at Bolton-le-Sands. In all likelihood, Polly could not afford to stay in the pleasant little cottage, even with William Carter's stipend coming in from China, and with the arrival of autumn the threesome moved from their cottage at the seaside to the industrial city of Lancaster. Peggy found herself in an environment that she had never before experienced. In the early part of the twentieth century, Lancaster was one of the most active trading ports in England and had a very transient population. As early as the seventeenth century, writer Celia Fiennes had described Lancaster town as "old and much decay'd"; by 1906, it was also very visibly a coal-mining town, surrounded by coal pits, slag heaps, mill chimneys, and row upon row of smoke-blackened terrace housing. Aunt Polly rented one of those houses in a dreary, working-class district, the best she could afford, and started letting rooms to lodgers to help with the bills, while she and the children lived in rooms at the back of the house.

Things went from bad to worse for Marjorie. A small, enclosed back yard of dark, damp blacktop provided the only area for the children to play. The little girl lived in terror of the mournful drawn-out cry of the rag and bone man as he drew nearer to the house – everyone knew that he would take away badly behaved children in his sack, to become bones themselves and never to be seen again. There was not enough money to pay for heating, let alone for outings or treats, and Marjorie was always cold, becoming so seriously ill with pneumonia and whooping cough as a result that on one occasion she nearly died. A diet of porridge and cheap food did little to help with her poor health. She was also subjected to treatment that she had never before experienced: physical punishment for any miscreant behaviour. Aunt Polly was a tall, temperamental woman plagued by worry over debt and no doubt resentful of the direction her life had taken, in contrast to her brother's exciting life and career. Peggy later wrote in her memoirs that her angry aunt would take out her frustration on her formerly pampered niece by boxing her ears or locking her in the coal cellar as a punishment. This may have been an accepted form of discipline for the times, but it was still not looked on kindly by many – and the neighbours, at least, were horrified. In any event, the self-contained little Marjorie suffered no obvious long-term effects from these punishments. The coal cellar was a peaceful, warm place to take a nap, and it held no fears for her. The self-sufficiency she was developing, and her ability to handle adversity and rough circumstances with such equanimity, would also prove invaluable in later life.

In the meantime, unbeknownst to his English relatives, William Carter's health had worsened rapidly. Less than a year after Mabel's death, the young architect died in Shanghai, bankrupt and his career in ruins. Toward the end, his daughter's future evidently troubled him more than it had previously: Carter managed to extract a promise from two of his friends, a Dr. Goode and one David Nesbitt, that she would be cared for properly. It gave Peggy comfort in her later years that, at least at the end, her father had demonstrated this affection and concern for his small daughter. She certainly bore no ill will toward him; instead, she retained a strong sense of pity for the attractive and personable man who was too weak to control his own impulses. She was also determined never to demonstrate any such weakness on her own part. If anything, her experience had the opposite effect: she maintained a rigid sense of duty and adherence to proper behaviour throughout her life.

The implications of her father's death did not have an immediate impact on Marjorie or her circumstances. William Carter's friends had arranged for his burial in Bubbling Well cemetery in the British concession in Shanghai. They also raised a collection in order to keep sending funds to England, at least in the short term, while they considered what to do about the orphaned child. Money continued to arrive from China, which everyone assumed was coming from William's estate, and despite some discussions taking place among the Blackburns about making alternative arrangements for Marjorie's care, Aunt Polly declared adamantly that she "could not bear to part with her dead brother's only child." As Peggy could not recall "a single caress or sign of affection, or even a gentle action" toward her on Aunt Polly's part, her cynical conclusion, as an adult, was that the attraction lay in the stipend that her aunt was receiving for her upkeep — and what Aunt Polly imagined would be coming to her by way of Marjorie's inheritance.

As 1907 dawned, the four-year-old's prospects looked bleak. Although Aunt Polly didn't know it yet, no inheritance would be coming from China. Unless the Blackburns were prepared to take her back, there was no reason to believe that Marjorie's life would not simply unfold as that of a working-class girl from the industrial slums of Lancaster, unwanted and unloved, with limited educational opportunities and even more limited future options for marriage or a career. It was, in Peggy's own words, not an auspicious beginning.

2

The coming of
the unicorn

"My adoptive mother's...consuming desire was to make me believe — so that ultimately she could come to believe — that I was her own flesh-and-blood child."

— PEGGY ABKHAZI, *A Dragon Aunt Remembers*

THROUGHOUT PEGGY'S LIFE, VARIOUS GUARDIAN ANGELS, CELESTIAL OR earthly, intervened from time to time to rescue her from undesirable circumstances. This time, it was her father's old friend, Dr. Goode. Taking his promise to William Carter seriously, he did not wash his hands of the affair when he learnt that little Marjorie was being cared for by her Aunt Polly. Dr. Goode had understood the state of William Carter's financial affairs well before William's family realized the truth of his bankruptcy. He knew that Carter had had no family money behind him and that there would be no more money going to England from China for the child's upkeep. Although Dr. Goode was a confirmed bachelor with little interest in children, some notion of the orphan's miserable future, by comparison with what it could have been, must have compelled him to keep pursuing the matter.

Dr. Goode discussed the problem at length with his friend David Nesbitt, the little girl's other notional "guardian." A possible solution presented itself when David Nesbitt's wife, Lucy, suggested to her best friend in Shanghai, Florence Pemberton, the idea of adopting William and Mabel Carter's orphaned daughter. At the same time, while Florence and her husband Thomas agreed to think it over, Aunt Polly and the Blackburn family in England were beginning to understand that Marjorie had inherited from her father nothing but unpaid debts. The notion that someone else might take Marjorie must have been very attractive, and it was much discussed in whispers and behind closed doors. "Like a dog, I became aware of something in the air...an impending change, like a change of weather," wrote the adult Peggy much later. "And I clearly remember hearing for the first time in my life the word 'adoption' being bandied about. I had no idea what it meant. To this new word was added the interesting statement: 'Rich people from China'." Although the little girl could not possibly know it, if the Pembertons' answer was to be "Yes" to the proposal to adopt her, then Marjorie's fortunes were about to reverse again, dramatically. Thomas Pemberton, a Shanghai "taipan," and his young wife, Florence, were very wealthy. They were also reputable, moved in all the right social circles, and had no children of their own. It appeared that they would make ideal adoptive parents for the little girl.

Thomas Pemberton originally came from a Cheshire farming family but seems to have had no desire as a young man to carry on the family business. In 1863, at the age of eighteen, he instead joined the British shipping firm of Shaw, Ripley in Liverpool and shipped out for the four-month journey to Shanghai, yet another young trader on the way to make his fortune. It took some adjustment for the young Englishman to adapt to the heat and customs of Shanghai. In the comfort of his eventual success, Thomas used to enjoy relating the story of his first meeting in China with his new employer. The young man had smartly dressed himself for the meeting in traditional Liverpool attire: top hat, woollen pinstriped suit, and cut-away coat. In the humid heat of a Shanghai August morning, when Thomas had politely removed his top hat, the entire top layer of skin underneath came away with it. But Thomas Pemberton adapted to China with little other difficulty, and his business career in Shanghai was extremely successful. In 1907, when he was sixty-two years old, he was already considering retiring to enjoy the fruits of his success. Almost certainly, he had not planned to adopt a child at that stage of his life, but to please his beloved wife Florence, he would not hesitate if that was what she wanted.

Florence Pemberton, a former contemporary and acquaintance of Mabel Blackburn Carter, was much younger than her husband. Still only in her thirties, she was an intelligent, flamboyant woman with a vivid imagination and a highly emotional temperament. Deliberately vague about her background, Florence intimated to her acquaintances that it was well-to-do, with hints of an English country lifestyle, horses, stables, dogs, and formal social occasions. In reality, she was born in Stratford-upon-Avon in England, one of several daughters of the local tavern keeper, and had attended a village school. In many ways, however, Florence was very similar to Thomas when he had been younger. Yearning for a better and more interesting life, at the age of seventeen she had left her family to join the "fishing fleet" – young Englishwomen in search of better opportunities for marriage overseas, where youth and availability often took priority over class and background. Travelling to Shanghai, Florence had become a governess to the two young children of a wealthy British trader. It was the mother of those children who, many years later, revealed to Peggy the true story of Florence Pemberton's origins.

After being in China for only a year Florence had married a young English storekeeper in Hongkew. The marriage was brief, unhappy, and childless. Within a short time, her husband died "of drink." Only nineteen years old, Florence was stranded in Shanghai, a penniless widow with no social background to fall back on and no employment. But she was not without assets, for she was still beautiful, flamboyant, and charming; and her rescuer came in the form of forty-eight-year-old Thomas Pemberton. He fell in love with the vivacious and amusing young woman and married her in 1893. The marriage was an excellent one for both of them, despite the age difference. Thomas was kind and gentle, and he adored his young wife, indulging her every whim. Florence in turn devoted herself to caring for her husband and making him happy.

The one thing lacking, for Florence, was a child. It was unlikely that Thomas and Florence would have one of their own. Their marriage, while perfectly contented, was not physically intimate, according to Peggy. But

Florence was attracted to the idea of having a daughter. Her memories of her own former dire circumstances and the unexpected good fortune that had come her way may also have resurfaced fifteen years later as she considered young Marjorie's situation. With relatively little hesitation, even though she had not seen Marjorie, Florence decided that they should adopt the little girl; and Thomas, who was quite comfortable with children despite his age, indulgently and unhesitatingly agreed. Although he would keep some business investments in China, he immediately made his retirement official; and the Pembertons decided to leave Shanghai, collect their new daughter in person rather than send for her, and settle at least temporarily in England. Neither Aunt Polly nor Marjorie's grandfather raised any objections to the adoption, and the transaction could be executed quite simply – no papers had to be signed, no formalities were required on anyone's part. Peggy marvelled at this all of her life. It was, she remarked, as if the Pembertons had simply acquired a new puppy or a kitten.

Marjorie Carter was only four years old at the time of her adoption, and had no real understanding of the momentous decisions being made around

Thomas and Florence Pemberton, Peggy's adoptive parents, are in the foreground of this photograph. Date unknown, but likely early 1900s. University of Victoria Archives

her. On July 26, 1907, a hot and sticky summer day in Lancaster, the little girl was dressed up in her finest clothes, in readiness to meet "the rich people from China," and warned to be on her best behaviour. She was to be presented to them in Aunt Polly's version of the "drawing-room," a stiff, formal room that had always been forbidden to her. Marjorie still had no idea what was happening — as far as she was concerned, it was simply another day, but one on which her aunt was even more tense than usual, in anticipation of the visitors coming. Completely wound up in a situation she did not understand, and suffering from the heat in her long dress, the child washed herself obsessively over and over, throughout the day, while waiting for the "rich people." By the time the Pembertons finally arrived, Marjorie was soaking wet, a hot, sticky, damp, and confused little child. She was already sporting a robust Lancaster accent and had had no training in etiquette or good manners. What the Pembertons thought as they arrived at the little rented house in the slum districts of Lancaster, to be presented with this vision of their prospective future daughter, will never be known; but as Peggy recollected it many years later: "My first authenticated conversational gambit to my future parents was 'Pooh, I'm sweating,' and, in spite of that, they adopted me."

There is no record of the Pembertons' thoughts, but little Marjorie's impressions, on the other hand, were very vivid. "I doubt if I can in any way give you the least conception of the impact that this extraordinary woman had upon [me]...she was literally a being from another world...beautiful, wearing lovely clothes — her hat was enchanting, turned up dashingly on one side with a gorgeous arrangement of birds' wings. She was warm and soft when she put her arm around (did she notice how wet I was?) me, and she smelled lovely...(Roger et Gallet's 'Violette de Parme')." The child's impressions were not without substance. Florence Pemberton was a beautiful, dramatic, and very intelligent woman, although she had had little formal education, and she was charming, gay, and generous. These were the qualities that had also captured Thomas Pemberton's heart. In contrast to Thomas's height — he was six feet, four inches tall — Florence was tiny, always beautifully dressed, with shining black hair, dark, outstanding grey eyes, and a vivid complexion. Little Marjorie fell instantly in love with this vision of a "fairy godmother," barely noticing the handsome, kindly, quiet man next to her. Typical of the men in Peggy's adult life, Thomas Pemberton played a shadowy,

Peggy Pemberton's adoptive mother, Florence, date unknown. The small child was captivated by the strikingly beautiful, vivid woman who had adopted her. UNIVERSITY OF VICTORIA ARCHIVES

background role throughout their relationship.

The couple did not say anything, but they took in the situation very quickly. It was clear to them that Aunt Polly no longer wanted the child, and they did not hesitate. They left Lancaster immediately, taking Marjorie and her meagre belongings with them. The little girl's life was changed irrevocably: starting with the acquisition of a brand-new name, Peggy Pemberton. And for the first time in her life, Peggy also had the undivided attention of an adult who cared about her. She was in heaven. For the first few days, the little girl and her adoptive mother, whom Peggy was instructed to call "Mamma," had to be quite forgiving of each other's flaws. Florence, completely inexperienced with children — loving, charming, but also hot-tempered — had to learn Peggy's routine, but young Peggy was very generous with her because she knew that her new Mamma had never had a little girl before. Florence, for her part, swallowed her horror when she found that not only were all Peggy's baby teeth thoroughly decayed but that her head was crawling with head lice. Inexperienced as she may have been, Florence also seemed to have a natural ability with the child and loved her passionately from the beginning. This combined love and intuition, and the return to a normal, happy childhood in pleasant surroundings, eventually restored the solid ground under Peggy's feet. Florence would allow Peggy to cry if she hurt herself or was sick, but if Peggy did not have any good reason,

Peggy Pemberton, aged four, with her new adoptive father, Thomas Pemberton, and friend Mattie Nesbitt at Bournemouth, 1907. ROD BREEN/MACKENZIE FAMILY

Florence would punish her: not with some physical penalty, but by withholding a treat, such as a bedtime story. Within a few weeks Peggy's self-control returned, and the bouts of silent weeping disappeared, never to reoccur. In postcards that she wrote to her new Mamma in 1907 and 1908 Peggy continued to assure Florence proudly, in her beautiful copperplate handwriting, that she had not been crying at all.

After collecting Peggy from Lancaster, the Pembertons travelled first to Bournemouth, a seaside resort town on the south coast of Dorset, where the new family rented rooms for the summer in a boarding house that they were to share with David and Lucy Nesbitt and their two children, Mattie and

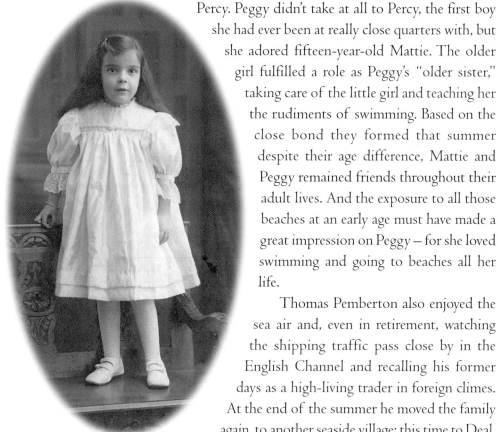

Peggy Pemberton in Deal, England, aged four or five. ROD BREEN/MACKENZIE FAMILY

Percy. Peggy didn't take at all to Percy, the first boy she had ever been at really close quarters with, but she adored fifteen-year-old Mattie. The older girl fulfilled a role as Peggy's "older sister," taking care of the little girl and teaching her the rudiments of swimming. Based on the close bond they formed that summer despite their age difference, Mattie and Peggy remained friends throughout their adult lives. And the exposure to all those beaches at an early age must have made a great impression on Peggy – for she loved swimming and going to beaches all her life.

Thomas Pemberton also enjoyed the sea air and, even in retirement, watching the shipping traffic pass close by in the English Channel and recalling his former days as a high-living trader in foreign climes. At the end of the summer he moved the family again, to another seaside village: this time to Deal, a small town near Dover, in Kent, known for its bracing climate. A furnished house was rented, and for the first time in her life Peggy enjoyed having a regular home and routine, full of affection and fun. A new black kitten named "Fluffy" was acquired, exclusively for Peggy to play with. On Saturday afternoons she could take her weekly pocket money of one penny and purchase sweet buns, or flowers, or candy – the choice was hers. A pleasant live-in maid named Edith Buddle provided additional enjoyment and security in the child's life, and she would take Peggy on walks through the quiet village streets when she had leisure time. It was easy to please Peggy and Edith: "It was a gala outing for both of us if we encountered a funeral…the more wreaths and the longer the floating black crepe, and the veils, the better." The two thoroughly enjoyed each other's company; the difference in their ages dispelled any difference in their status.

Although the legend on the back of this photograph suggests that it was taken in Shanghai in 1906, it is more likely that it was taken in England, either that year or the following year, on the occasion of Peggy's fifth birthday or a friend's birthday. Peggy is kneeling in the front.
UNIVERSITY OF VICTORIA ARCHIVES

Peggy's physical health improved, as did her state of mind. Her adoptive mother conjured up surprises, games, and treats, and she made Peggy a new wardrobe of pretty dresses. By the time Peggy turned five, on December 12, 1907, her life had changed from one of apparent emotional neglect to that of being loved and well cared for. Until then, no one had ever celebrated her birthday with her — she had not even known on what day it fell. But on the morning of her fifth birthday, the little girl awoke to find next to her bed a doll's bed, complete with spotted muslin curtains tied back with blue ribbon, elegant linen, and seated upon it the most beautiful doll she had ever seen, dressed in a lace-trimmed blue silk replica of one of Peggy's own dresses. Peggy's Mamma had made all of the clothes and linen herself. It was the most blissful morning that Peggy had known in her short, but eventful, life.

3

Halley's comet

"*Flexibility, adaptability, and curiosity are the three
most blessed gifts I was born with...to which must
be added an enormous amount of good fortune.*"

— PEGGY ABKHAZI, LETTER TO PHILIPPA, JULY 6, 1970

HER ADOPTION BEGAN WHAT PEGGY DESCRIBED AS AN EXTRAORDINARILY
happy childhood – an old-fashioned but informal upbringing for the times.
She was able to come and go far more freely than many of her contemporaries
were. The Pembertons were fond of the outdoors, and Peggy enjoyed many
summers walking and swimming and playing in the fresh air. Until the outbreak
of the First World War in 1914, her life continued to be nomadic, as she
travelled with her new parents back and forth to Shanghai, Japan, Europe, and
Scotland, staying for only brief periods in England. She developed a great
love for the places she visited – although once again, Peggy had no spot that
she could define for more than a few months at a time as a home of her own,

nor individuals her own age that she could befriend on anything but a temporary basis. However, she could, for the first time, feel secure in the love and support of both of her parents.

In Florence's case, though, there was a price to pay by Peggy if she wished to see her highly strung new Mamma remain the charming and gay woman she had appeared to be at their first meeting. Florence Pemberton clearly loved her adopted daughter passionately. Consciously or unconsciously, however, she demanded from the beginning that the love be returned, or at least demonstrated in equal intensity by Peggy. As an adult, Peggy reflected that Florence had wanted desperately for her new daughter to believe that her Mamma was her own flesh-and-blood mother. Florence in all likelihood did suffer from some insecurity that she was not Peggy's natural mother; she may also have been trying to compensate for the unsettled and migratory lifestyle that the family were living. Peggy was enormously grateful to Florence for rescuing her from misfortune and was enchanted by her Mamma's charm and wilfulness, but as she had already discovered, Florence was also selfish, domineering, and hot-tempered. She demanded that Peggy behave exactly according to her wishes at all times. Her vivid imagination could lead her to flights of fancy that bordered on the irrational, and sometimes to the making of wild and unfounded accusations. Thus Florence's uncompromising desire to be a "perfect" mother and her exacting requirements of Peggy led to an emotionally controlled upbringing for the child, informal though her childhood was in many other ways. The impact on Peggy's adult character and behaviour of this apparently free and idyllic childhood, coloured by Florence's demands for love and unquestioning compliance with her wishes, becomes more obvious when the path of these early years of her life is followed. The disproportionate balance of power in the intense relationship that Florence formed with Peggy in those early years was to dictate every aspect of Peggy's life for the next thirty years, and indeed it influenced her own approach to relationships for her entire life.

While it was Florence who figured most intensely in young Peggy's daily life, Thomas Pemberton, by contrast, was a kindly, much older, and relatively unknown figure in the background of her new existence. Although she understood that his presence equated with her new sense of security, Peggy paid him little attention, even avoided his company if intimacy with her new

Papa might be required. This was not due to any fear or dislike of Thomas, but occurred for the simple reason that he sported a luxurious moustache that reeked of the strong tobacco and cigars that her new Papa favoured. It was an odour the little girl could not bear. Too young to let gratitude or affection overcome her distaste, the moustache proved to be "an insuperable barrier...to a close relationship." Peggy withheld any physical affection from Thomas, refusing to kiss him good night or good morning. Thomas wisely did not press her. Photographs of the two of them, young Peggy smiling broadly up at her Papa, show that they enjoyed an easy companionship when they were together. But Peggy regretted greatly and far too late that what she described as "an absurd whim" on her part "stultified a relationship that would have greatly enriched both his life and mine." It was only after Thomas died a few years later that she came to realize what an enormously calming influence he had exerted on his young wife's temperamental behaviour.

In the meantime, Thomas's gentle authority did temper his wife's conduct – although he could not restrain Florence entirely. The child had already learned the art of being invisible in order not to attract unwanted attention. Now she acquired other skills in order to stay out of trouble. Taught not to argue with her elders, Peggy "tended to develop a sort of self-protective want of candour – [which] with the passing of time, became the grounding for tact." In a letter she wrote several decades later, commenting on a friend's rebellious young daughter, she remarked: "Mercifully, children are not as docile nowadays as my generation was forced to be. Undoubtedly our manners were admirable, but most of us, self included, went through a period of being highly accomplished liars." Nevertheless, Peggy was too young then to be much troubled by any of this. She was enjoying the novelty of love and attention, having her own pretty toys and belongings for the first time, and was having many delightful experiences. Florence's demands were a relatively easy price to pay for what, on the surface, appeared to be a freedom of movement. Peggy's life continued to be interesting and blissful, especially after her final encounter with Aunt Polly and her cousin about a year after her adoption.

Peggy's memory of leaving Lancaster and Aunt Polly and Daisy behind in 1907, having lived with them for nine months, or most of her conscious life, was completely blank. She had remembered "no goodbyes, no tears, no apprehension as to the unknown future with strangers...nothing!" The detached, self-contained little girl, already used to sudden changes, did not seem to have even felt relief at her escape from her situation. Florence Pemberton must have had some notion of it, but the fact that Peggy's former life must have been a miserable and frightening experience only came completely to light for the Pembertons during the summer of 1908. It seems that Aunt Polly had continued to correspond with the Pembertons – perhaps out of a genuine desire not to lose contact with her brother's only child. Upon learning that the Pembertons would be travelling by train to Edinburgh through Preston, near Lancaster, Aunt Polly arranged that she and Daisy would be on the railway platform at Preston when the train pulled in, in order to see Peggy. But Peggy was immediately and obsessively concerned about this proposed encounter; and Florence, perhaps hoping that Peggy would forget her biological family altogether, also wished to minimize the encounter, and she pretended that they would not be able to get out of the train because the doors would be locked. When they stopped at Preston, there were Aunt Polly and Daisy, holding a basket of strawberries and waving. In terror, Peggy recalled, she "clung dementedly" to Florence, trembling frantically. The meeting was brief – just long enough for the cousins to see each other and exchange a few words – and then "the train gathered speed – we were off...I was safe!" The Pembertons made sure that Peggy never saw her aunt or cousin again. As far as Peggy knew, Aunt Polly subsequently got married again, to the local butcher, and later emigrated with her new husband and Daisy to an unknown destination.

The train that Peggy was on in that summer of 1908 when she last saw Aunt Polly and Daisy was headed for Kennet, a hamlet at the headwaters of the Firth of Forth in the county of Clackmannanshire in the south of Scotland. Kennet was built in the nineteenth century on the estate of Lord Balfour of Burleigh, an old friend of Thomas Pemberton. It was a regular retreat for the Pembertons during the hot summer months, when the beach resorts in the south of England were flooded with tourists, and the 1908 visit was the first of many for Peggy over the years. The little girl was very taken with the noble family she encountered in Kennet. For her, it was like meeting a family out of one of her storybooks. There was the handsome, white-haired Lord Balfour, dressed always in very formal clothing, and Lady Balfour, attired to match; a married Countess daughter, and a handsome dark-haired young Laird in a kilt, with whom five-year-old Peggy immediately fell ardently in love; thin, sad, spinster daughter Miss Jean and tall, plain Master John, the younger son, who, when the handsome young Laird subsequently died during the First World War, became the next Lord Balfour; and Peggy's favourite, the youngest, Miss Victoria, who had enviably curly black hair and a pack of big dogs always following submissively at her heels. Kennet House itself was suitably large and impressive, with the proportions of a castle for a small girl with an active imagination, and with multiple entrances, lodges, and a huge rhododendron garden surrounding it.

Peggy was even more enchanted by the tiny village of Kennet, a place of tranquillity and amiability such as she had never before experienced. Like a toy town built expressly for a child's pleasure, the entire village comprised a simple row of stone cottages with low stone walls — very suitable for sitting on to have a rest — a general store selling everything from shoelaces to kerosene, and, of course, a cozy little inn. There were no cars or buses, and the butcher and the fishmonger each called twice a week in horse-drawn carts, coming from Clackmannan or Alloa, the nearest towns. Breton onion sellers and Italian ice cream vendors with their tinkling bells and colourful clothing would pass through occasionally, hawking their wares on their way to the bigger markets. In these peaceful surroundings the Balfour daughters taught Peggy how to make bread and scones and soup, and how to knit and crochet. On wet days she could read to her heart's content, an activity that became one of her lifelong loves. On fine days there might be picnics, and walks through the country lanes surrounding the village, picking mushrooms, wild roses, and honeysuckle. The lanes were bordered by farmers' green fields, full of vegetables and young corn under the soft northern summer sun, a perfect place for a little girl to play and chase butterflies and listen to birdsong in the peaceful afternoons. The only rule that was ever applied rigidly was the requirement to attend church twice on Sundays — a four-mile round trip on foot each time. "No strength left for sinful thoughts," remarked Peggy. It was a small tariff that she was more than willing to pay for this perfect summer holiday.

But like all holidays, it had to end. Thomas Pemberton had some outstanding business that he wanted to conduct in China. When the summer in Kennet was over the family gathered its possessions together and returned to Shanghai, where they were to remain for more than a year. The timing of the Pembertons' return to Shanghai at the end of 1908 coincided with the

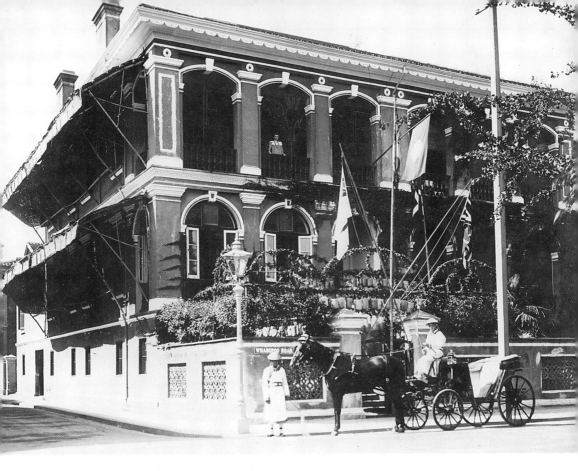

The Pembertons' residence in Shanghai, China. UNIVERSITY OF VICTORIA ARCHIVES

declining years of the ancient Chinese empire and the slowly rising star of the revolutionary Sun Yat-sen. China was at the brink of a series of huge upheavals that its people would continue to experience for the next forty years, but the luxurious lifestyle of wealthy foreigners in Shanghai continued unabated in the meantime. Little had altered in the International Settlement in the two years that had passed since Mabel Carter had taken her daughter back to England with her. Peggy, too young to understand the massive political changes brewing around her, was of course oblivious to the intense concerns occupying the minds of the locals. As far as she could know, she was surrounded by a household of contented Chinese servants, beautiful to behold in their long, colourful silk coats and neatly braided queues, and happy to be there to see to her needs. The Pembertons were duly installed in a large, imposing rented house, managed by their previous "Number One Boy," Tze Tsoong. His first task was an important one: it fell to Tze Tsoong to find an amah to look after

Peggy, aged six, with her Papa, Thomas Pemberton, on the racecourse in Shanghai, 1909. ROD BREEN/MACKENZIE FAMILY

the new addition to the family. It was one thing for Florence in England to care for Peggy herself; in Shanghai, at least as far as Florence was concerned, things were done differently. Peggy did not mind — and to her great satisfaction the new amah, who struggled unsuccessfully with Peggy's name and affectionately called her "Pigga" instead, immediately replaced the silver bracelets that had been lost to Daisy.

Life was as it should be for a young, privileged English girl in Shanghai — peaceful and normal. Peggy attended kindergarten, which she enjoyed, although having spent almost her entire life among adults, she found other children of her own age immature and uninteresting. She also attended dancing classes, held by a teacher who later taught the young Margot Fonteyn in the years before Fonteyn became an international ballet star. Peggy was to have no such career in her future: she was a robust and vigorous little girl and could walk for miles with her parents, but she was also completely uncoordinated. Although she enjoyed the pretty dresses and the silk dancing shoes, she disliked dancing class intensely, the more so because it involved little boys, who terrified her. But dancing was only a winter activity. To escape the sultry summer, the family travelled to cooler seaside resorts; and in 1909 Peggy visited Japan for the first time, staying at the coastal town of Kamakura, on the Miura Peninsula southwest of Tokyo. Although it had been the ancient capital of Japan, by the early twentieth century Kamakura had sunk into relative obscurity and was merely a pleasant rural village. It would in later years again grow and become a popular resort, but when the Pembertons visited it few people were aware of its charms as a seaside retreat.

Peggy at the age of six, in Japan. PHILIPPA PROUDFOOT (NÉE DAVYS)

Peggy loved the beach and swimming in the warm sea, and she was enchanted by the little town and the rural Japanese landscape. To her young eyes, the countryside and its small towns had not yet suffered from modern urbanization or the industrial development spreading from Tokyo. The local Japanese people, wearing traditional dress rather than western clothing, made Peggy feel as if she were visiting a perpetual fairyland.

By the early spring of 1910 Thomas Pemberton once again concluded his business affairs in Shanghai. Perhaps he foresaw and feared the revolution that was coming to China in the near future. Much as he loved the country that he had lived in most of his life, staying was becoming too big a risk, especially at his age; although he was apparently content to leave some investments in Shanghai. The Pembertons left the International Settlement once more, this time, they thought, for good. Thomas was looking forward to settling down again in some tranquil spot on the south coast of England, but he decided that the family would first take a scenic and leisurely route back home. They travelled through the Suez Canal, a part of the world with which Peggy would become greatly, although unintentionally, familiar nearly twenty-five years later. They disembarked at Marseilles during the height of the spring mistrals, wind storms that blew from the north. From there, the Pembertons caught the train to Paris. It was Peggy's first encounter with the city that in her sixties she would describe as the love of her life: "We then took the train up to Paris…and I began my lifelong love affair with that city…its light and spaciousness, the trees and the parks…and the food! All so different from anything I had hitherto experienced."

Thomas was less than enamoured with Paris, however, and the family soon continued on their travels, spending the summer of 1910 in Switzerland. It was another wondrous experience for Peggy, piled onto the many she had already had in such a short time. She found the country to be another fairyland, not unlike Japan, with snow-capped mountains and bright sunshine, alpine meadows where she could indulge herself without restraint in picking violets and daffodils to bring to her Mamma, lakes for her to swim in, and pretty, comfortable hotels. Florence, who was a dog lover, did not have any qualms in giving Peggy permission to play to her heart's content with a basketful of fox terrier puppies attached to one of the pensions they were staying in. It was Peggy's first exposure to dogs, and she fell hopelessly and uncontrollably in love with them – and another of her lifelong passions was born.

Two events of global significance that occurred in 1910 also registered themselves on Peggy's consciousness, less in their own right but because of the minor impact they had on her life at the time: the death of King Edward VII of England, and the appearance of Halley's Comet, last seen in 1834. Because of the King's death, sober clothing had to be worn, much against the indulged child's wishes; and when the comet appeared, a sleepy Peggy was

Florence Pemberton and Peggy, aged seven, with an unidentified friend in Switzerland, 1910.
PHILIPPA PROUDFOOT (NÉE DAVYS)

hauled from her bed to admire it, protesting against being disturbed in her slumbers. Neither of the two events meant much to such a young child – in fact, Peggy admitted in her memoirs that she could not truthfully say that she ever saw the comet. It was not until later in life that she appreciated both occasions for their own sakes. But if she failed to comprehend the events taking place on the world's stage, Peggy's perceptions about her situation in life were growing. She already understood, in her own naïve way, how vulnerable she was to her adoptive mother's charm and impetuosity. She had also already started to learn how to play into Florence's domination and demanding ways. And, now well used to the transience of her daily life, she immediately embraced every new situation and location so as to enjoy it to the maximum before she had to move on once more. Like the flowers she loved to pick in huge bunches everywhere she went, Peggy seemed already to know that the pleasure in each new experience would be fleeting, would soon have to be relinquished in favour of the next move. Still only seven years old, she also possessed a self-containment and a deceptive passiveness that were well beyond her years, and a sense of self-preservation that allowed her to pay little attention to things that did not affect her or that she could do nothing about.

In the meantime, however, Peggy's life was about to become somewhat more settled. As the autumn of 1910 approached, the family continued on their journey to England. Although they stopped briefly in Croydon, southwest of London, the climate did not suit the Pembertons, and both Florence and Thomas were eager to move quickly on to the coast. Peggy and her Mamma were both suffering from severe colds when Florence read an advertisement, placed in the newspaper by two elderly ladies, for a sunny, south-facing bungalow to rent on the English Channel. As Peggy recalled: "Mamma must have been desperate, because normally she made all the decisions…poor, kind Papa was sent (by train, in those days a two hour journey) to inspect 'Channel View' at Sandgate, near Folkestone, Kent – where I spent the next ten years of my life, apart from various school holidays spent here and there. Papa came back with glowing reports of house, garden and the Misses Green, but above all, of the glorious December sunshine which greeted him, in contrast to Croydon's hideous winter weather." Florence did not hesitate. The family packed their bags once more, and Peggy celebrated her eighth birthday at Channel View cottage, her new home.

Peggy always loved dogs - her love affair began when she found this basketful of puppies to play with at a hotel in Bex-le-Bains, Switzerland, in 1910. ROD BREEN/MACKENZIE FAMILY

Peggy, aged seven, walking with her adoptive parents Thomas and Florence Pemberton in Champéry, Switzerland, 1910. ROD BREEN/MACKENZIE FAMILY

4

Une jeune fille bien elevée

"I was delighted with the wild garden and I was given a kitten and a doll's house, and couldn't imagine ever wanting anything more."

— Peggy Abkhazi, *A Dragon Aunt Remembers*

Sandgate, a tiny dot on the map of southeast Kent about halfway between Dover to the north and Dungeness to the south, is a gentle seaside town built during the early nineteenth century. Photographs of the town taken between 1907 and 1912 show a peaceful, elegant village, stretched along the edge of the stark, chalky hills of this part of Kent. A broad, treeless strand faces the stony beach, dotted with benches for sightseers and locals to rest their tired feet. The benches and bathing shelters are intermingled with wooden capstans, for pulling fishing boats up onto the sand. On the High Street, tidy three-storey brick buildings and wrought-iron gas lamps line one side of the wide thoroughfare, and a solid row of trees has been planted along the other side. In the grainy black-and-white images, horse-drawn buggies are pulled up underneath the trees, available for hire by passersby. At the famous Sandgate Lift, wooden cable cars carried tourists up the steep cliffs at the back of the town to enjoy the views; on busy days in summer, as many as three thousand people would take the short ride each way. The town was big enough to boast its own school, which Peggy would attend once the family was properly settled. Sandgate also had a castle, once occupied by King Henry VIII – possibly with his bride, Ann Boleyn, whose family was from Kent. The town's claim to literary fame was local resident H.G. Wells, born and bred in the county, who had moved to Sandgate during the 1890s. By the time the Pembertons arrived in town, the author had already produced two of his best-known works: *The Time Machine* and *The War of the Worlds*.

The ten years that Peggy Pemberton was to live in Kent were the most stable period that she had yet known in her life. Although she did not reminisce a great deal about Kent, it is quite likely that living so many of her formative years in the county known as the "Garden of England" had a significant influence on her. At the very least, some interesting coincidences exist among the lifestyle, people, and events in Kent and the interests that Peggy developed later in her life, especially her great love of plants and gardening. Because of its Mediterranean climate and rich soil, Kent's many gardens flourished in all seasons, and Peggy would have been exposed as a child to some of the most famous gardens of her time. There was Chartwell, with its azaleas, Japanese cedars, and auracania, where Winston Churchill later made his home; Sissinghurst Castle Gardens, near Goudhurst in the southwest; and Holwood Park, with its magnificent trees. It was under an oak tree in Holwood Park that William Wilberforce, the English politician who campaigned successfully for the abolition of the British slave trade, had a discussion that he recorded in his diary thus: "1788. At length, I well remember after a conversation...at the root of an old oak tree at Holwood...I resolved to give notice on a fit occasion in the House of Commons of my intention to bring forward the abolition of the slave trade." (It is the stuff of local legend in Victoria, British Columbia, where Peggy spent much of her later life, that when she was in her eighties she and her former neighbour and close friend Sheila Anderson had planned to have an oak tree in her garden proclaimed a "heritage tree." It was grown, Peggy is said to have claimed, from an acorn from the tree under which William Wilberforce sat in 1788.)

Richard Church, who was a boy in Kent when Peggy was growing up there, later wrote of the rich soil of Kent that "everything grown on that chalk soil, quick and savage, takes a double dose of colouration. To look into a flower from that earth is to look into an element of coloured flame, fierce and primordial." The warm, soft Mediterranean climate, much like that of Victoria, also helped define Kent's lifestyle. Church described Kent as "more European than any other part of England…it is the front door of England." From high up on the cliffs above Sandgate, on a clear day, it is possible to see the coast of France. It was yet another connection to a country that as an adult Peggy loved above all others. Historically, there were also close relations between the residents of coastal Kent and their French cousins. As far back as Julius Caesar's day, the Roman emperor noted, although perhaps sarcastically, that the inhabitants of Kent were "as civilized as those of Gaul."

The first acquaintances the Pembertons made in that winter of 1910 were somewhat less than civilized, although this was not immediately evident. Ethel and Winifred, the Misses Green from whom "Channel View" had been rented, lived at the back of the house and saw to all of the housekeeping details. Once a week an accounting would take place, and Thomas Pemberton would pay the rent to the Misses Green, along with the sums due on bills for groceries and services supplied by the butcher, the greengrocer, the coal merchant, and all their other suppliers. Peggy was usually unaware of the existence of her parents' landladies. She had a garden of her own to play in and her new kitten to play with. Her Papa was contented, happy to spend hours watching the Channel's shipping traffic, and her Mamma had made new acquaintances to play badminton and bridge with and was continuing to enjoy having a small daughter to bring up properly. The house itself that they were living in did, however, have some small drawbacks. Although it was pretty enough, built of wood painted white with green trim, it was bitterly cold during the winter months. The Pembertons were also surrounded by some unexpected neighbours. When Thomas Pemberton had rented the house he had not noticed that much of the seafront was occupied by convalescent homes for tuberculosis sufferers. These homes had been opened by an enterprising businessman, taking revenge on the local council for refusing him permission to build a hotel on the waterfront. By this means, the businessman hoped perhaps to pressure the council into changing its decision. It did not; and not until 1914, when the government commandeered the houses for military purposes, were the last T.B. patients relocated to a less popular location.

In the meantime, it was slowly dawning on the Pembertons that something else was also amiss. The local tradespeople were treating them shortly, sometimes downright rudely, and Thomas and Florence must have started to have severe doubts about the community they had chosen to live in. The penny finally dropped for the Pembertons when the milkman's wife lost her temper with them at last, demanding that they pay their long-overdue bills immediately. It seemed that from the very beginning, Ethel and Winifred Green had been pocketing the housekeeping money that Thomas was paying to them instead of using it to pay the accounts. Horrified, the Pembertons immediately paid all of their outstanding bills in full; and the tradesfolk, to their relief, were completely satisfied.

Thomas and Florence were remarkably forgiving: in the face of the tearful remorse expressed by the two elderly ladies, they did not move their residence or take any further action against the Misses Green, except to take over payment of the accounts directly. Otherwise, things continued much as before; but only for a brief time. Unfortunately, the Pembertons' tolerance and compassion went unrewarded. On the summery June day in 1911 that the family went to London to see the coronation of King George V, Ethel and Winifred held a celebration of their own in the dining room, and the Pembertons returned to a scene of "much revelry and many bottles – and worst of all – Mamma's most elaborate lace and embroidered table linen was not looking too good." It was the last straw, and this time the family moved, almost immediately, to "Compton House," a drearier and more formal home with no garden on the High Street.

Peggy was very forlorn. She had lost her private playground and her views of the sea; and this was in addition to her despondency at being enrolled in a proper English school for the first time in her life. She started her formal education at Easter term, 1911. "I loathed school from the first despairing day when I laid my head on a table and wept noisily and shamelessly until the last day when the school moved to Bath…five years later as a result of the first German air raid on a civilian town during the 1914–18 war." Owing to the circumstances in which she was brought up, Peggy had been a loner from the beginning, more often in the company of adults than of other children. Throughout her life, she was never happy to coexist at close quarters with crowds of people. Now, at the age of eight, she became one of a large class of her contemporaries, none of whom had much sympathy for the rich little "foreign" outsider who had joined their ranks. To make matters worse, Florence Pemberton had no intention of letting her adopted daughter look like the offspring of the common townsfolk. While Peggy's heartfelt desire, if she could not escape the rigours of school life, was at least to look exactly the same as her classmates — wearing gym tunics and black stockings and having tightly braided hair — Florence was equally determined that Peggy be attired appropriately as "une jeune fille bien elevée." Dressed accordingly in kilt, sweater, and woollen socks and with her long hair hanging down and a large black bow on top, Peggy found herself teased unmercifully by her classmates.

The child gravitated naturally to the nearest sympathetic adult — her young teacher, who encouraged Peggy in her musical studies and started her on piano lessons. The teacher also introduced Peggy to botany and encouraged her love of wildflowers; Peggy credited this young woman with greatly influencing the development of her tastes. And her school days were not entirely a desert of despair: along with excellent teachers, the curriculum of the classes was also, by and large, enjoyable. The school put much emphasis on languages and history, subjects to which Peggy was well inclined; even at that young age, she claimed, she was able to read with equal pleasure in English or French Dumas's *Count of Monte Cristo* and *The Three Musketeers*. Peggy also soaked up poetry, retaining the ability well into her eighties to quote long sections of poems that she had learned in her school days.

Her nemesis was sport. For a child who loved playing outside and who often went on long walks with her parents, her complete and utter lack of coordination made games, like her earlier dancing classes, a nightmare for Peggy. A combination of factors was at play in this. Peggy had had great difficulty making the transition from the informal and varied life she had so far enjoyed with her adoptive parents, to the strict routine and repetitive discipline of being in classes every day. The long walks to school and back, the noise and confusion of the classroom, and her boredom with some of the required subjects and all the tedious rules left her with little energy to devote to games. Peggy also simply could not fathom the British love of team sports, with all their rules. Neither could she understand why they were played in all weathers, fair or foul; the only rationale that she could come up with was that at least all the running around served to keep the players warm.

Peggy's recollections of her school days were therefore of five years of chronic lateness and disorganization, of lost books and a constant sense of rushing and noise, in which she could never find a comfortable place to fit among her peers. So she employed the strategy that had worked for her on other fronts: she became invisible. By hanging around the periphery of activities, trying to look otherwise occupied, she avoided having to join in anything. She also found another avenue for escape from both the games and the classroom, with the encouragement of her influential young teacher: entering into every Royal Academy of Music subject that she could. Eventually, Peggy was able to justify being excused from games altogether.

Life at home, on the other hand, continued to be wonderful for Peggy. Her devoted parents remained dedicated to ensuring that she received a broader education beyond the classroom. The Pembertons also wanted her to enjoy the ordinary pleasures of childhood. For her tenth birthday, Peggy was allowed to keep the best present that she had ever received, one that had been given to her by the Pembertons' cook, Mrs. Castle – a Yorkshire terrier puppy that she named Prince. At Christmas, the Pembertons went to London for the theatre and attended pantomimes and children's plays like *Peter Pan* for Peggy's benefit. During school holidays the family would travel to Kennet, or to Devonshire or Wales. And in the spring of 1913, to Peggy's great delight, she and Florence returned to Paris for a vacation. Peggy recalled it as three weeks of "unadulterated bliss." A friend of Florence's had arranged for the pair to stay with a French family in a beautiful apartment on Avenue Victor Hugo, and the family treated Peggy royally. The daughters, Genevieve and Germaine, made Peggy dresses for her doll; and le Monsieur would take her for a walk every afternoon to the Bois de Boulogne or to the Tuileries, there to enjoy ice cream as a reward for their efforts. The food, she recalled fervently, was "heavenly."

In the meantime, the Pembertons finally purchased a home of their own in England. It is not certain what triggered their decision, but Thomas was getting older, and he may have decided that the time had finally come to give up living as a nomad, with all of his belongings permanently kept in storage.

"Channel View" was for sale, and the Pembertons briefly considered buying it. But they were cautious, given their previous experiences with the Misses Green; and their prudence was justified when it was discovered that the property's mortgage was held by someone else. Florence found instead an acre of land with two semi-detached houses on it, and with the help of an architect had them joined together and renovated into a modern home in an elaborately landscaped garden. The house came complete with a new cook and a parlour maid. The garden "was ruled over by a red-haired, fiery tempered genius, single-handed." Peggy's love of picking flowers put her into immediate conflict with Bignell, the genius gardener: she had a talent for picking the particular specimen that he had been saving for his own purposes. Although Peggy was at first terrified of him, she and Bignell eventually became lifelong friends and correspondents through their mutual passion for gardens.

The Pembertons moved into their new home in the autumn of 1913. For one more year at least, Peggy's world would feel safe and untroubled by anything more than the minor woes of her daily existence. One that occurred in short order was the loss of Prince, the Yorkie puppy, who had come off worse in a battle with a passing bus. He was suitably mourned, and promptly replaced by Pegs, a gorgeous standard poodle. Such ordinary traumas and joys, including the ups and downs of her school life, fully occupied Peggy's mind. As well travelled as she already was, the eleven-year-old could have had little understanding of the momentous world events about to take place. The summer of 1914 was, for Peggy, simply one of the hottest and most beautiful English summers she had yet experienced. Not until many years later would the words of the British foreign secretary, Sir Edward Grey, resonate in her memory: "The lamps are going out all over Europe. We shall not see them lit again in our lifetime."

There was little immediate impact on Peggy's day-to-day life when the Great War broke out at the end of 1914. But Kent, and little seaside towns like Sandgate looking toward the southeast, were facing the conflict over in Europe directly. Peggy watched long lines of khaki-clad troops marching north toward nearby Folkestone, to be temporarily housed in the fancy hotels and boarding houses that had been redesignated as camps. At Shornecliff Camp, half a mile from the Pembertons' home, the Canadian troops and medical corps were gathering prior to their departure for Europe, and British naval battleships were a constant sight as they patrolled the Channel from Dover to Portsmouth. With the wind coming from the southeast, the heavy vibrations of bombing across the water could be felt, if not heard; and as time went on, the bombing came closer to home. Merchant ships in the Channel were being attacked, and sometimes they were sunk as horrified onlookers on shore watched.

Not until 1916 did the first bombs fall near Sandgate. In her eighties, Peggy still remembered the first Zeppelin raid, but she told two different versions of the incident. In one version she was watching her schoolmates play hockey, taking her usual role of off-field "hanger-on," when shrapnel started to fall. The girls were quickly hustled into the pavilion to take shelter, but the gamesman, the husband of the Pembertons' cook, waited outside until he was sure that they were all safe. Before he could take shelter himself, he was killed by a piece of shrapnel. In the other version, Peggy recalled instead that the cook's husband had been the victim of shrapnel falling in the High Street of Folkestone. Either way, it was a horrifying event and, fortunately, the only really direct experience Peggy would have of the long conflict.

The more mundane impact on the Pembertons was the rationing of fuel and of food. In addition, poor Bignell was called up to serve in the army, and the two maids went to work in munitions factories. The family did not suffer particularly—there were plenty of vegetables and fruit growing in their garden, and dairy products and meat were readily available if one was willing to go directly to a farm. But the seriousness of the international situation told on Thomas Pemberton's health. He was extremely worried about Britain's position, and he was certain that his country would be defeated by Germany, particularly if the United States of America continued to refuse to enter the war. Unnoticed by Peggy, her Papa's health grew worse and worse.

There was one happy result for Peggy of the Zeppelin raid in that summer of 1916. As an indirect result of the raid, Peggy met the second person that she later considered to have had a lifelong influence upon her; and she received the first real intellectual stimulus that she had ever encountered. Following the raid, a decision was made to relocate all the private schools on the coast a few hundred miles away to the northwest of England, where it was still considered safe. Peggy's school was to be moved to Bath, in Somerset. She was horrified: if day school had been bad, she could not even begin to contemplate what boarding school would be like. During the first half of her life, Peggy usually allowed other people, particularly Florence, or else the prevailing circumstances, to dictate what she would do. However, there were two or three watershed moments in those years when Peggy was not only adamant about what she wanted but willing to do just about anything to achieve it — and this was one of those watershed moments. If forced to go, Peggy declared, she would run away with Pegs, the standard poodle. She had no idea how she would go about it, but to her relief she never had to work it out: "Mamma was, of course, enchanted by my attitude for though I was unable to recognise it at the time, looking back I can see that her deep love for me was already becoming coloured by the devouring possessiveness which caused us so much unhappiness during the [next] twenty years of our life together." That unhappiness lay in the future, however. For now, Florence quickly and happily agreed that Peggy did not have to go away; and Peggy, in turn, was elated.

Some alternative to complete her education was needed, however, so once a week Peggy was to travel to London with Florence for music lessons, while for the remainder of the time she would have to be privately tutored. A local clergyman who had taught at the school before it had been moved was hired, and Peggy's world was suddenly, and gloriously, opened up to whole new vistas. Peggy credited John Ferguson as being the man who taught her to think: "His aim was to develop in me a 'well-furnished' mind." A Scotsman brought up by crofter parents, Ferguson had been educated in Aberdeen. He had a Celtic love of words, tempered by his harsh experiences working in the slums of Glasgow, and a pragmatic view of human nature. It did not take him long to assess the hold that Florence Pemberton had over the fourteen-year-old girl in his charge. While he naturally encouraged obedience, John Ferguson also introduced to Peggy the novel concept that she did not have to simply subscribe, without question, to her adoptive mother's views and opinions; for the first time, the notion was awoken in Peggy that Florence might not represent the sum of perfection. Although she did not suddenly enter into a period of teenage rebellion, Peggy did experience a conscious awakening of independent thought. "It was, intellectually and imaginatively, as much a 'rescue' as was the rescue of hot damp little Marjorie Carter by the Pembertons from Aunt Polly's clutches ten years earlier." The enthralled student and her stern but affectionate teacher happily studied literature, language, and the humanities, in a program that they had designed together to fit their mutual love of words.

Florence, surprisingly, sensed no challenge to her authority, and did not interfere with the arrangement.

This happy state of affairs, unaffected by the war, continued unchanged for the next two years. But Thomas Pemberton's declining health did not improve, and in the summer of 1918 Peggy's gentle, kind Papa died. It almost seemed to come as a surprise to Peggy: she had paid so little attention to the sick, elderly man in the background of her life. But having supported Florence in her decision to adopt Peggy, Thomas Pemberton then had the next largest impact on Peggy's life in his dying. With his sudden absence, Peggy almost instantly, and with huge regret, realized just how much Thomas had contributed to the stability of her existence. Florence

John Ferguson, the Scottish tutor who opened the teenage Peggy's mind to independent thought for the first time. UNIVERSITY OF VICTORIA ARCHIVES

Pemberton, who had been devoted to her husband, was devastated by her loss. Only in her early forties, she seemed to be a ship without a compass; and the young teenage daughter at her side, with all of her teenage problems, seemed to add to her confusion. Without Thomas, "Mamma's wilder flights of fancy gradually were transformed into total unreasonableness." As Florence groped uncertainly for what to do next, Peggy watched mutely. There was little else she could do.

 and frivolity

A BEAUTIFUL BLACK AND WHITE CAMERA PORTRAIT OF SIXTEEN-YEAR-old Peggy, taken by Dorothy Wilding of London, shows a sombre, unsmiling teenager, one hand cupping her face, her other arm folded across her chest. It is an unusual photograph for the era. Peggy's air is casual, but also completely resigned. Peggy was a lonely and unassuming young woman, still just a teenager, whose life had suddenly taken an unexpected turn: the death of her adoptive father, Thomas, initiated the irreversible loss of childhood ignorance, joy, and freedom. It was also the beginning of the painful disintegration of her once-loving relationship with Florence Pemberton.

Peggy was too young to have made any independent acquaintances or to have entered "into society"; she had no real friends that she could call her own. As Florence drifted, anchorless, trying to decide what she should do and simultaneously avoiding having to do so, Peggy kept close to her side, dutifully trying to help her mother. Peggy's view years later was that Florence, and others of her generation, must have been significantly disoriented by the social and economic upheavals generated by the First World War; far more than Peggy and her generation would be affected twenty-five years later by the Second World War. Whereas the latter were to experience a great liberation from the strictness and rigidity of previous years, someone like Florence Pemberton only faced confusion and a huge upset to the equilibrium of her life that she had once thought unshakeable. Also, Florence had taken Thomas's death very hard; her husband had been her best friend and constant ally. Without him, there was no one to indulge her whims and eccentricities, no one to be the adoring mirror reflecting her beauty and charm back to her constantly. Although she had friends, none of them were particularly close. They all had lives of their own, and Florence was not their first priority. Florence was also not about to turn to her family for support, given her apparent embarrassment about her original background and the illusions that she had spun around it. In fact, as far as it can be determined, Peggy never became acquainted with any members of Florence's family.

With Thomas gone, Peggy was the only stable person in Florence's life. Thus there seemed never to be any consideration that Peggy should now be free to return to school or to attend any kind of finishing school in another country, as was often the custom. Consciously or unconsciously, Florence drew Peggy closer to her side, and from that time they were rarely out of each other's company. Increasingly paranoid that Peggy might also abandon her, Florence started to exert a degree of control over her daughter that far exceeded anything that Peggy had previously experienced. To her dismay, over the next few years Peggy would watch Florence's beauty slowly turn to bitterness, the eccentricity to escapism, and the escapism into an incredible selfishness: and, from time to time, Florence's love turn to fury. But Peggy was determined never to quarrel with her adoptive mother. She felt that she owed Florence a huge debt of gratitude for her adoption. Complying with Florence's wishes and remaining by her side, cheerful and obedient, was the "only possible way of trying to repay an un-repayable debt." No doubt, at the tender age of sixteen, Peggy thought that it would only be for a few years at most.

Florence had no desire to remain in the house at Sandgate without Thomas, and accordingly in the fall of 1918 Peggy and her mother closed up the house and moved to London. The one clear goal that Florence seemed to be able to focus upon was ensuring that Peggy pursued her musical studies, and this was the primary objective of the move. Thanks to that first teacher at the school in Sandgate, Peggy had already developed a great love of music, and even though she regarded herself as "no heaven-born genius," she promptly enrolled in an ambitious program at the Royal Academy of Music. There she rubbed shoulders with students and teachers who would go on to win international acclaim—Warwick Braithwaite, then unknown but in later years a world-class conductor, was Peggy's accompanist for her examinations. In this heady environment, the young woman studied piano and violin and played in one of the Royal Academy's orchestras as well as a chamber music class. Encouraged by Florence, Peggy for the first time entertained thoughts of becoming a concert pianist, one of the few acceptable occupations for a well-bred young Englishwoman in those days; and she threw herself diligently into her work. The long hours of practice and study of theory left her little time for any other diversion or schooling or to pay much attention to her still-grieving mother.

Florence had arranged accommodation for Peggy and herself with a widowed friend whom they had known in Shanghai. They shared a flat in Hampstead, not far from London. Their mutual Shanghai experiences and recent bereavement provided a bond for the two older women, who were both looking for a useful way to occupy their time. While Peggy studied and practised industriously, the two friends became active volunteers, serving in railway canteens as thousands of soldiers moved through London on their way to or from France in the post-war "cleanup" period. For pleasure and relaxation, they played bridge, one of Florence's favourite games. "But after a few months," Peggy later wrote, "the inevitable quarrel occurred." This quarrelling with erstwhile good friends was a pattern that Florence Pemberton was to repeat for the next decade and a half: an unconscious but constant alienation of people who could have provided her with the comfort and support that she needed. At her still relatively young age, Florence probably suffered a great horror of being relegated to a widow's status, confined to stuffy and dull drawing rooms for the remainder of her days, with no other diversion but the playing of bridge with other older women — and subconsciously may have behaved in a way calculated to provoke arguments and invite rejection. Combined with her growing inclination to unreasonableness and unfounded accusations against those nearest to her, it was a certain recipe for destroying her relationships in short order and one that was to become the norm.

The reason for the quarrel with the Hampstead flatmate is not known, but it was sufficiently serious that after the two widows argued, Florence and Peggy retreated to the house in Sandgate. Florence was determined that Peggy should not give up her music studies, however, and permitted her daughter to travel to London by herself on the train four days a week in order to attend classes at the Royal Academy. It was quite extraordinary that Florence was prepared to give Peggy this latitude, given her obsessive desire to control her daughter: Peggy remarked that it must have caused her Mamma much "soul-searching." But Florence also had a genuine desire to please Peggy when it came to things musical, and it was the one subject on which, usually, she was prepared to indulge her daughter's wishes. It was a temporary liberation that provided Peggy much relief, as well as offering her first opportunity for illicit rebellion. Despite her unusual childhood, Peggy was, after all, a typical teenager. She spent her daily lunch money on cheap beauty magazines and facial creams, forgoing nourishment in favour of such frivolous items; hiding her treasures in her music case, she carried them back and forth with her to London on the train, crossing her fingers desperately against their discovery by Florence on the weekends.

Ironically, it was not the unveiling of this actual deception, but rather the incident of an imagined wrongdoing, that marked the permanent change in Peggy's relationship with Florence to one based almost entirely on duty and gratitude rather than love. It was a profound moment, one that caught up with her unawares. Peggy returned home one evening from a day in London and walked in the door of their home to find Florence waiting within, in a towering rage. Without greeting her, Florence began to hurl accusations against Peggy that she had been seen loitering on the streets of London, against her mother's direct instructions. Peggy was dumbfounded. Her beloved Mamma railed at her about her abuse of trust and about how much she "owed" to Florence. "She was completely out of control of herself. I was embarrassed — as if I had seen her naked for the first time — and at that moment my childish bewitchment by Mamma ended." The episode had of course been entirely innocent on the teenager's part. She had simply decided to take advantage of the beautiful day and ride the bus, instead of taking the underground train, to the Royal Academy. A neighbour from Sandgate had seen her waiting on the street and had unwittingly commented upon it to Florence, unaware of the reaction her remark would provoke. Florence had immediately panicked, interpreting the incident as Peggy's first step away from her control. Her reaction shocked Peggy and brought the teenager face to face with a sudden, hard reality: "This is the cruellest…sentence I shall ever write about poor Mamma. At that moment, I lost my admiration – and with it my love – for her…I hope that I do not delude myself, but I do not think that she ever noticed the difference."

Shortly afterward, Peggy concluded her first year of musical exams, achieving two bronze medals and honours in her theory subjects. Florence decided arbitrarily that she wanted to return to Shanghai, of all places – ostensibly to check on her late husband's investments. She may have been influenced by fears that she seemed to have lost some control over Peggy, but Florence also had other plans for her adopted daughter: in particular, making her ready for her formal debut into society. Florence thought that the International Settlement of Shanghai, with which she was more familiar than London, would be the best place to do it. Peggy seemed to have no objection – it had to be more interesting than staying in Sandgate – but even if she had, it is doubtful that Florence would have changed her mind. The waiting lists for tickets were very long, however, due to the shortage of passenger vessels after the end of the war, and it was another eighteen months before she was able to obtain passage for the two of them to China. That left plenty of time for a seventeen-year-old girl to dream about the exciting and romantic life to come in Shanghai. The teenager fantasized about elegant clothes that would be the talk of the city, handsome young men bearing bouquets of flowers, unchaperoned dances at which "bathtub gin" was served, and going to jazz parties, all the latest rage. Peggy thought of herself then more or less as an ugly duckling, hoping magically to become a swan. "I don't really know what I expected…I would become beautiful? And a touch tragic? And popular and witty and elegant overnight?" she wrote decades later, in the comfort of her old age and long after the sting had gone out of the memory of quite a different outcome.

If the reality was less than the dream – Florence's idea of a suitable social launching was vastly different from Peggy's fantasy, and many tears would be shed later by Peggy as a result – the preparation helped to pass the time pleasantly. It also served to mend, at least temporarily, the day-to-day relationship between Peggy and Florence as they enjoyed assembling Peggy's debutante outfit together. As a young woman Peggy always had a great fondness for beautiful clothing. The accumulation of her wardrobe for the forthcoming trip was one of her cherished memories – especially the articles of clothing themselves, which more than sixty years later she was able to describe in detail. Although the new wardrobe was not quite the splendid romantic ensemble that her heart desired, it was a vast improvement on the tweeds and wool that she was used to. Peggy rejoiced over a hoard of silk stockings, with open work down the front, or "clocks" up over the ankles, and crêpe-de-chine lace-trimmed underwear; including an adored boudoir cap that was a "wisp of lace and ribbon" that she could dream of wearing "when my unimaginably handsome dream-husband would kiss me good morning" (although she did not recall ever wearing it). Two evening dresses also adorned the collection, one of white crêpe-de-chine, and the other an apricot georgette with blue glass-bead trim. To go with the white dress, Peggy had white silk stockings, white elbow-length kid gloves, and a white ostrich feather fan. It was not the dashing and décolleté flapper outfit of her wishes, but she was quite contented and ready to launch herself on society, come what may.

While Peggy was mooning over her romantic future and neglecting her music studies in favour of her daydreams – she failed all of her second-year exams in complete ignominy, but apparently with little regret – Florence was attending to the closure of the last details of their life in Sandgate. She no longer wanted to keep the house that she had so carefully designed, with its memories of her life with Thomas, and she sold it to friends in the summer of 1920. Yet another quarrel with these friends was provoked by Florence, or ensued in some fashion, and both house and friends were lost forever after it was over. As contradictory and impulsive as ever, Florence then decided to share a rented flat with her old friend Lucy Nesbitt and her daughter Mattie. Lucy was by now also a widow, and again, it seemed a natural fit. The Nesbitts could care for the dog while Florence and Peggy were away in China, and they would have an established place to come back to at the end of their trip.

As now seems inevitable, it was not to be. This time, the cause of the quarrel that Florence provoked is known: she took exception, of all things, to young Mattie Nesbitt's boyfriend, and made her views known in no uncertain terms to Lucy Nesbitt. Her instincts were correct – the young man turned out to be no good – but the old and dear friendship between Florence and Lucy was ruined permanently. In a cool and unforgiving atmosphere, Peggy and her mother awaited word of their departure to China. It finally came in November 1920. The pair departed on a P & O liner, SS *Plassy*, for the six-week journey to Shanghai. One way or another, Peggy was finally launched.

OPPOSITE: *Peggy Pemberton at sixteen years old. The portrait was taken by photographer Dorothy Wilding of London.* PHILIPPA PROUDFOOT (NÉE DAVYS)

6

Going to the decadent city

"My vague dreams of drifting around in some of my new splendours
were squelched…by Mamma who said…it would look and be vulgar. I
reluctantly obeyed, and wore my flat heels and less-than-ravishing
garments whilst envying a beautiful, rich and seductive Mrs. Montefiore
who was on her honeymoon with a sad looking little Mr. Montefiore.
Every evening she made a grand entry into the dining saloon in a
different and more glorious glory. Never mind, if I was unable to
compete with Mrs. M., I did win the first prize at the Fancy Dress Ball.
I went as a Red Indian…coloured feathered headdress, face coloured
with brown shoe polish (drastic measures needed to remove same) and the
prize was a pretty piece of amber mounted as a pendant on a black
ribbon. I had it for years — but somewhere along the way it disappeared."

— Peggy Abkhazi, *A Dragon Aunt Remembers*

Peggy very much enjoyed her six-week trip on the *Plassy*. It
offered a temporary escape from the tedious reality of her life in England
with Florence. Despite the drawbacks of travelling with her watchful Mamma,

it was still exciting to see once again the ports and cities that she had last been in as a child, and to observe the elegant passengers in their daily excursions on deck and to the dining salon. But not everything was unqualified fun: although Peggy was starting to harbour doubts, Florence was still proudly certain that her daughter might yet make a concert musician and wanted Peggy to practise on the ship's piano daily. Much as she enjoyed her music, it was a mortifying experience for the teenager, who did not seem to mind playing for an audience but could not bear to practise in public. It was the one topic relating to her music on which apparently Peggy could not persuade Florence otherwise; but she was at least able to convince her Mamma that she should not inflict violin practice on the other passengers, and she confined herself to the privacy of her cabin for that exercise.

While Peggy was suffering minor anguish over her piano practice, Florence was dealing with a much more difficult decision, one that was required only as a result of her vivid imagination. Many people on board the *Plassy* were from Shanghai, and plenty of them knew Florence Pemberton and her daughter. Even if the acquaintance was minor, these people were likely to be familiar with the history of Peggy's adoption. But Florence had convinced herself that Peggy thought of her as her biological mother. In her overwrought state she was also convinced that Peggy would learn this "secret" from a stranger, and Florence decided that she must confess the truth to Peggy. With her usual fondness for melodrama, Florence staged a dramatic scene for unveiling the secret, no doubt expecting to have to comfort the young woman and provide her with assurances of her maternal love. In doing so she may also have subconsciously expected to gain even greater control over Peggy. But, if so, Florence was greatly disappointed by her adopted daughter's pragmatic and dismissive response. Peggy was under no illusion that her Mamma was really her mother, and her strongest reaction was mild astonishment that Florence should believe that Peggy would not remember her childhood prior to her adoption.

The exchange set back their relationship once again. Florence must have been greatly wounded that Peggy did not think of her as her real mother, after all she had done for her. Peggy on the other hand was starting to experience a growing frustration that she and her adoptive mother could not enjoy a friendship and simple affection based on their enjoyment of each other as individuals. Their relationship was instead becoming cemented in the notion of the debt of gratitude owed by Peggy to Florence for her adoption out of unfortunate circumstances. Nevertheless, Peggy was still young enough to entertain great hopes for the future and to think of her current circumstances as a temporary interlude, until the natural time when she would meet her dream husband-to-be and leave Florence Pemberton's side. When that happened, the relationship might return to normal. In the meantime, the lifestyle the two women adopted on the passage to Shanghai would become the norm — and Peggy must have hoped fervently that the interlude would be a short one.

At much the same time as Peggy was sailing to Shanghai on the *Plassy*, a young Irish-Canadian woman named Muriel Langtry, from Victoria, Canada, was also en route to Shanghai, on board the vessel SS *Empress of Asia*. Unlike Peggy, she was travelling by herself and enjoying her more informal lifestyle at sea a great deal. Writing home on April 29, 1921, to her brother in Duncan, British Columbia, Muriel excitedly described her daily routine thus: "By Monday we were all feeling very frisky and started deck tennis at which we all became very expert before the end of the voyage. We had some very keen matches and played every day from breakfast until lunch, then after lunch till 4 o'clock, when we danced and had afternoon tea little of the latter until 6 o'clock, then more tennis till seven when there was a wild rush for baths and dress for dinner, then dancing from dinner till 10.30 p.m. then some refreshments. It was a most wonderful trip."

Muriel Langtry did not disembark in Shanghai, although she would return later; as she watched her erstwhile deck-tennis partners leave the ship, she more soberly observed: "The tender takes the passengers up the river as the ship just anchors at the entrance to the Yang-Tsze [*sic*] which is a dirt filthy muddy river. Crowds of dirty Chinese fishing boats come alongside the vessel with long poles with a net at the end, begging for money or food. The poverty is very remarkable at Shanghai. Hotel accommodation is very difficult to get so I did not get off at Shanghai." She continued to Hong Kong, and less than a year later, Muriel married David Roderick Mackenzie, a commercial agent with the trading firm of Jardine Matheson and Co. Although she settled in Shanghai with her new husband, it was almost twenty years before Muriel and Peggy were introduced to each other. When they did finally meet, they became almost instantly the best of friends, which they would remain for the rest of their lives. Muriel was also the catalyst that would later influence one of the most significant choices of Peggy's life after the Second World War. The two women were bound up by many coincidences of fate, both major and minor: one of Peggy's most cherished memories from her teenage years was sharing a train carriage to London one day with the famous Lily Langtry — who was, according to one of Muriel's descendants, her second cousin. For now however, the two future friends were fated to simply pass close by, each completely unaware of the other's existence.

Muriel Langtry Mackenzie as a young woman, date unknown but likely circa early 1920s.
ROD BREEN/MACKENZIE FAMILY

Peggy and Florence were met at Hongkew wharf by that constant guardian angel of Peggy's, Dr. Goode. Rooms had been arranged for them by Dr. Goode at the Burlington Hotel near Bubbling Well Road, not a very comfortable establishment but sufficient for their purposes. Now in his early sixties, the shy Dr. Goode had remained a confirmed bachelor, but holding true to his long-ago undertaking to William Carter he was determined to ensure Peggy's comfort and well-being, even if this meant having to deal with two such emotional and difficult women. Florence Pemberton and Dr. Goode, who were of extremely different temperaments, took a dislike to each other — but Florence also recognized that both she and Peggy needed his help, and Dr. Goode was made of sterner stuff than to allow the flighty Mrs. Pemberton to put him off what he saw as his duty to his old friend's daughter. Peggy was greatly endeared to him immediately, despite the shyness on both sides.

Florence continued the pattern that had already been set for all of Peggy's and Florence's travels together. "Mamma adopted the same system as that of the Duchess of Kent (Queen Victoria's mother) who, until the day of Victoria being proclaimed Queen, insisted upon their sharing a bedroom. I found this very difficult…twenty-four hours a day at such close quarters, year in and year out, with someone belonging to another generation. I have often wondered why she did not find it equally trying," commented Peggy. The one consolation for her was that she no longer had to practise her piano music in public but could do so in the privacy of her room. This arrangement with her mother, however, also made it impossible for Peggy to become the social success that she had been dreaming of. She could certainly not return unnoticed to the hotel from an engagement. It was also difficult to return hospitality, and although money did not appear to be a problem for Florence, for some reason she refrained from participating in many of the lavish social circles of Shanghai, especially resisting the wealthy foreign taipans from Jardines and other big commercial enterprises. Perhaps, given her humble origins, and without Thomas Pemberton at her side, Florence felt insecure and incapable of holding her own in that environment. In any event, she was certainly not about to permit Peggy to join in that kind of fun.

And fun it certainly must have been, in those heady days of the early 1920s in Shanghai. Money was the theme for everything: it was easy to make, and even easier to spend. The First World War had had little negative impact on Shanghai; it had boosted the fortunes of merchants and industrialists in China's largest port. The factories and the godowns were bursting with trade goods, and the economy was thriving. Around the International Settlement the activity was ceaseless, as workers toiled twenty-four hours a day in mills and factories and engineering plants. New banks were springing up to handle the cash flow, and new buildings were constantly under construction on Shanghai's swampy soil. The war had also opened up opportunities for the local Chinese to participate on a level footing with European merchants for the first time. Chinese millionaires placed their funds at the new Bank of China and built themselves magnificent homes that outshone the largest foreign mansions. With all of this money flooding the city, vast department stores were opened for the first time offering an array of goods from around the world. The Shanghainese became enthralled with hunting for the latest novelties and luxuries, and in shopping as a recreational activity. These huge stores foreshadowed the mega-malls of modern North America, providing an array of theatres, restaurants, games rooms, casinos, even cabarets and hotels. Chauffeur-driven new motorcars appeared on the streets, alongside the throngs of yellow rickshaws, delivering their occupants to the International Race Club, to afternoon tea dances at one of the hotels, or to lavish all-night parties that were hosted continually. Renegades rubbed shoulders with mandarins at these events; an American divorcée like Wallis Simpson could party freely in the company of Dukes and Duchesses — and she did.

A somewhat darker, underground world also existed alongside these more acceptable, if still risqué social occasions. With the influx of large numbers of refugee White Russians into Shanghai in the aftermath of the 1917 Bolshevik Revolution, the city's nightclubs and brothels took on a new life. The Russians, having lost their citizenship, did not enjoy the same extraterritorial protection from the Chinese government as other foreigners in Shanghai. Having also lost their land and most of their material possessions in the flight from Russia, they were forced to engage in any enterprise that would enable them to survive, and this was often easiest to do in the entertainment industry. Many new jazz clubs and bordellos were created by the refugees, who employed their compatriots as musicians, bartenders, cooks, and hostesses. Some of the wealthy foreigners in the International Settlement were horrified to see white men and women in roles normally associated with the Chinese population — but for those who wanted new diversions, and there were many, a fascinating and exotic nightlife in the new clubs started up by the Russians was readily available.

Beneath the surface of this free-wheeling and lascivious lifestyle the growing discontent of the Chinese population was brewing, and an intellectual and cultural revolution was under way. The most visible sign of change in the ten years since Peggy had been in Shanghai was the absence of the long, pig-tail braided queues formerly worn by her Chinese servants. One of the first government orders of Sun Yat-sen's bloodless "democratic" revolution in 1911 had been that all Chinese men must cut off their queues. Sun's order had the effect of breaking a cultural tradition thousands of years old; many had resisted, only to have their hair forcibly removed. It was just one manifestation of the upheaval to come. In the meantime, the cost of all the industrial activity and production supporting the high lifestyle of the foreigners and wealthy Chinese was poor wages for local labour, and even worse working conditions. Coolies, or *kwei-li* — meaning "bitter strength" — were at the very bottom of the chain, earning a few cents a day in appalling circumstances.

Strikes broke out sporadically, and labourers were clearly looking for a channel to vent their growing anger, but the Chinese leadership offered little hope to them. Sun Yat-sen's revolution had foundered in corruption and ineptitude. Sun had been forced to flee the country, returning to Canton subsequently to try and establish a rival government to the warlord regime in Peking. At the same time, Shanghai had become a political centre for various factions competing for prominence, and by 1921 Sun had moved to the city in an attempt to accumulate power. The one issue uniting most of these factions was continuing fear of a Japanese infiltration of China. In July 1921 the Chinese communist movement was born in a near-empty schoolroom in the French Concession. It was founded upon the May Fourth Movement — an overwhelming protest stimulated earlier that year by the revelation that the Versailles Treaty of 1919 proposed to hand over to the Japanese all of the German Concessions in China. Sun Yat-sen was made chairman of the new Communist Party, and Chiang Kai-shek, Sun's military aide, was sent to Moscow for military training.

Peggy, nineteen years old and focused entirely on making her social debut a raging success, was still blissfully unaware of the seething political and cultural environment she was living in. Florence was equally determined that her daughter — debut or not — would not get involved in the hectic and flamboyant Shanghai scene. Poor Peggy's social life was therefore limited to staid and elegant dinner parties at her guardian's apartment, in the company of her Mamma and proper young married couples, and wallflower appearances at a couple of suitably sedate balls. She was also allowed to attend one of the more decorous regular tea dances at the French Club on Sunday afternoons, but neither of her pretty party dresses were permitted an airing — low-heeled shoes and a blue serge suit were the dress that Florence dictated as being suitable. Peggy gazed in hopeless envy at the "wild American girls," hatless and wearing gorgeous filmy frocks to the tea dances, and she sank into her shy invisibility again.

At musical evenings she played accompaniment to the singing, feeling ridiculous as she carried around her violin case and music: "I would so much rather have been beautiful and witty and fascinating than playing piano

Peggy Pemberton's horse-riding days, Shanghai. According to her mother's rules, she was not permitted to dismount when in the company of men in case it encouraged overfamiliarity. SUSAN HAMERSLEY/
MACKENZIE FAMILY

accompaniments and violin solos," she mourned. For some reason, Peggy did not place any blame for this situation on her mother – rather, she assumed that her lack of social success was entirely her own fault. Golf and tennis lessons arranged by Florence were met with Peggy's usual despairing lack of coordination, precluding a good opportunity to meet and mix with suitable partners her own age. And despite her best efforts, Florence also lost the battle to teach Peggy how to play bridge, another acceptable social diversion. Peggy was not interested in the game and could not learn its nuances, no matter how much she practised. "Eventually," remarked Peggy, "she was defeated by my stupidity – but I lost the war, for I was condemned to playing rummy with her every evening of our lives, unless we were going out to a concert or to the theatre."

The only diversion Peggy was truly able to enjoy was riding, which she was allowed to do unchaperoned, provided she did not break the cardinal rule never to dismount from her horse – voluntarily, at any rate. She was frequently

Peggy Pemberton with riding companions, Shanghai - Peggy's handwritten note, opposite, tells the tale of Peggy breaking the rules! SUSAN HAMERSLEY/MACKENZIE FAMILY

thrown, but loved riding nonetheless. There are many photographs of Peggy atop her horse, smiling broadly at the camera — there are even some pictures showing that she did, in fact, break the cardinal rule, as she is seated in front of the horses in the middle of a group of several men. Dr. Goode also attempted unsuccessfully to help with Peggy's social life, introducing her to a middle-aged bachelor friend of his named John Henry Green. But Peggy paid little attention to the shy and unassuming older man, who nonetheless appears to have fallen quietly and quite hopelessly in love with her. She was not aware, at least then, of his affection for her. She was only nineteen years old, after all, and her sights were still set on an ideal in her mind's eye of what her dream husband might eventually be like. John Green hung around the edges of her existence and did not give up hope; which was just as well for Peggy, for he was to become very important to her in later years.

Although Florence and Dr. Goode had little time for each other, in the summer of 1921 she allowed herself to be persuaded by him that she and Peggy should take a two-month tour of Japan to broaden Peggy's mind and experiences. Dr. Goode made arrangements for a Japanese guide, Nakasan, to take the mother and daughter on a three-week hiking trip of the lake country around Mount Fujiyama. Peggy relished every moment of her second visit to Japan. Florence was pleased to have a change from Shanghai and shared Peggy's enjoyment of walking, and the two had an extremely happy summer together, with none of their usual tensions and pressures. They walked, as Peggy remembered it, up to twenty miles a day with Nakasan, who spoke little English. The Japan of the 1920s was still remarkably undeveloped: "We never touched a highway, never saw another European, we climbed and descended passes and mountain footpaths, our sensible boots held together only because Nakasan each morning laced Japanese peasant straw sandals over them — one bounced along on these 'cushions' and never felt the roughness of the tracks." In the evenings, the pair would have a hot Japanese bath and sleep at an inn. Peggy loved not only the simple food, but also its elegant and stark presentation. She was also very taken with the grace and charm of the Japanese people she met. Nakasan personified charm and diplomacy, and he managed never to offend Florence, as Peggy had feared he might — at least, until the moment of farewell, when he expressed his hope

Do you recognise Neville Trueman & your somewhat liberated Dragon Aunt? I suppose the ratio of 4-1 was safe enough for me to dismount?!

to guide them again next summer, with "the young lady's husband-to-be." Florence was not pleased with the implication and the tour was never repeated, but Peggy cherished the memories of it for the rest of her life.

Not least among the memories was the treasured experience of the last truly happy journey with her adoptive mother. By contrast, of the remainder of that year and much of the early part of 1922, Peggy had no memory at all. To some degree, this reflects her general state of denial about her circumstances. For Peggy – ostensibly privileged, well educated, and wealthy, a young woman poised on the brink of great potential and opportunity – life in one of the most exciting cities on earth was almost unbearably dreary and restricted. Despite her dreams, she was starting to lose hope that she would soon meet that ideal husband of hers: "I was still the misfit of my generation." Florence certainly had no motivation to promote any opportunity for Peggy to abandon her side by introducing her to eligible young men; if anything, she actively discouraged it. Peggy had neither the money, nor, at that age, the personality, to strike out independently. She was still very much a conformist – simply following her mother's directions – and could not even begin to think of stepping aside from what she considered to be her duty to support Florence in favour of enjoying herself. The risk was that Florence might disown her, although it is unlikely that Peggy consciously formulated this thought. More likely, she tried to rationalize her growing misery by concluding that this was mostly the result of normal mother–daughter tensions.

Peggy threw herself into her music, which more and more was becoming her solace and "food for the soul." Within her general state of wretchedness, it was slowly starting to dawn on Peggy that this unhappy situation might continue for a long time. There seemed to be little room for optimism.

7

The crazy years

"Even years later, when 'life with Mamma' became exceedingly difficult —
when the gaiety had changed to a self-centred and dictatorial attitude and
manner and the imaginative flights of fancy became masterpieces of self-
deception, that charm would flare up from time to time and one would
forget the biting tongue and the unreasonableness. (And nearly sixty years
ago, even Nico was conscious of this charm!)"

— Peggy Abkhazi, *A Dragon Aunt Remembers*

In 1922 Peggy experienced several events that were to have a lifelong impact upon her, in ways both great and small. Early in the year Florence, impulsive as ever, had decided it was time to return to Europe to continue "broadening" Peggy's interests. The real excuse, Peggy felt certain, was to prevent them becoming too settled in Shanghai. Her temperamental mother was easily and quickly bored — in all likelihood she was also fearful that the longer they stayed, the more probable it would be that Peggy would meet and fall in love with a young man who would then take her away from Florence. Earlier the Pembertons had been invited to visit, of all places, a remote farm in Saskatchewan, Canada — the home of Bromley Hill, who was the son of an old friend of Florence and Thomas Pemberton and who had visited them in England during the war. Thus, almost a year to the day that Muriel Langtry had passed through Shanghai on the *Empress of Asia*, Florence and Peggy embarked on the same vessel, this time returning to Canada. As it turned out, Muriel was once again on the boat, travelling to Victoria, British Columbia, for a visit to her family with her new husband. The two young women still did not meet: Muriel, a few years older than Peggy and still in a state of new matrimonial bliss, did not seem to notice the shy younger girl who did, however, notice Muriel. She stared at Muriel from the shadows, fascinated and enchanted by her beauty, vivacity, and gaiety. Peggy was too intimidated to introduce herself to this vision of feminine confidence and happiness, and another opportunity for the pair to become acquainted slipped away.

On this trip Peggy had her first glimpse of Victoria, the city that would eventually play such a large role in her later life, when the *Empress* tied up briefly at the city's passenger wharf at Ogden Point, on its way on to Vancouver. Peggy had no chance to explore, and remembered little, if anything, of her initial impressions. She was however certainly far from impressed with her subsequent visit by train to the prairies of Canada. Their "dreary awfulness" prejudiced the young woman so thoroughly against Canada that she promptly vowed that she would never live in that country.

In the fall of 1922 Florence made another impulsive decision, this time one that was to result in a much happier existence for Peggy over the next couple of years. If Peggy was ever to become a concert pianist, Florence insisted, then she must live and study in Paris, France. With some wariness, given her previous experience, Peggy listened to Florence outline her great scheme. They would once again share an apartment with an old friend from Shanghai days – this time, a pleasant and kindly older woman named Florence Struve, with whom Florence Pemberton had much in common and who seemed better able to manage the other woman's temperamental outbursts. Peggy was thrilled at the thought of returning to her favourite city, especially to study the music she loved – the possibility of becoming a concert pianist had not yet been dispelled from her catalogue of hopes – and to live there for an extended period of time, so she swallowed her fears. The pair moved into Mrs. Struve's attractive apartment in Auteuil, a quiet tree-lined residential district in the 16th arrondissement, in the west end of Paris. Peggy found it a glorious and tranquil place, a semi-rural European setting like that of Kennet in Scotland or of the Alpine villages of Switzerland already so dear to her heart: "Even in those days, goat herds used to bring in their goats early on a spring morning, blowing on their flutes enabled the apartment dwellers to run out on to the sidewalk, jugs in their hands, and have the goat milked straight into the jug! And yet it was only fifteen minutes by underground to the centre of Paris. Once again I was enchanted by the lovely city and its special atmosphere."

Paris in the ebullient 1920s was definitely as Peggy as found it – a place with a very special atmosphere. As she studied her piano lessons with Isidore Philippe, who was said to have studied in his youth with one of Chopin's own pupils, she was surrounded by the inhabitants of "les années folles," the crazy years of Paris. With the relief of the end of the First World War still fresh for everyone, freedom was literally in the air, both politically and artistically. It was impossible to walk down the streets of Paris without tripping over writers, artists, dancers, and musicians, as well as political activists and philosophers, all testing the waters of liberal and artistic democracy to the fullest extent possible. The French currency was so weak that it was possible to buy a month's supply of bread with one American dollar, and the city was flooded with young and aspiring writers from the United States,

Mrs. Florence Struve, December 30, 1921. It was through Mrs. Struve, who was an old friend of the Pembertons from their Shanghai days, that Peggy Pemberton first met Nicolas Abkhazi in Paris in 1922.
ROD BREEN/MACKENZIE FAMILY

sampling the pleasures of Paris and searching for someone to sponsor their writing of a great novel. F. Scott Fitzgerald wrote *The Great Gatsby* in Paris in 1925, in good company with many other well-known foreign writers then living in the city: Ernest Hemingway, John dos Passos, Gertrude Stein, Ezra Pound, e.e. cummings, James Joyce, and T.S. Eliot graced the literary hallways of Paris from time to time over those tempestuous years. In 1922, the year that Peggy arrived, Joyce produced his *Ulysses*, breaking all the rules of English novel-writing. In the cafés and bars, Jacques Prévert and Jean Cocteau were both writing their lyrical poetry. Les Ballets Russes were active, under the leadership of the flamboyant Sergei Diaghilev and frequently accompanied by the great composer Igor Stravinsky, who was already famous for his controversial modernist work *The Rite of Spring*, which had provoked riots when it first was performed, even in that modern and thoughtful city. Jazz, especially black American jazz performed by great artists like Sidney Bechet, was becoming hugely popular, and Cole Porter and his contemporaries were performing in the best nightclubs. Pablo Picasso, Joan Miró, and Marc Chagall all kept studios in the bohemian art district. Cubism was no longer avant-garde, and even art deco was giving way to the new trend towards surrealism. American photographer Man Ray was photographing the artists and musicians and their friends, and gaining his own following in the art world, while Frenchman Henri Cartier-Bresson, in his moment of epiphany, defined the principle of the "decisive moment" of making a photograph and changed the concept of photography forever. Followers of the extreme anarchist Dada movement, inspired by the ridiculous and the insane, searched tirelessly for ever-crazier stunts to pull off and prove that this new artistic and philosophical world had no limits or, indeed, sense to it.

Women were also embracing the new freedoms, especially after France's women were finally enfranchised in 1919. The French feminist movement was very strong, and women were encouraged to be independent. Fashion promptly followed the new freedom, and in Paris, Coco Chanel hit town, introducing a simple new fragrance in a plain glass bottle with black lettering on the side, a new concept for presenting perfume that had never been tried before. Thus Chanel No. 5 was born and was soon followed by another of the designer's signature items, the mass-produced essential Chanel "little black dress." Actresses and dancers flocked to the city, seeking diversion, if not employment.

In 1927 American dancer Isadora Duncan died, famously, when her long, trailing white scarf was caught under the wheels of her accelerating convertible and instantly snapped her neck, moments after she had driven off, calling to her friends, "Adieu, mes amis, je vais à la gloire." There were also many single American women in Paris, lonely heiresses looking for an impoverished European aristocrat to marry, someone willing to trade their title for a fortune. And there was plenty of opportunity: as well as numerous European counts and barons, there were many Russian and Baltic aristocrats who had chosen Paris as their place of refuge after the 1917 Bolshevik Revolution.

A large community of expatriate Georgians who also had been victims of the revolution were living, for the most part, in the 15th arrondissement – only the wealthier ones could afford the more luxurious 16th arrondissement. The Georgians considered themselves rather different from the Russians, having never fully accepted Russia's annexation of their province in the previous century, and they lived somewhat apart from the Russians' rather dissolute expatriate lifestyle. For one thing, the Georgian community assumed that their stay in Paris would be brief – that before long, the Bolsheviks would be defeated and that they would be restored to their rightful aristocratic heritage. Among this group of Georgian refugees at the time that Peggy arrived in Paris in the autumn of 1922 was a young nobleman, Prince Nicolas Abkhazi. Born in 1899 in Tiflis (modern-day Tbilisi, in southeast Georgia), the twenty-three-year-old Georgian prince was the last surviving son of a line of ancient kings of Abkhazia, a region on the Black Sea near the Turkish border. His great-grandfather had been the last King of Abkhazia at the time the tiny kingdom joined the Province of Georgia, and was then annexed by the Russian Empire in 1864. On joining that empire, such small states became principalities and their princes became part of the government of the provinces. Nicolas's father, General Prince Constantin Abkhazi, had remained in Russia after the 1917 revolution to protect his title and his estate; but fearing for the safety of his wife, Princess Héléne, and his then eighteen-year-old son, he had sent them out of the country in the company of a friend, who had brought them to Paris.

In France, the members of the refugee Georgian community generally seemed to be at a loss as to what to do with their lives. Hoping to return to Georgia soon, they had filled in the time in various leisurely ways. It was, remarked Peggy several decades later, a sad waste of their days. Many believed they were simply going through an unpleasant but temporary period that would soon pass, and accordingly few of them made an effort to become established in Paris until they realized, years later, that they were in France to stay. By then it was too late to do anything very meaningful with their new lives. Prince Nicolas Abkhazi, on the other hand, appeared to be an exception; he almost immediately enrolled at the Academy of Paris to study law. He was young enough to justify seeking an education, even in France, and was not intimidated by the foreign university – he also wanted to prepare himself to govern his province, if it should come to that. But it was just as well that he had chosen a course of study that would give him other options. On May 23, 1923, Abkhazia's Prince Constantin was brutally executed by the Bolshevik government. Nicolas never returned to his homeland, nor did he ever receive his rightful inheritance.

Nicolas Abkhazi's mother was Princess Hélène Abkhazi, or "Elene" in her native Georgia. She was an elegant and gracious woman whom Peggy held in great awe. UNIVERSITY OF VICTORIA ARCHIVES

OPPOSITE:
Nicolas Abkhazi's Georgian passport. Nicolas is twenty years old in the photograph. UNIVERSITY OF VICTORIA ARCHIVES

REPUBLIQUE GÉORGIENNE

PASSEPORT № *6741*

Les autorités chargées de maintenir l'ordre dans les Etats sont priées de laisser passer librement Monsieur *Nicolas Abchazi* citoyen géorgien, demeurant à *Tiflis* allant à l'étranger et de lui accorder aide et protection en cas de besoin.

Signalement:

Taille *moyenne*
Cheveux *bruns*
Yeux *noirs*
Visage *rond*
Signes particuliers

Signature de porteur

En foi de quoi le présent passeport lui a été delivré à Tiflis le *25 septembre 1919*

Le Directeur de la Chancellerie du ministère des affaires étrangères

Prince Nicolas Abkhazi in Paris, France, July 15, 1922 (front row, far left). The photograph was taken a year before his father's execution by the Bolshevik government in the Soviet Union - his companions are unidentified but are likely to be fellow Georgian refugees. UNIVERSITY OF VICTORIA ARCHIVES

This sad event was still several months away, however, when Peggy settled into her music studies in Paris in earnest. In Florence Struve's apartment, she had a room of her own, and she relished the newfound privacy that it offered. Her Mamma seemed quite content living with Mrs. Struve, and the two older women appeared to be enjoying each other's company. Peggy's Mamma even agreed when Mrs. Struve suggested that Peggy should really be taking advantage of living in Paris by visiting the art galleries and museums and attending concerts. Mrs. Struve had in mind her young friend, the same Prince Nicolas Abkhazi, as an eminently suitable escort for Peggy. Wisely, she did not suggest the idea immediately to Florence; she simply made occasional casual references to a "Georgian prince," with only the vaguest of implications that he might be someone that they should eventually meet. Peggy paid little attention, assuming that her mother would quickly squash any notions that might involve her getting to know an exotic Georgian prince; until the night Mrs. Struve surprised both Florence and Peggy by inviting Nicolas to the apartment for refreshments and suggesting to him that he might escort Peggy to some of the interesting parts of Paris on his free Thursday afternoons. Peggy was thoroughly embarrassed, but Nicolas readily agreed; and to her utter astonishment, so did her mother. Florence Pemberton appeared to be hypnotized by Nicolas's old world charm and raised no objections, despite the fact that it was quite a breach of proper etiquette for a young man and woman to be unchaperoned on such outings. The only rules that Florence imposed were that Peggy pay her own expenses, no doubt a relief to the charming but impoverished Nicolas, and that the two should not sit down together at any time. Determined not to lose her daughter's companionship just yet, presumably Florence imagined that by keeping Peggy standing or walking she could minimize the risk of any romantic relationship ensuing.

Peggy passed a pleasant winter and spring of 1923, studying hard and enjoying her weekly excursions with Prince Nicolas. The pair did not embrace the raging and outrageous cultural revolution sweeping through Paris, preferring innocent ramblings through museums and galleries, gardens and parks; never once, of course, sitting down together. Nicolas spoke no English then, and Peggy's conversational French became near-perfect as a result. Despite the idyllic situation, Florence had nothing to worry about – romance did not yet appear to enter into the equation. Peggy was only twenty-one and had her mind on other things, including her music. She may also have not thought of an impoverished Georgian aristocrat, title or no title, as the ideal husband that she continued to dream about. For his part, Nicolas was heavily engaged in his studies and he would not obtain his licence to practise law until March 1924. Still in his early twenties, he may not yet have given up hope of returning to rule Abkhazia some day. At any rate, his mind was very unlikely to have been on marriage at that time. His passport photograph shows a dashing and handsome young man, whose charm had already been demonstrated to be hypnotic with women of all ages. In photographs of Nicolas from this period, he is almost always in the company of attractive young women – and none of them are Peggy.

The lack of a romantic attachment may have been a great relief to Princess Hélène as well as to Florence. Although she approved of her son's young companion, she was also unlikely to have wanted their relationship to develop beyond friendship. Nearly sixty years later, Peggy jokingly recounted that Nicolas's mother did not want him to marry anyone not Russian and royal, and that her Mamma did not want Peggy to marry a foreigner, as she assumed

Princess Hélène Abkhazi, date unknown. UNIVERSITY OF VICTORIA ARCHIVES

that all foreign men were fortune hunters. As it would turn out, it was unfortunate for Peggy that Florence had not had that perception with regard to Englishmen instead. But what the two mothers thought appeared to be irrelevant. The two young people formed a firm platonic and intellectual friendship based on their weekly excursions and their mutual love of art and literature, and they appeared to think nothing more of it at the time.

As the summer of 1923 approached, both university classes and Peggy's music lessons came to an end for the season, and Peggy and Florence prepared to return to Sandgate and Kennet for the summer. Peggy looked forward to a relaxing summer and to resuming her studies and her excursions with Prince Nicolas again in September. But seemingly out of nowhere, over some trivial and long-forgotten thing, came the long-dreaded quarrel between Florence and Mrs. Struve. It occurred only a few days before the Pembertons were due to leave for England, and there was no time to repair the friendship between the two older women. Peggy would not be able to get in touch with her kind benefactor for almost twenty-five years. Worse, she temporarily lost contact with her other good friend, Prince Nicolas, with whom mutual contact had been kept through Mrs. Struve. It would not have "done" at all for Peggy to initiate contact with the young man directly, and Florence almost certainly would not have permitted her to break the conventions in attempting to do so.

Florence and Peggy did return, briefly, to Paris in late 1923, but the idyll

Prince Nicolas Abkhazi with his mother, Princess Hélène, in France, 1920s. Nicolas was managing a large estate for an American couple named Kelly. It is possible that this estate is the location of the photograph. UNIVERSITY OF VICTORIA ARCHIVES

of the previous winter was not to be repeated. Peggy may have contrived to see Nicolas, despite her mother, but it seems unlikely. Her mind seemed fully occupied with her music and dealing with Florence. They stayed in Paris only long enough for a few more piano lessons, which proved fruitful for Peggy because she learned through her teacher that it was possible to purchase a portable "silent" keyboard to practise upon while travelling. No longer would she have to endure practising her piano music in public as she roamed the world with Florence. The keyboard that she promptly bought was to be her most useful possession over the next ten years of her life.

8

To travel
hopefully

*"One always has to pay, in some manner, for
everything that one receives in life."*

— Peggy Abkhazi, letter to Philippa, January 8, 1970

In December 1923 Peggy turned twenty-one and entered her
majority. She had not known about it, but Mabel Blackburn Carter had left
her daughter an inheritance of jewellery in trust, to be given to Peggy on her
twenty-first birthday. Florence and Peggy travelled to London to meet Peggy's
Aunt Agnes Blackburn and another of her uncles and to receive her inheritance
— a starburst diamond brooch of
substantial value, which Peggy thought
quite beautiful. As pleased as she may
have been with the brooch and much to
Florence's delight, Peggy — by now used

*Peggy's twenty-first birthday portrait.
She celebrated her birthday with Florence
Pemberton in Folkestone, England.*
PHILIPPA PROUDFOOT (NÉE DAVYS)

to mixing in more sophisticated circles – was snobbishly unimpressed by her relatives. It was to be her last meeting with any of her Blackburn family; she never contacted or heard from any of them again. Given her experiences as a small child, her biological family, with the possible exception of the young mother who had died before Peggy could really know her, meant little to Peggy. "Being a lone wolf, I haven't the least conception what a 'blood relationship' means – or if it really means anything at all," she wrote in a letter to her goddaughter nearly fifty years later.

For the next ten years of her life Peggy rarely stayed in one place for very long. Florence roamed the world restlessly, with her daughter always close to her side. Despite all their travels, the Pembertons seemed to have been astonishingly well insulated by their wealth and lifestyle from the significant events of that decade. In her written reminiscences of those years, Peggy was completely self-absorbed – she simply recorded the day-to-day events of her travels and her reactions to the places she visited, and occasionally recounted the increasing tensions of her relationship with Florence. Peggy was constantly trying to deal with her own difficult emotional position with regard to her adoptive mother. There is no indication that Peggy was even slightly interested in, or affected by, the significant political, social, and economic issues of those years: the Japanese threat in China; the growing German influence in Europe; even the onset of the Great Depression in 1929 all went by without so much as a passing remark from her. This may partly have been a reflection of her relative youth; as the years went by, Peggy became much more aware of her environment. In 1966, after reading Malraux's *La Condition Humaine*, she marvelled at the fact that in 1927 she had been completely unaware of the violent struggle taking place around her in Shanghai between Chiang Kai-shek's militia and the communists. But even forty years later, she preferred to imply that the absence of modern media and communications was to blame, rather than the intellectual isolation of her wealth and lifestyle at the time.

On the surface, the lifestyle that Florence and Peggy led was certainly luxurious and attractive – travelling the world on sumptuous ocean liners, staying in first-class hotels, and being waited on constantly. But beneath the surface of that privileged and insular existence, Peggy could not escape from her problems. The excitement of travel could not make up for the lack of a stable home or of any real freedom. A young Englishwoman of Peggy's class was not expected to seek employment, much to Peggy's later regret, and she therefore completely relied on Florence for an income. The constant moving around made a discouraging joke out of any aspirations for Peggy to ever become a concert pianist. Most regrettably, she was rarely able to make enduring friendships with people of her own age. Peggy remained at Florence's side as her Mamma's closest social companion, bound by her ironclad sense of responsibility and of the debt of gratitude owed by her. It was a painful and disappointing way for her to spend those long years of her youth.

Immediately after her daughter's twenty-first birthday, Florence had decided that it was time once again to return to Shanghai, but this time by way of an extended South Seas tour through Australia, New Zealand, and Hawaii. The trip "followed the usual pattern of life with Mamma during these years…a shared bedroom in some hotel, strict chaperonage at any party or outing, and gin rummy every evening. I often felt that one might as well have stayed put in one place; the alleged 'broadening effects' of world travel did not seem to operate very well in my case." Peggy was not totally numb to her environment, however. By now well established in her preference for warm sunshine and beach resorts, glamorous European or Asian cities, and pretty rural settings, Peggy was appalled by the backward, dull Antipodean countries she visited. Australia she described as a "nightmare" place. She disliked the topography and the food, and had difficulty adjusting to the fact that Australia, like New Zealand, was a country ruled by the middle class and one in which people were not accustomed to having servants or hired domestic help of any kind. Notwithstanding her own middle-class origins and her apparent boredom with her lifestyle, Peggy had well and truly become one of the idle rich. The way of life in this British corner of the South Pacific was not at all like the life she was used to in China, where a ready supply of local labour was always available at her beck and call. The Australian coast was as hot as Shanghai, but completely without the conveniences at hand in that city: the right kind of clothing, and servants to wash the clothes daily, "even if you changed four times a day." There was in her view no suitable food to be had anywhere in Australia, and in any event there was no ice to keep what food there was fresh. And "as for the so-called 'outback', it was hideous – hot, dusty and frightening – with peculiar indigenous animals, sort of leftovers from the dinosaur period…ugh!" New Zealand she found a little more hospitable, and she enjoyed

Peggy and Florence Pemberton on a hiking trip in the 1920s, probably in New Zealand.
UNIVERSITY OF VICTORIA ARCHIVES

the spectacular scenery, but Peggy found the young cities there backward and tedious beyond belief by comparison to the mature, sophisticated metropolises of Europe and Asia. Had she not had a significant reason to return to that country many years later, it is doubtful that she would have ever given New Zealand any further thought.

When she arrived in Honolulu with Florence in June 1924, however, Peggy was instantly enraptured. Here were all the ingredients to please her sensibilities: a warm, tropical climate, lanes and cottages lined with sweet-smelling frangipani and a multitude of other colourful, fragrant flowers, and dazzling white beaches, where she could swim in the clear, intensely coloured water of the Pacific Ocean among an array of bright tropical fish. Peggy was back in an environment that she loved: "I was enchanted by this atmosphere of soft warmth and idleness and no hurry and all the time in the world for courtesy – and the beauty of the place, and the beauty of the mixed-race Orientals... Chinese/ Polynesian/Japanese...an atmosphere in which I felt at home."

Peggy and Florence installed themselves in a unique little hotel called the

Melbourne, Australia, 1920s. Florence and Peggy visited the city on their travels during that period, but Peggy thoroughly disliked everything about Australia.
UNIVERSITY OF VICTORIA ARCHIVES

Peggy Pemberton in Hawaii, 1924-25. SUSAN HAMERSLEY/ MACKENZIE FAMILY

Halekulani, comprised of six cottages built on Waikiki Beach. Here all of the modern amenities were on hand, notwithstanding the hotel's relatively remote location in those days. The most marvellous innovation to Peggy's mind was the Halekulani's American "hostess," a woman who played a role similar to that of a liaison officer on a modern-day cruise ship — ensuring that all of the guests were suitably entertained according to their needs. For Peggy, the hostess was a godsend. On meeting the two Pembertons, the charming and diplomatic woman intuitively assessed the situation and immediately took the younger woman under her wing. She tactfully subverted Florence from insisting upon the nightly rummy games with Peggy by persuading her that she was an essential fourth for playing bridge with some other guests. It was Florence's favourite game, and apparently she could not resist the flattery. Peggy was left free to go to the nightly beach parties instead, accompanied by the hostess, who assured Florence that she would chaperone. The motherly hostess also took the opportunity to give Peggy some much-needed advice, bypassing Florence altogether to take the young woman shopping for a more suitable bathing suit than the one she owned — and for Peggy's very first bra. Florence, born in the corset-wearing era, had always dismissed bras as suitable only "for actresses and such like" to wear. Those three months in Waikiki — "full of delightful laziness and swimming and the agreeable company of my own age group" — were happy for Peggy, but she knew by now that they would be fleeting. At the end of September she said goodbye to her new acquaintances and friends, and continued the prolonged journey with Florence to Shanghai.

Little occurred to mark the following year in Peggy's memory. It followed the usual routine of music practice and the reinstituted rummy games, interspersed with visits to family friends at Tientsin, in northern China (now called Tianjin) and Peitaiho, a seaside resort for non-Chinese close to Tientsin; and to Peking, a city that Peggy instantly loved, comparing it to Paris. She enjoyed most of all staying with the friends at Peitaiho and the relief of having something like a home life there, with pets around, home-cooked food, and a family atmosphere. To Peggy's resignation, it was once again short-lived — apart from the usual quarrel between Florence and her hostess that ended the visit abruptly, Peggy's much-loved guardian, Dr. Goode, suddenly died of a heart attack in Shanghai, and she and Florence returned immediately to the International Settlement.

Back in their hotel in Shanghai, Florence attempted to console her grief-stricken daughter with an unusual gift, considering her tendency to keep Peggy under her eye: a red Morris Oxford car. Although Florence was selfish and often irrational, she also loved Peggy and had always responded positively to what she considered was legitimate anguish on her daughter's part. So, while she would still not let Peggy wear "unsuitable" clothing or attend "improper" social functions, she also allowed Peggy to purchase her own horse, an elegant chestnut that Peggy rode every day. The daily rides afforded her some welcome relief from Florence's company, and she met a number of eligible young men who pursued her in an ad hoc fashion. But her spirits were so low that Peggy did little, if anything, to encourage them, feeling it was futile. Her circle of single girlfriends provided some diversion and support, but like the fictional Bridget Jones, with dismay she watched the circle grow ever smaller as, one by one, those friends became engaged and moved on. Looking back on this period of life many years later, Peggy found it hard to believe that any modern twenty-three-year-old "would be so spineless," simply waiting passively for something, or anything, to happen to make her life change.

Peggy's music offered her the only real solace and sense of purpose in a life that otherwise felt increasingly pointless. It was also a topic on which it was apparently still relatively easy to convince Florence of anything that Peggy wanted: by 1927 she had decided that she wanted to study the German school of technique and interpretation. Florence acquiesced, and the pair immediately began preparations to move to Vienna, the "city of melodies." Stopping for a few days in Paris to collect a letter of introduction from her former music teacher to the great Viennese pianist Emil Sauer, Peggy managed to briefly renew her acquaintance with Prince Nicolas, despite the breach of convention. She must not, after all, have been quite as spineless as she thought. In the years since they had last met, Nicolas had received his law degree and embarked upon his career as a lawyer. When Peggy and Florence passed through Paris, he was managing the large estate and associated affairs of a wealthy American couple named Kelly. This time, eager not to lose touch again with such a good friend, Peggy must also have obtained a mailing address for Nicolas. From then on and for the next few years the two continued to correspond sporadically, and they were even able to meet occasionally whenever Peggy and Florence were in the city.

The Pembertons spent nine months over the winter and spring of 1927 and 1928 living in the district of Hegelgasse, just behind the Vienna Opera House and not far from the Danube River. Many wealthy expatriate British people lived permanently in Vienna at the time, taking advantage of the city's rich musical heritage; but beautiful as it was, Peggy disliked Vienna and never became accustomed to what she described as its dreary oppressiveness. The cold blackness of the European winter could not have helped; nor did the visible poverty that was the legacy of the Versailles Treaty's dismantling of the Austro-Hungarian Empire. Vienna was left with an enormous population — well over two million people — but little in the way of natural resources to support the Austrian economy, and even less in the way of foreign exchange to purchase imported food and goods. What the city had not lost, thankfully, were its musical, artistic, and architectural riches, and in these Peggy revelled. If she could not enjoy the mood of the city itself, she did take great pleasure in the magnificent Gothic, Renaissance, and Baroque buildings that she visited. She recalled with awe the Hofburg Art Gallery, where, in 1928, visitors could still examine by hand the original sketches of Michelangelo, Raphael, and Dürer — an unimaginable privilege now. She also immersed herself in her music lessons, in hour upon hour of daily practice, and in as many concerts, choirs, recitals, and operas as she could attend. She found the glorious music of Bach, Haydn, and Mozart "a perpetual festival." She sank into the pews of the Hofkapelle, the Hofburg Palace Chapel, to listen to the most perfect acoustics she had ever experienced. Vienna itself may have left her cold, but its music filled her soul and warmed her heart. The stay marked a turning point in Peggy's appreciation of music, from enjoyment of simply playing it herself — mostly at social engagements — to an indelible passion for hearing the perfect compositions and the master practitioners of the art performing them. It was a passion that she retained for the rest of her life, and one that eventually would replace any trace of a desire she may ever have had to be on the concert stage herself. The conscious closing of that door was still to come, however; in the meantime, Peggy embraced her music and continued to practise and to play — hour after hour, day after day, year after year.

OPPOSITE: *Peggy and Florence hiking, 1920s. Their companion may be Peggy's former tutor, John Ferguson.* SUSAN HAMERSLEY/MACKENZIE FAMILY

PAGES 98-101:
China, 1920s: scenes from Florence and Peggy Pemberton's travels. SUSAN HAMERSLEY/ MACKENZIE FAMILY

Florence Pemberton is in the foreground
of this photograph.

ABOVE: *Peitaiho, China, mid-1920s. Florence and Peggy Pemberton with a daughter of friends at this seaside resort, which was exclusively for the use of Europeans.*

9

Flight of fancy

*"I made an eminently suitable marriage when I was
27. The net result was five months of unmitigated
misery for two people."*

— Peggy Abkhazi, letter to Philippa, January 8, 1970

PEGGY PLAYED THE PIANO TO ACCOMPANY HIM WHILE HE SANG. HE HAD
red hair and blue eyes, and he was very handsome and spirited. He was born
and brought up in Japan, but he was British; and by the late 1920s he was also
of increasingly limited means but of sufficient social standing to mix in Peggy's
upper-class circles. He was, perhaps, in character a little like Peggy's father,
the wayward William Carter. At evening entertainments he singled her out
and wooed her with determination. Peggy, the ugly duckling, the naïve, self-
described "elderly teenager," fell hard. Excitedly, she wrote letters and sent
photographs of him to friends. On the back of the one that she sent to her
friend Prince Nicolas in Paris, she wrote in French: "A group in our garden —

my fiancé is to my left." This time, Florence seemed unable to prevent the inevitable. Despite the warnings and objections her mother must have raised, Peggy was quite determined to marry the man, as he was her, and in 1929 they wed. And to give Florence credit, having been unsuccessful in changing Peggy's mind, she appears to have supported Peggy in her decision and even to have provided the newlyweds with an income.

Unfortunately, on both sides, the motivations were flawed. Peggy saw the means to escape from Florence's clutches and obtain the freedom to live a normal life. Her husband saw the solution to his financial problems. From the moment they were married, it seems, Peggy was virtually ignored – an inconvenient by-product of her husband's real objective in getting married. She was unceremoniously left at home while her husband resumed his lively social life, using his newly acquired funds. But if he thought that he had married a typically submissive young Englishwoman, bred to obey her husband, he was quite wrong. Peggy, despite appearances to the contrary, was not about to stay captive in a new life that was turning out to be worse than the old. With Florence, at least Peggy had the consolation of her adoptive mother's love and desire for her daughter's company. Within months Peggy left her husband and returned to her Mamma, saddened by the "rancour and squalors of a short marriage entered into, on both sides, for all the wrong reasons."

It was no easy feat to obtain a divorce in the early 1930s. Peggy's humiliation was twofold: first, that she had been so blindly misled by the man in question, and second, that she was forced to turn to her mother for help in buying off her husband. It took four years of demeaning negotiations to extricate Peggy from her predicament, but in 1934 she finally obtained her divorce papers in London, England. In Peggy's own eyes, she felt that she had failed greatly. It was an episode in her life that she did not attempt to hide, nor could she – she was required to disclose her marital status on legal documents, including her certificate of marriage to her future second husband — but neither did she ever discuss the marriage in any depth with even her closest confidantes. Many of her acquaintances later in life did not know of her first marriage at all, and there is no record of his name in any of Peggy's remaining papers; to be divorced in the 1930s was to have many doors automatically closed, so the subject was best not mentioned. Further, in making her poor choice of a husband, Peggy had contrived, in her own mind at any rate, to bungle her life even more. Rather than escaping from her mother, she now felt an even deeper sense of obligation to Florence for rescuing her – for the second time in her life – from deeply unsatisfactory circumstances. The bond of obligation, if not love, became even stronger.

At some point, Peggy stopped corresponding with her friend Prince Nicolas in Paris. Florence may have raised objections to Peggy writing to another man when she was getting married, or perhaps Peggy herself had eventually thought it unsuitable. It would be some time before she had the courage or inclination to renew the friendship. They met at least once again, in 1933, and continued to write to each other – but it was the last time that the two friends saw each other for thirteen years. Nicolas had accepted that a return to Georgia was not going to occur, and in May 1930 he became a

Florence and Peggy Pemberton with unidentified friends in their garden in Shanghai. To Peggy's left is her fiancé, whose name is unknown. ROD BREEN/MACKENZIE FAMILY

The Great Wall of China, 1930s. Florence Pemberton is in the foreground.
SUSAN HAMERSLEY/MACKENZIE FAMILY

naturalized citizen of France. Apart from this one commitment, he seemed to float, disconnected, in a sea of indecision. Still unmarried, Nicolas had moved from estate management into a variety of occupations, ranging from perfume merchant to chicken farmer. His path, although confined to Paris, seemed just as aimless as Peggy's.

Of these exceedingly miserable four years in Peggy's life, there is little written or said. Florence and Peggy continued their travels, keeping an eye on divorce proceedings in London in the meantime. The stress of recent events was starting to tell, and the endless round of hotel rooms and travel schedules became more tiring than entertaining. Settling back in England held little attraction for Florence, however; she was more accustomed to the

Florence Pemberton, Shanghai, 1931.
ROD BREEN/MACKENZIE FAMILY

Peggy Pemberton in a Shanghai garden, with tame pigeons, circa 1930. PHILIPPA PROUDFOOT (NÉE DAVYS)

excitement of living in a lively international community. In 1934, for someone with money, it was still possible to live in one of the few remaining international expatriate enclaves scattered around the globe in a style in which the most pressing decisions concerned which social engagements to accept or how many servants would be required. The political realities of a world teetering toward a second global conflict could be ignored in such places, if they were even considered. But this was increasingly difficult to do in London or Paris; and the more remote parts of the world, such as New Zealand or Australia, were still far too dull and pedestrian to contemplate. So Florence decided to return to Shanghai yet again with Peggy, and to settle down for a period. She remembered her previous life there with great pleasure, and it seemed as if it could be resumed with no great difficulty. Still completely cowed by her experiences of the last few years, Peggy appears to have raised no murmur of dissent. As soon as her divorce papers were obtained in early 1934 Florence made plans, and within a few

OPPOSITE: *Peggy Pemberton in Shanghai, 1930, immediately after her engagement to her first husband.*
PHILIPPA PROUDFOOT (NÉE DAVYS)

weeks the Pembertons boarded a German cargo boat and set off once again from London for Shanghai. They did not know it at the time, but it would be a full ten months before they reached their destination. The trip would also, finally, spell the last of their travelling days together.

On the day that their vessel arrived in Port Said, at the Mediterranean end of the Suez Canal in Egypt, Florence suffered a severe stroke. Peggy did not recount the events leading up to the stroke but simply referred obliquely to the fact that the journey up until then had been a "very difficult situation" for both of them. Florence and Peggy had been spending twenty-four hours a day together, throughout their travels. The stress must have been enormous; and on the ship, with little room to escape each other's company, it must have been intensified further. Given Florence's inclination to provoke arguments, she and Peggy may well have quarrelled, or perhaps she simply wound herself up to the point of having the stroke. Regardless of the cause, Florence's condition required immediate medical attention and it was impossible for the Pembertons to continue their journey.

They were landed in Port Said under the charge of the port's doctor, "a charming but slightly tricky Greek, who rejoiced in the name of Skouphopoulis." Dr. Skouphopoulis, despite Peggy's less than flattering description of him, was the respected and undisputed leader of the port's medical community and initially housed the Pembertons in one of the local convents, possibly the famous Bon Pasteur. There, Florence was attended to by the nuns, who were also competent nurses. Eventually, as Florence's health and mobility improved slightly, Dr. Skouphopoulis moved the pair to less austere surroundings, a pleasant hotel run by a Madame Caffes, who was part Greek and part Arab. Peggy implied that the good doctor may well have supplemented his legal fees with a commission from the referral, but if so, he earned it — Peggy found it a delightful establishment, and the pair were very comfortable. They had two large, airy rooms facing the Mediterranean and were well fed on excellent cuisine, something Peggy never failed to appreciate. And with Florence being attended to by Dr. Skouphopoulis and assorted nurses, Peggy had greater freedom than usual to roam.

Far from being a city containing "the concentrated essence of all the iniquities and all the vices in all the continents," as Kipling had described Port Said in 1890 in his novel *The Light That Failed*, Peggy had the sense rather of living in a pleasant French provincial town and, despite its relative youth, a reasonably sophisticated one. The climate was warm enough to suit her tastes, and despite the city's industrial origins, it had beautiful white sand beaches on the Mediterranean coast, with clear water safe for swimming and close enough for her to enjoy. Port Said, now known as Bur Said, was born not so much from commercial and industrial imperatives, but, as was so common in the nineteenth century, political motives. Egypt had not been a major player on the world's stage in the early 1800s; France and Britain were under pressure from commercial interests to provide a more direct, and safer, shipping route to the east. The two European powers also were locked in a continuing intense political and imperialist rivalry. France had the upper edge, given its longstanding connections with Egypt. Many high-ranking Egyptians were educated, as a matter of course, in France, and its language had already become the lingua franca of the region. Thus, at much the same time that the Erie Canal was under construction in New York state in the 1820s, the notion of building the Suez Canal was first seriously discussed in Paris.

Not until 1859, however, was Port Said actually founded by the French Canal Company to begin ten years of canal construction in the swampy delta at the north end of the Isthmus of Suez. It named the city after the Viceroy Said Pasha – "Said" in Arabic means "happy" – and established a pleasant residential district on the far bank of the canal at Port Fuad, providing elegant housing and parks for the French company executives and their families to enjoy. By the 1930s, when Peggy and Florence were staying in Port Said, it enjoyed many elegant homes, hotels, and municipal parks. The city by then had more than 100,000 people, and although it was much smaller than Shanghai, Peggy may have enjoyed it particularly for its similarity to that city – the style of construction of its buildings was also dictated by their swampy foundations, there was a distinctly continental atmosphere to the city, and it too had a very multicultural population.

There was far less rush and bustle in Port Said, however, than in the bigger Asian city. Sylvia Modelski, in her book *Port Said Revisited*, remarked of the city in the 1930s: "Heavy toil and maniacal haste...[are] not normal on the ground in Port Said where distances are so short that an unhurried gait is cultivated to foster the illusion that one is getting somewhere." But for a "sleepy provincial town," as Modelski described it, Port Said also enjoyed a cultivated lifestyle. It offered several elegant hotels, dancing and concerts, café terraces, and smart, well-stocked emporia. For strolling, there were popular promenades in parks like La Pepinière, laid out in the classic French style, and along the beautifully constructed stone West Jetty to the old lighthouse; and every kind of boating club imaginable, including the popular rowing club, Le Cercle Nautique. In the summer, French families would come to enjoy the resort facilities on the beautiful Mediterranean beaches west of the town. Amazingly, even as late as 1934, when the Pembertons were in residence, the city was a British protectorate, seized in opportunistic fashion immediately after the First World War on the pretext of protecting the Suez Canal. It would not be returned formally to Egypt until 1936.

It was, therefore, a pleasant enough city for two English refugees to have been cast ashore in. However, it was eight months that Peggy spent in yet another state of limbo, and she must have felt relieved when her mother eventually quarrelled with Dr. Skouphopoulis over his bills, which seemed to Florence to be excessive. This falling-out with one of the city's prominent citizens made their continuing presence in Port Said awkward, and Peggy felt the fact that Florence was fit enough to have a heated argument was a sign that she was certainly well enough to travel. Peggy decided that she and Florence had remained in port long enough, and they resumed their interrupted journey to Shanghai, arriving there late in 1934.

That decision marked a significant change in the relationship between Peggy and Florence. For the first time, other than in her unfortunate choice of her first husband, Peggy made the decisions that would affect them both; and Florence had little choice, or incentive, but to go along. It was a subtle shift, but an important one. From that time on, Peggy was no longer the silent partner. Rather, she was the one who initiated and implemented the decisions. It was perhaps the only way in which the thirty-three-year-old Peggy could continue to justify to herself the life she was leading. She was not about to abandon Florence at that stage of her mother's life, but taking control was probably necessary to make sense of her existence: "All in all, it was a lonely life during these years…along the road Mamma had lost all the friends of her generation, and of my age group, all were busy with their lives, husbands, and babies." Only the faithful John Henry Green, the middle-aged bachelor to whom Dr. Goode had introduced Peggy back in 1921, would remain at close hand. Still quietly in love with Peggy, he provided a rock of support for her to lean on through the next difficult three years, and beyond. Peggy obliquely implied later that she had not understood that poor, faithful John had been so in love with her. Upon her second marriage, many years later, John met Peggy with her hew husband just once, but chose never to visit her again; and she coyly remarked in her reminiscences, "It was years before I realized why." It is difficult to imagine that an intelligent, divorced woman in her thirties, no matter how naïve, could have not even once suspected that this devoted friend – her companion at social engagements, her "man around the house" at times of need – wanted desperately to be more than a friend. More likely, she turned a blind eye to the situation. It was flattering, it was convenient, and it filled an emotional if not a physical need in her life during what would otherwise have been a desolate period. Peggy did at least admit: "I do not know how I could have managed without him during those barren years."

In the meantime Peggy had settled Florence back into Shanghai in comfortable quarters and acquired a dachshund, Flush. The Pembertons were now in the good care of their new Number One Boy, Li. Shanghai was little changed since the late 1920s, and Peggy's awareness of the realities of life for the Chinese remained as limited as ever. She continued to live in a world completely bound up by her own comforts and wealth, her frustrations at her situation, and the care of her ailing Mamma. She was in little position to enjoy the ongoing high social life of the expatriate community in Shanghai, which continued to rollercoaster onward, regardless of the effects of the Great Depression elsewhere and the gathering darkness in Europe. For most foreigners still living in this city of three million people, it remained a vibrant and exciting international community, a unique environment where each nation set its own agenda, regardless of the Chinese. Dora Carney, a Canadian journalist who arrived in Shanghai in 1933, found the city an "exhilarating and bewildering experience." In an article she wrote for a Toronto newspaper, Carney enthusiastically described the excitement of living in a place where, despite the growing threat of war elsewhere, a collection of different nationalities was able to live in harmony and successfully manage their common issues.

And yet, beneath this supposed harmoniousness, Chiang Kai-shek's thugs continued to systematically and brutally eliminate members of the Chinese Communist Party, even within the sacrosanct walls of the International

Settlement; and the grounds of Lunghua Prison, on the outskirts of Shanghai, echoed daily with the rifle shots of executions. The Japanese continued to amass power on the borders of China, and an almost hysterical fear was growing among the Chinese people. Peggy remained apparently oblivious to it all. Of the Japanese invasion of August 1937 she makes absolutely no mention, despite the fact that even the International Settlement was heavily bombed, destroying buildings and homes — including the Palace Hotel that William Carter had designed thirty-five years earlier — and killing hundreds of civilians, with thousands of refugees pouring into Shanghai from the rural districts. Surely she was aware of the chaos, but she did not seem to be affected by it. Most foreigners left Shanghai, including Dora Carney. But many of the British chose to stay, despite warnings from their consulate. In her book about the origins and history of Shanghai, *The Rise and Fall of a Decadent City*, Stella Dong writes: "Many of the British women 'should have taken advantage of the opportunities to leave with their children,' remarked one Englishman, but stayed because they 'preferred the easy life of the Orient with numerous servants and chose to remain hoping that nothing serious would happen to them.'" But, even if she had wanted to, Peggy may not have been able to leave. By 1937 Florence's health was seriously failing, and doctors had diagnosed terminal cancer.

It was a bittersweet time for Peggy. Facing imminent death, Florence dropped all her pretences and affectations, and her finest qualities came back to the surface. For the first time in many years Peggy not only felt a genuine affection for her mother but, in caring for her, also regained a sense of purpose in life. Florence needed her, and Peggy responded accordingly. By the spring of 1938, however, it was clear that her mother did not have much longer to live. Peggy took her to a rented bungalow at the beach in Peitaiho, one of Florence's favourite spots, with an entourage including Li and a Russian nurse named Maria, and Florence died peacefully there three weeks later, on June 22. She was buried in a small cemetery near the village. "Maria and I and the clergyman, followed by Li at a respectful distance, conducting Flush on her leash, walked there soon after the dawn of a lovely June morning for a simple graveside service — to me, it was the essence of the peace and serenity which that poor woman never found during her lifetime." Florence was seventy years old when she died, after a life quite different from the one that she may have imagined unfolding for herself when she joined the "fishing fleet" so many years previously. In Peggy's memory, Florence remained "that extraordinary woman – a human being of more extreme contradictions than any other person I have ever met during my long life. Generous – and the opposite. Kind – and cruelly selfish. Full of charm – and quarrelsome and domineering. Only her physical good looks (in spite of illness and great suffering) remained unimpaired until the end."

Peggy was thirty-five years old. Although she was a mature woman who had had more unusual experiences than many of her contemporaries, she was still the "elderly teenager," quite unfamiliar with the social customs and behaviours of the late 1930s. Florence's death finally set her free to behave as she wished, and three quite significant changes occurred almost immediately – two of her own making, and one that was simply a happy coincidence of fate. Peggy immediately changed her name, adding a hyphenated "Carter" back to the end of it. It was a salute to her origins but did not eliminate the most influential people in her life, Thomas and Florence

Florence Pemberton in her sixties - always a striking, elegant woman. SUSAN HAMERSLEY/ MACKENZIE FAMILY

Pemberton. It was also, in all likelihood, a reclaiming of her identity. In addition, Peggy realized that there was more to life than endless piano practice in preparation for a career on the concert stage that was never going to happen. Music was still a passion, but it was no longer the "food for the soul" that it had once been, consoling Peggy in her emotional limbo. She closed the door once and for all on a musical career, and from then on she played the piano purely for her own pleasure, and only occasionally.

The third significant event in her life at that time was an invitation in Peitaiho to afternoon tea with her dentist's wife, Maud Evan-Jones. Mrs. Evan-

The Mackenzie family and Peggy (seated far right) at Peitaiho Beach, China, 1938. ROD BREEN/MACKENZIE FAMILY

Jones insisted that there was someone that Peggy should meet, a person whom she felt would be a kindred spirit for Peggy. Peggy was not inclined; she was not only unaccustomed to going out to tea but did not much expect to like someone who was in the habit of going to such formal functions on a beautiful hot summer's afternoon. The other guest, for her part, was cross at having to put on a dress and go to tea with a complete stranger on such a lovely day, but both she and Peggy liked Mrs. Evan-Jones and reluctantly complied with her wishes. Only when she arrived did Peggy instantly recognize with delight the beautiful young Muriel Langtry Mackenzie, whom she had last seen on the *Empress of Asia* in 1922, but who now had two small daughters in tow.

The two women took an instant liking to each other that resulted in a firm lifetime friendship. Muriel drew Peggy into her family and circle of friends, introduced her to the simple pleasures of picnics and parties and just spending time together walking and talking, and they became inseparable. For the first time since she had been a child, even more than when she had become engaged, Peggy was completely happy. She finally had an intimate female friend of her own generation. As she jokingly remarked, now she could actually sit down with a gentleman, alone, if she chose. And she could wear gorgeous clothes and dance all night, without remonstrance, which she did. "My life was so unbelievably changed that sometimes I thought that I must be

Peggy Pemberton and a friend at a club in Shanghai, 1938. ROD BREEN/MACKENZIE FAMILY

dreaming — and yet the events were all perfectly normal for a woman in her late thirties. I made friends, met pleasant acquaintances, wore elegant clothes, fell in love…more or less seriously, and was fallen in love with…also more or less seriously." Here, she is being coy once more; she never elaborated, to anyone, about who these lovers may have been.

They were lighthearted, those days of 1938 and 1939, in a time when lighthearted days were soon to vanish. Peggy, like the fabled grasshopper, paid little heed.

Peggy Pemberton and Muriel Mackenzie (left) with a friend at Peitaiho Beach, China, 1938. ROD BREEN/MACKENZIE FAMILY

10

Dragons, cherry blossoms, and barbed wire

"One is only too ready to fall, under the hypnotic effects of the drab routine of internment, into the belief that nothing can be happening outside, and that nobody can possibly still be alive and not in a Civilian Assembly Centre."

— PEGGY ABKHAZI, *A Curious Cage*

*E*VEN THE OUTBREAK OF WAR IN EUROPE IN SEPTEMBER 1939 DID LITTLE to discomfort Peggy. She was enjoying her new life so greatly that she drifted along, vaguely aware of the horror happening thousands of miles away, but unaffected by it. While other foreigners were by then leaving Shanghai in droves to return to their homelands — including the Mackenzie family, who left for Canada early in 1940 — Peggy stayed on, convinced that nothing could cause difficulty for British citizens with extraterritorial rights in China. She was financially independent and may have assumed that she would have ample means to leave quickly if she ever needed to. She did not, however, take the precaution of moving any of her Chinese investments out of the country. Peggy seems never to have envisaged leaving.

And where would she have gone, in any event? Britain, in 1940, was not an attractive option. Not only was the country at war, but its lifestyle did not appeal to Peggy. She had not lived in England for many years, and she seems not to have retained any substantial connections to family or friends there or in Scotland. Friends outside China were scarce, too. The Mackenzies were living in Canada, and by the late 1930s Peggy had resumed her intermittent correspondence with Prince Nicolas Abkhazi in Paris. It is extremely doubtful, however, that by 1940 she would have thought of going to Paris, especially in light of the war – she had had plenty of opportunity to do so in the year after Florence's death in 1938. As for Canada, Peggy had vowed never to live in such a desolate country, and nothing had yet appeared to change her view.

But Peggy, quite simply, probably never contemplated leaving. She was happy in Shanghai, where she had a pleasant home and a Chinese staff, including the faithful Li and his daughter, Ah Ching. She felt as responsible for her servants as if they were her dependants, which to a great extent they were – in addition to receiving a salary, they lived and ate in Peggy's home, and their medical and school bills were paid by her. She did not want to abandon them, nor did she feel any need to. Peggy felt so little concern about the international situation that she even felt comfortable enough to take holidays. By May 1940 the war had not yet reached the Pacific, nor did she have any sense that it would; and she decided to journey to Canada to visit Muriel and Rod Mackenzie, and stay with them for several months. The Mackenzies had settled with their young daughters Elizabeth and Maureen in Victoria, the congenial capital of British Columbia, at the southern end of Vancouver Island. It was a small and charming city with a Mediterranean climate and was heavily populated with British expatriates. Muriel and Rod Mackenzie had strongly encouraged Peggy to come and see them in their new home in the suburb of Oak Bay and to get to know the city. The Mackenzies had a generous ulterior motive: they wanted her to come and live permanently in Victoria and were eager to sponsor her stay. The hindsight of wishing that she had stayed with them while she had the chance must have been agonizing for Peggy later, but the clarity of that vision was to remain obscured for another eighteen months.

She had been visiting with the Mackenzies for only a few days in June 1940 when they learned of the fall of Paris. Peggy had heard no news from Prince Nicolas or his mother, Princess Hélène, since the outbreak of the war,

Peggy Pemberton-Carter with Muriel Mackenzie in Victoria, 1940. SUSAN HAMERSLEY/
MACKENZIE FAMILY

and she became very concerned for their safety. She did nothing immediately, but when she travelled to New York City for a few weeks in October to enjoy the concerts and theatre, she inquired of the Swiss Red Cross there what could be done to send funds to Paris to assist them. The organization advised her against trying to send money to Europe, thinking it unlikely that the Abkhazis would receive it under the German occupation. Instead, the Red Cross deposited the funds in an American bank account on trust and sent a cable regarding the money to Princess Hélène in Paris. If she and her son Nicolas could find a way to get to America, the funds would be waiting for them there. No response was received while Peggy was still in New York — only much later, when she was back in Shanghai, did Peggy receive a reply from Princess Hélène, once again through the medium of the Red Cross. Nicolas, the princess reported, had enlisted immediately with the French army when war was declared, but he had been captured and was being held captive in a German prisoner-of-war camp. Hélène herself was very ill and had no means to escape by herself to New York in order to obtain the funds held there for her and Nicolas. It seemed there was little else that Peggy could do, and she heard nothing further from either of the Abkhazis for the duration of the war. In the meantime, Peggy returned from New York to Victoria briefly to spend a happy Christmas and New Year holiday with the Mackenzies. In early 1941 she boarded a passenger liner to return to Shanghai.

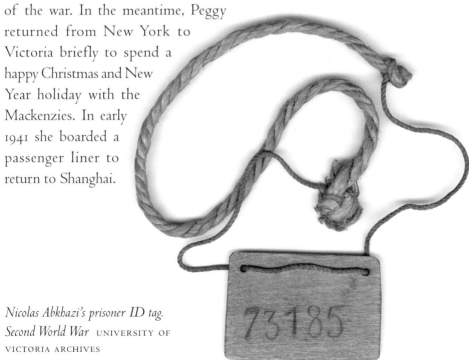

Nicolas Abkhazi's prisoner ID tag. Second World War UNIVERSITY OF VICTORIA ARCHIVES

"Captivité" - German soldiers with French prisoners of war, including Prince Nicolas Abkhazi, September 1940. UNIVERSITY OF VICTORIA ARCHIVES

Peggy had planned a quiet, relaxing voyage home. Since she could easily afford to do so, she had booked a stateroom with its own piano, to while away the long, slow hours of the journey across the Pacific. But also on board the ship when Peggy embarked in Victoria was a handsome forty-one-year-old New Zealander, a man named Stanley Davys, who was working in the New Zealand cable service and had been in the United States on a steel purchasing foray for the New Zealand government. Now he was on his way to China en route to his home. Davys was a colonial "rough diamond": a Kiwi who had left school at the age of sixteen and gone directly into the wire communications business. By the time he was eighteen, he claimed, he was handling all of New Zealand's external cable communications for the government, and he dined out frequently on the story that he had been the first person in New Zealand to hear the news that the First World War had ended. It was an exciting business to be in, especially in wartime, and despite his lack of formal education Stanley

Davys was an engaging and attractive man who appeared to have no shortage of female admirers.

As Stanley recounted it to his children many years later, he walked past Peggy's stateroom one afternoon to hear glorious piano music coming from within, and he stopped to eavesdrop. Realizing that the pianist was the glamorous Englishwoman that he had been admiring ever since she had boarded the ship, he introduced himself humbly and asked for permission to continue listening. Charmed, Peggy consented, and Stanley spent every remaining day of the voyage listening to Peggy play the piano.

Stanley Davys. PHILIPPA PROUDFOOT (NÉE DAVYS)

Nobody knows what Peggy's and Stanley's relationship really involved during those few weeks of the voyage to Shanghai and the month that he stayed in the city after their arrival. But Peggy certainly enjoyed his flattering attention, even though Stanley was clearly not an intellectual match for her; nor did he have the social background or manners that she was used to. There was, however, a strong mutual attraction, no doubt stimulated by the romantic shipboard atmosphere and flavoured with the dangers of wartime. Stanley did try to persuade Peggy that she should not stay in Shanghai, because of the danger, but whether he attempted to persuade her to come to New Zealand is unknown. One of Peggy's confidantes in her later life claimed that Peggy had told her that Stanley had proposed, but that she turned him down. Whether or not this is true, certainly for his entire life he held her in high esteem, portraying her to his daughters as a "brave, elegant and wonderful" woman whom they should regard as a great role model; in 1947, when his first daughter, Philippa, was born, Stanley also insisted that Peggy, whom his wife, Jean, had not yet met, be made Philippa's godmother. Peggy and Jean Davys did meet and become friends eventually, but their relationship was always formal, if not exactly cool – Peggy and Jean were two very different people, and Stanley's outspoken admiration for Peggy must surely have been trying at times for his wife.

Peggy clearly did not dismiss her attractive admirer at the beginning of 1941. On the contrary, she enjoyed the attention and the protectiveness, and at the very least formed a strong emotional attachment to Stanley Davys. But she may simply have been keeping her options open. After he left Shanghai, she sent him several letters throughout the remaining four years of the war; and at Christmastime in 1943, when she had the opportunity to send a radio message to someone outside China, she chose Stanley as the recipient. And even though she did not receive replies either to her letters or to the message, one of the first long letters she wrote after the end of the war was again to her New Zealand admirer: "San Francisco, November 16, 1945. My dear Stanley, here I am in the land of the living again, and I wonder whether you are in Wellington…I wonder whether you ever got any of my…letters I sent from time to time from Lunghua. I haven't heard from you since the autumn of 1941, but I hope that you are well and happy, and that everything goes as you would wish. I also hope that I shall hear from you soon, one of the major pleasures of this return to life is getting into touch with one's friends again." She closes the letter by repeating: "I do hope that I shall hear from you soon…I wish we could hear the Chopin Etudes again…With love and all good wishes, from Peggy." But by the time Peggy heard back from Stanley he was married; and any question of a different relationship between the two could never be contemplated again.

Peggy settled back into Shanghai in the spring of 1941. Her lifestyle was little changed, but the growing menace of the Japanese could no longer be entirely ignored. Their foothold in China was strong; by 1937 the Japanese had already captured the capital at Nanking from Chiang Kai-shek's Kuomintang and taken control of the north of the country and most of the Pacific coast. Tensions were increasing between Japan and the United States, whose concessionary ports were being blockaded by the Japanese. The United States retaliated with an oil embargo, breaking its trading agreement with Japan, and demanded that the Japanese withdraw from China and Indochina. General Hideki Tojo, who had become the premier of Japan in mid-October, refused and instead prepared for war.

Stella Dong writes in *Shanghai: The Rise and Fall of a Decadent City*:

"The event that many of Shanghai's westerners thought they would never live to see occurred on December 8, 1941. That morning, shortly after four o'clock Shanghai time, Shanghailanders living near the Bund woke to the sound of a half-dozen explosions. Thinking the noise came from firecrackers set off by people celebrating an unknown Chinese holiday, some went back to sleep. But when the blasts continued, they called their friends with penthouse views or went up to their roofs. What they saw was the British gunboat *Petrel* on fire from stem to stern and Japanese bluejackets, bayonets and guns in hand, massing on the Bund and moving their lines into the business area. Simultaneously, Pearl Harbor was being bombed, they soon learned from their wireless sets."

Peggy awoke three hours later to find the International Settlement under the control of the Japanese and her extraterritorial "rights" useless. It was far too late for any regrets. A small number of British citizens and other foreign nationals were almost immediately expatriated by the Japanese, but Peggy was not among them. She and her friends, now classified as enemy aliens in an occupied war zone, became players in a strange theatre of civilian life. Allied nationals could, notionally, continue to go about their daily business. But they also were required immediately to register with the Japanese police and were issued with red armbands, stamped with the initial letter of their nationality and an identification number. Peggy received armband number B2268, which she was to wear in public at all times. At the same time, the freedom of movement of enemy aliens was severely restricted and their bank accounts frozen. The currency "went to glory," as Peggy described it, devaluing daily; but Allied nationals were expected to be able to live and function on a small and static monthly allowance.

Peggy's long years of experience in stoically accepting events beyond her control and staying invisible in order to keep out of trouble now stood her in good stead. Despite the chaotic events occurring around her, she kept a journal of her activities, thoughts, and feelings, which many years later would appear as a book called *A Curious Cage*. Written in the form of a "never-to-be-posted"

As an "enemy alien" living in Shanghai, during the Japanese occupation, Peggy Pemberton-Carter was required to wear her red armband with its identification number at all times in public.
UNIVERSITY OF VICTORIA ARCHIVES

letter to her friends the Mackenzies, it was a means, she said, of keeping her thoughts coherent. The journal is an interesting collection of facts and anecdotes, clearly circumscribed in its breadth by Peggy's fear of censorship and possible punishment. Its most interesting aspect is not written, but clearly revealed in the journal: Peggy's strength of character, her resourcefulness, and her determination to survive all came to the surface. The war appears not so much to have changed her as a person, as simply to have stripped away pretence and superficiality, allowing Peggy's down-to-earth core to emerge, really for the first time in her life.

Peggy did not attempt to continue life as it was before; she was too pragmatic for that. There were certain aspects of the enforced simplicity of her lifestyle that she quite enjoyed: "I must say one's sense of appreciation is sharpened to the most acute degree, and we are certainly all liberated from taking things just for granted. It is quite amazing how much one's interest is turned towards food and warmth. It doesn't take much or long for one to shed the finer intricacies of thought or imagination. On the other hand there is a great sense of comradeship with everyone, and a natural friendliness which I have never experienced before, excepting with one's very dearest. The absence of irritation or impatience at long and cold waits is something that makes me smile; I used to be amongst the world's worst waiters." She enjoyed the slower tempo of life without cars on the roads, and the "delightful leisureliness" invoked by having to cycle or walk everywhere, as well as the healthy appearance brought on by a lack of cigarettes, alcohol, and sweets. Peggy also embarked enthusiastically on a joint venture with her good friend, Bob Lang — a pig farming business — hoping to obtain a supply of fresh meat and make some money on the side. She strongly wanted to immerse herself in some physically exhausting activity, to keep her mind away from mental and emotional stresses; and the hard work of the pig farm, a lengthy bicycle ride away from her home, fitted the bill nicely.

Bob Lang was yet another man who played an important role in Peggy's life. Like Nicolas Abkhazi, John Green, and Stanley Davys, he fulfilled her emotional needs at a time when she desperately needed attention. Given how romantically barren her youth had been, she seemed justifiably proud of having so many admirers as a mature woman. But in the years since her failed marriage, despite the dalliances she mentions in her reminiscences, Peggy did not appear to want to make any of her relationships permanent. The right person and the right time seemed to have not yet coincided in her life. In the meantime, people like Lang provided to her much-appreciated male companionship. In her journal at the time she wrote of him: "We both know the limitations on both our sides, but he fills up many of the superficial chinks of my loneliness — very many of them, and I give him a kind of companionship he has never had before…He has taught me much, and I should miss him greatly in these days, but beyond that, our paths will always be miles apart." Her resolve was not always so strong: "Truly the man is an irresistible mixture of poet and child…Perhaps I am feeling indulgent this evening but in these days of what seems to be perpetual cold, petty economies and unglamorous clothes it is nice when one has succumbed to the extravagance of a fire, and the lure of silk next to the skin, to be phoned up and told 'You looked lovely' — even if…oh blast it all!"

There was little time, however, for such thoughts to continue as the war over the Pacific Ocean progressed. The hard physical labour needed to manage the pig farm occupied most of Peggy's days, as did trying to keep warm during the freezing winter of 1942 and looking after friends in greater need than she. The Japanese appeared to be triumphing over the Allies, and the occupying forces became increasingly arrogant, making life difficult for the enemy aliens in Shanghai. Food was also in ever-shorter supply. More and more civilians were taken to internment camps, including John Green and several other of Peggy's friends. Bob Lang and Peggy decided to close down the pig farm; it was becoming too dangerous to travel even the relatively short distance from what was once the International Settlement. Fearful of being called up for internment at any moment and of running out of food, Peggy desperately started to seek a home for her dog. She was fortunate to find one; many of her friends were forced to have their loved pets destroyed. It was either that, or seeing them starve.

As a result, it was a relief when Peggy received notice on March 3, 1943, that she was to report to the Civil Assembly Centre in Shanghai on April 5, to be transported to an internment camp. Pragmatically, Peggy believed that she too would have starved if she had not been sent to a camp. Preparation in the days leading up to her scheduled internment date was nonetheless a strange sensation: "During these last days of quasi-liberty, life has taken on a queer, unreal complexion, as though one might be living at the bottom of the sea," she wrote. The internees-in-waiting had previously been given a surprisingly extensive list of what they could bring to the camp, and generous instructions had been provided on how to store their other remaining possessions in Shanghai. The latter instructions were regarded somewhat cynically, as the Japanese had already confiscated most assets of any substantial value. Peggy had, however, managed to hold on to some jewellery and clothing, and rather than utilize the Swiss Consulate, as recommended in the instructions, she stored them with Hansons, the law firm that had been looking after her affairs.

One of the precious items that she put into the safekeeping of Chinese partner T.S. Yeh was a diamond bracelet that she had had made with diamonds from the original starburst brooch that her mother Mabel had left her, together with some other diamonds she had inherited from Florence Pemberton. T.S. Yeh would subsequently trade the bracelet for a far more useful and inflation-proof gold bar, which he could liquidate in a series of small pieces, thus keeping Peggy supplied over time with much-needed extra food rations in the internment camp. It was a transaction, as it turned out, that had far greater meaning for Peggy than simply keeping her fed. Forty years later she remarked: "I find it to be a touching — or a strangely complete conclusion — that the diamonds belonging to the mother who gave me life, and to the [other] mother who, during the years when nobody else wanted me, cherished that life, should have contributed to the prolongation of that same life during a period of considerable hardship and some danger." And, stoic as she may have been, Peggy certainly did feel threatened during those years. In a moment many years later when she was baring her soul on a number of matters to her goddaughter, Philippa, she wrote: "You have never known cruel treatment as a child, of not being wanted or needed by anyone – or years of harsh discipline which was administered in the honest belief that it was maternal love – nor have you known years of poverty, nor hunger and thirst and physical danger, with a brutal death a very real and constant possibility."

But in the meantime, her relief that she would at least be fed and sheltered dominated her fear. Peggy collected some warm clothing, some precious books and papers, and a store of food, relying on the rumours being transmitted back from the camps for her selection of things to take with her; and on April 5, 1943, she was taken by bus from Shanghai to Lunghua Middle School, her new "home" for an unforeseeable period of time. Forced to share quarters with dozens of other women, which was anathema to the self-described "lone wolf" that she had become, Peggy quickly marked out her territory in the dormitory and set herself up to survive as best she could. In fact, while the environment of the internment camp was cramped and squalid and often freezing, the situation was nowhere near as bad as it might have been. The camp commander was a well-educated and pleasant man who had been the Japanese ambassador in London, England, when the war broke out. Not intending to be humorous in any way, he explained to the internees that he, too, had been interned in London, at the Savoy Hotel, and he urged them to "cherish" their new quarters, as he had, being the only home they now knew. Although his advice was met with cynical laughter, he was much appreciated by the internees as a kindly man who attempted, as much as possible, to smooth the way for them in difficult circumstances.

What wore the internees down, remarked Peggy, was not "physical torture or rape – but unending mindless bureaucracy, hunger, thirst, dirt, smells – extreme cold and heat – that's what internment largely consists of…I still marvel at our escape." She described it as her university education, albeit a liberal one, having learned during her time there so much about "the art of living." There is no question that her thinking, abilities, and actions evolved in response to the challenges she faced. In many ways, although she never forgave the Japanese government for her internment, she thoroughly appreciated the skills that she acquired: learning how to plant a garden from new soil, using hand tools (she cultivated a little wildflower garden outside her dormitory window, the first she had created entirely by herself); acquiring the first job she had ever had, as quartermaster in the camp's hospital; and notwithstanding that she preferred the company of the cats that she had managed to acquire to that of her human companions, she also had to learn to live with "every imaginable type of human being from all different backgrounds." Usually philosophical, practical and down-to-earth at all times, she resolutely adapted to her circumstances and managed to maintain a blunt sense of humour about the ruder aspects of life in camp. In her journal she described the regular Saturday routine of taking an enema, in an effort to counteract the stodgy camp diet: "But there being neither privacy nor reticence in camp life, upon my return [to the dormitory], looking rather less like a gasometer than usual, up goes the ribald chorus: 'She's de-beaned...!' And I laugh too, and hate and loathe the squalor and want of privacy until I can discover something else ridiculous to laugh at."

But as the long war years wore on, there seemed less and less to laugh about. By the end of 1944 the tide was starting to turn against the Japanese, but with the rising hope of Allied victory came the real fear inside the camp at Lunghua of Japanese retaliation against the internees. The extra food parcels started to come less regularly, and with their meagre contents, it was becoming harder to deal with the cold and the constant sickness. And as the food shortage became increasingly acute, Peggy had all but one of her cats put down, a huge blow to her morale. Even the news on May 7, 1945, that the Allies had been victorious in Europe supplied only temporary relief; and in some ways it made each passing day even harder for the internees to get through. Rumours and speculation were rampant, and despite the presence of an illicit radio in camp that allowed the internees access to some international news, no one really knew what to believe. Heavy threats were made by some of the Japanese guards that if they were forced to withdraw, they would first kill all the civilian prisoners. By August 11, 1945, when the internees learned the good news of Russia's declaration of war against Japan, they were so worn down with tension that they no longer had any idea how to balance their hope against despair.

II

rom

war to peace

"Some of the young girls of the hut rushed in shouting and laughing — 'The war is over! The war is over!' And then miraculously one heard the same cry echoing from the whole camp. And yet if you asked how they knew, or who had told them, nobody could say…"

— Peggy Abkhazi, *A Curious Cage*

Although Peggy and her companions first heard the reports that the war was over on August 11, 1945, it took several more days for the war in Asia to draw to its slow and anguished conclusion, and at least another month for all of the internees to be liberated from Lunghua. In the meantime, while Peggy's most immediate sensations on hearing the news were relief and joy, they were tempered by confusion as conflicting reports continued to circulate in the camp. The camp commander continued to insist that the fighting would carry on, unless terms of peace satisfactory to Japan could be settled upon — but the reports on the secret radio were indicating otherwise. Peggy did not know what to think. Nevertheless a certain amount of reckless joy permeated the camp, and most of the internees threw caution to the winds, celebrating by feasting upon their last remaining carefully hoarded stores. They had been living with such great fear and tension for so long, that perhaps they could simply no longer keep it hidden. Their tension exploded in a frenzy of unrestrained jubilation, even though they continued to be surrounded by heavily armed and intensely frustrated Japanese guards.

The memories of her fear during that intense time stayed with Peggy for decades, long after the temporary sensations of joy and relief had dissipated. Twenty-five years later she recalled vividly in a letter her "strange feelings" then – likening them to animal intuition – that the Japanese guards would become more and more unreasonable and brutal in their treatment of the internees, as they sensed imminent defeat in those last few days. With the progression of the war the prisoners had become intensely dependent on their secret radio, which was "our lifeline and our defence against their propaganda news of perpetual victories." At the same time Peggy became increasingly fearful of the potential consequences if the Japanese should discover the radio. She and the other internees were constantly hearing tales of the instant and arbitrary decapitation of innocent prisoners in retaliation for any infringement of the rules.

Peggy's "strange feelings" were vindicated many years later, when she learned that the commander in chief of the Japanese forces had chosen September 7, 1945, as the day on which all enemy prisoners were to be executed, regardless of the circumstances. Even after all those years, it shocked her hugely that she had been a mere three weeks away from certain death, but for the dropping of the atomic bomb on Hiroshima. And although it had meant her salvation, Peggy was also very troubled by the deaths of the innocent Japanese civilians living in Hiroshima, writing in a letter to Philippa Davys in 1971: "[It] has lived in my mind as a moral problem for all these nearly twenty-six years. Thousands were killed and maimed – so that *I* could live? My mind never found an answer, but my heart has tried, as a poor expiation, to ask forgiveness of those killed, and it has also tried to show me how to try and live these years so as to a little justify my escape from being murdered."

As she prepared to leave Lunghua, however, the full impact of Hiroshima was still relatively unknown, and Peggy was far more concerned with her immediate survival. In those first few days after the war had ended, she had no idea whether she had any money or investments left, or whether any of her friends were still alive: in China, or anywhere else in the world. Peggy's emotions bounced daily from exhausted despair to energetic enthusiasm, depending on events. She marvelled at the kindness of the Chinese, who showered the internees with gifts of food and money and offers of assistance; but she sank to the depths of gloom when she contemplated her own potential financial situation. She said farewell to her remaining and beloved cat, Timmy, with great sadness, seeing him off to a new home in the country. At the same time, with her by-then typical sense of humour, she watched her erstwhile companions from the camp revel hysterically in all the newly available luxuries – soap, cigarettes, proper hair-dos – laughing at herself as well, because she was also prepared to pay the outrageously inflated cost of such "luxuries." A pound of peaches cost $35,000 in the failed Chinese currency; an ice-cream, $50,000; hotel accommodation, in the millions.

While still in Lunghua, Peggy wrote to her friend Muriel Mackenzie, whom she hoped was still living in Victoria, Canada: "altogether life has a flavour of the opera 'comique' these days, which is as well, because there is behind all the joy of the approaching return to normal life a feeling like that of blood returning to a frozen limb. I suppose it is natural, because I found that for myself the only way to make a success of camp life was to put all emotions and memories and plans and desires into cold storage...So," she went on, "though I feel weepy at any kindness from strangers or sign of affection from those I haven't seen for all these years, I'm also filled with the most tremendous zest for life, and am not mentally exhausted as are those who have all along fought for their rights as individuals instead of sinking themselves into this limbo-like existence." In the same letter, Peggy remarked that "I can honestly say that I'm not afraid of anything that life can offer from now on...more than that, I'm going to be able to enjoy or at any rate be interested in anything that is going to happen. Moreover, being stripped of everything does not change the essential 'me'...of that I'm sure."

At the time that she wrote to Muriel, Peggy was three months short of her forty-third birthday. Although she never commented on the fact in her journal, which she stopped keeping a few days after the war ended, her release from internment also set her free to build a completely new life. The war had changed life for women in general, and there was no longer any expectation that they had to conform to certain expected social roles and behaviour in the way that they had in the earlier decades of the twentieth century. Peggy could do as she chose — and her letters of the time reveal a strong determination not to make the wrong decision and fall back into any old, undesirable habits. Her Chinese lawyer, T.S. Yeh, made arrangements for her to be accommodated in a medical facility in Shanghai while she thought about her next steps. She could not return to her home: the house had been completely destroyed, the trees cut down, and latrines and trenches dug throughout what used to be the garden, and the place was beyond recognition. Although her Chinese investments were almost entirely depleted, her other meagre possessions were at least safe in storage. Peggy had also managed to hide a few hundred dollars' worth of traveller's cheques throughout her internment, which had never been discovered by the Japanese. Her British funds, and other substantial foreign investments in South Africa, India, and South America, were intact. She simply had to decide where she wanted to go.

But that was a very big decision. England? Canada? Possibly New Zealand? While Peggy was considering her options, the letter that she had written to Muriel Mackenzie from Lunghua on August 26, 1945, crossed with one that Muriel wrote from Victoria, dated October 10. Muriel had not received any of Peggy's letters that had been written since the end of the fighting and was frantic with worry for her friend's well-being. She was terribly frustrated by the lack of mail service between Canada and China, and even more frustrated with "the Americans, who won this War, [who] are just B. minded about everything and will not accept our letters to go by their boats." Begging Peggy to come and stay with her family in Victoria and to let her know what financial assistance they could provide to her, Muriel also tried to discourage Peggy from thinking of going to England. She had correctly guessed that that would be Peggy's most likely choice of destination, assuming that staying in Shanghai was no longer an option. But, wrote Muriel, "conditions [in England] are very bad, food so scarce, no heating in most of the houses and accommodation impossible to get, altogether life there is very difficult and the British people bless them, are tired and weary and now realising that the Labour Government cannot possibly give them all they promised." Victoria, she claimed, was much better off, with far fewer people and far more resources. The only noticeable thing lacking, noted Muriel, was "help of any kind," given that every available

able-bodied person had been working in support of the war effort. "Most of us," she wrote to Peggy, "have learned how to manage and run our houses without help, [and] many are going to continue as you know what domestic help in this country is like anyway!"

Despite Muriel's forebodings regarding conditions in Britain and her entreaties to Peggy to come to live in Canada, Peggy decided that England was where she would go. She was not particularly enthusiastic about it, but the bulk of her financial resources were based there as a result of tight post-war financial regulation. Although she certainly wanted to visit Victoria, and possibly to return there later, Peggy also felt a "great urge to clear up things, both actual and metaphorical, in England, with two perfectly good outlines of life to choose from...all the time allowing, as in past experiences, that Destiny probably has a third or fourth tucked up her sleeve!" Her plan, as she wrote to Muriel and separately to Stanley Davys, was to spend the winter in Victoria, continuing her recuperation, and then carry on to England in the spring. What "two outlines" of life she had in mind, she did not elaborate upon. As it turned out, capricious Destiny would behave exactly as Peggy had predicted. But at that point, Peggy did not care what was about to occur, writing to Stanley: "However, we'll see what happens. I must say that the sole constructive blessing of internment is that ANY alternative is delightful in comparison." Peggy was not about to allow destiny to make all of the choices, however. Perhaps the other blessing of internment, obvious to others if not to her, was the emergence of Peggy's unshakeable sense of determination to have her own way in the future whenever she could. For example, British subjects planning to leave China were under strict orders after the war's end to ship out directly to Britain – where, according to the regulations, their sources of funds were supposed to be. Peggy wanted to go to Canada first, via the United States. Accordingly, with her lawyer's help, she managed to circumvent the rules about going directly to Britain and instead to finagle herself a passage on the USS *Lavaca*, which sailed for San Francisco on October 13, 1945. In doing so, she demonstrated that she was no longer willing to allow anyone else to make those types of decisions for her if she could help it.

There was little left in the way of material things in Shanghai that meant anything much to Peggy as she bid a final farewell to the city of her birth, the place where once she had felt more at home than anywhere else in the world.

Her other friends were also dispersing themselves around the world, and many had already left. Peggy's greatest sadness came with having to say goodbye to the Chinese servants who had stayed loyal to her for more than ten years: Li and his daughter, Ah Ching; and her gracious and caring lawyer, T.S. Yeh. In the postscript to *A Curious Cage*, Peggy also gives us one last teasing hint at her relationship with John Henry Green, with whom she was briefly reunited the day before she embarked on the American transport ship: "It was a short and more moving reunion than I expected – but that is part of quite another story."

The *Lavaca* left Shanghai for San Francisco with more than two thousand troops and civilians on board, and Captain Walter S. Gabel at the helm. The quarters on board the ship were even more cramped than in Lunghua, with 150 people to a compartment and only canvas hammocks for the passengers to sleep in. All Peggy's luggage had been stored for the journey in the *Lavaca's* hold, and Peggy had only one change of clothes until the ship arrived in Hawaii and the bags could be retrieved. But she was quite composed and luxuriating in a sense of freedom and well-being after her internment. Lightheartedly she wrote to Stanley Davys of conditions on board: "I must say that they did everything possible to make the conditions more bearable, but thank goodness the Japanese had never seen some of the features or else they would surely have incorporated some of them into camp life for our greater discomfort!" And the weather was terrible the whole way to the west coast of the United States.

But the miserable passage was soon over, and by early November Peggy had cashed her traveller's cheques and was installed in a comfortable hotel in San Francisco. She indulged herself, with great delight and without having to pay a ridiculously inflated price for doing so, in all of the luxuries she had not enjoyed for years: long, hot baths, shopping for elegant clothes, going to concerts. The city was congested with transiting civilians and discharged

OPPOSITE:

Peggy shipped out to San Francisco after her internment on an American troop ship, the USS Lavaca. The captain and his crew did everything they could to make their passengers happy, including bestowing honorary appointments as "shipmates" upon them. Peggy made Coxswain.
UNIVERSITY OF VICTORIA ARCHIVES

U. S. S. LAVACA (APA-180)
C/O FLEET POSTOFFICE

TO ALL WHO SHALL SEE THESE PRESENTS, GREETING:

Know ye, that having participated in voyage on the United States Ship LAVACA, attack troop transport, between the ports of Shanghai , China and San Francisco, U, S, A., and that having successfully competed for deck space and in chow lines with innumerable Pacific Fleet Sailors and Okinawa Marines, and that having demonstrated a fine spirit of sportmanship and cooperation -

Mrs. Peggy Pemberton-Carter

is appointed to the rate of

Coxswain (Honorary)

And is entitled to all the emoluments, honors, and respect due this high office, and shall be accepted and acknowledged by all LAVACA Officers, Bluejackets, and Marines as a SHIPMATE.

Done this 24.5 day of October 1945, at Latitude 39°30'N and Longitude 180° E.W.

WALTER S. GABEL
Captain, USNR
Commanding.

The Canadian Red Cross Society

RED CROSS ENQUIRY BUREAU

139 QUEEN STREET   OTTAWA, CANADA

Rec'd
Feb 20/1946
Advt in newspapers

195 Prints Ghine
Home 3.
73875

MESSAGE TO LIBERATED PERSONNEL IN THE FAR EAST

NAME OF SENDER
in Canada .... Muriel Mackenzie

ADDRESS 424 St. Charles St., Victoria, B. C. Canada

RELATIONSHIP .... Cousin

Rejoice with you on release. Hope our long

separation nears end. How is your health? Expect

you here earliest possible moment. Your room

ready and great welcome awaits you. Children

wildly excited. What are your urgent needs and

how can we help you most? Be candid Peggy.

Affectionately, Muriel Mac.

ADDRESSEE

NAME Mrs. M.M.J. (Peggy) Pemberton-Carter

Unit or other particulars Lunghwa Civil Assembly Centre
Shanghai China

Identifying data Matriculation No. 20/61
Birthplace and
date of birth Shanghai about 1905

Addressee may reply on reverse side.

soldiers, and hotel accommodation was difficult not only to get, but to keep – after only five days, guests were required to vacate and find another room somewhere else – but Peggy revelled in the pleasant city with its warm climate and all the fresh food that she could eat. In the meantime, a flurry of letters went back and forth between Peggy and Muriel Mackenzie, the latter in an increasing fever of excitement and impatience at the delay in seeing her friend. Post-war bureaucracy required a permit even to visit Canada, and Peggy had no choice but to wait until she received clearance from Ottawa. Muriel wrote letter after letter to Peggy, assuring her that she had called on her forceful local member of Parliament, Nancy Hodges, to "hurry things up" in Ottawa, and rambling on excitedly about the heroine's welcome awaiting Peggy when she finally arrived. Muriel's teenage daughters, Elizabeth and Maureen, were also delirious with excitement and made all kinds of plans to entertain their "Aunt Peggy" in Victoria when she finally came.

Maureen and Elizabeth Mackenzie. SUSAN HAMERSLEY / MACKENZIE FAMILY

OPPOSITE:
Peggy's dearest friend, Muriel Mackenzie, was desperate to hear from Peggy after the war ended and to persuade her to come to Victoria. Peggy agreed, although her plans were to go to England afterwards. UNIVERSITY OF VICTORIA ARCHIVES

In her letter to Peggy of November 11, 1945, Muriel prevailed upon her again to change her mind about going to Britain, painting a bleak picture of conditions there and asking plaintively: "Peggy, why must you go and live in England? Is it on account of money, your Doctor friend, or is that where you particularly want to be?" Who she was referring to when she mentions the "Doctor friend" in England is not certain – it could well have been John Green – but Peggy did not mention him in her letters back to Muriel, and Muriel did not pursue the issue. Conditions were far better in Victoria than in England, she went on instead in her letter, but certain goods were in equally short supply. Muriel wrote twice to Peggy to advise her to get plenty of underwear and stockings while in San Francisco, as there were none of any kind – "wool, silk, cotton, or cheesecloth" – to be had in Victoria, let alone in England. Nor were there any sweaters or cardigans, men's socks, or nightclothes: "I saw an advertisement in the *Times*...two Shanghai night-dresses, new, what offer, above Two Guineas each. I can give you some of my Shanghai nighties to take home with you and you can sell them there and retire for the rest of your life."

That first post-war Christmas would also have to be celebrated in Victoria without the usual festive fare, save for a box of chocolates that Peggy promised to bring with her. Muriel was ecstatic at the thought of it, writing breathlessly: "We have not seen a box of chocolates for years, and have only been able to buy the most putrid stale chocolate bar about once a week, no sweets of any kind in this country certainly for the past two or three years, so you can imagine the excitement...The next day the sweet shop will be open is December 14 and then there will be about a dozen boxes and people will queue up hours ahead and the queue will be all the way around the block...We have no luxuries here at all," she continued, "all tinned fruits are rationed, no pineapple, have not seen any for three years, very few raisins or ingredients for a cake or pudding, no jellies or Jello Puddings in fact nothing but the simple ordinary food, but heaps of that and the other we have got along well without anyway, but the chocolates will be a real treat."

It was the last written exchange between the two friends before Peggy left San Francisco. On December 14, 1945, Peggy finally boarded a ferry in Seattle, arriving in Victoria a few hours later, into the loving and impatiently waiting arms of the Mackenzie family.

12

Semper liber

"Victoria isn't like any other town or place I have known... I would love you to see us in our own milieu."

— Peggy Abkhazi, letter to Philippa, October 13, 1968

THE WORLD THAT PEGGY CAME TO IN VICTORIA WAS DISTANT FROM THAT of her youth and former life not merely in terms of geography, but also in its culture and history. Later in life Peggy said she had heard that the city was welcoming of eccentric characters, and she certainly seemed to regard herself as one. If she knew about it at the time, perhaps Peggy was also taken with the city's motto, *Semper Liber* — "Always Free" — which she could well have adopted from then on as her own. In any event, coming to Victoria felt like a homecoming, despite the city's lack of familiarity, and her plans to go on to England were postponed indefinitely soon after Peggy settled in with the Mackenzie family.

For a provincial capital, Victoria was a relatively small city, with a permanent population of fewer than fifty thousand residents. On December 14, 1945, the day on which Peggy arrived, the *Victoria Daily Times* newspaper would have provided her with as good a picture of her new home as any guidebook or tourist brochure. It announced that the weather would continue to be cold and partly cloudy, with light to moderate winds – typical of Victoria's cool, rainy winters. The big local news on the front page was that window cleaner Hector A. Ignace had fractured his heels when he fell approximately twenty-five feet from an office window of the competing paper, the *Daily Colonist*; and a letter from Victoria to Vancouver, bemoaned the editor, had taken eleven months to reach its destination, less than one hundred miles away.

Notwithstanding Muriel Mackenzie's reports in her letters to Peggy of a dearth of dry goods in Victoria, Spencer's Department Store was running several full-page advertisements in the newspaper, enticing shoppers to purchase men's tweed sports coats for $18.95, men's "fancy socks" for 55 cents a pair, and street shoes for women for $4.50. Table lamps were going for $8.95; and an entire "Hollywood Bedroom Ensemble" could be had for $96 ("terms available"). The Royal Bank of Canada was touting its experience in dealing with South America: "Many of our staff are native South Americans," the bank assured its customers. Those in the market for a new home could purchase waterfront property close to the city for as little as $10,000. The neighbouring municipality of Oak Bay, an eastern suburb of Victoria, wanted to know if Victoria City Council would be in favour of laying a new water main from the Goldstream area, several miles northwest of the city, at a cost of $80,000. This measure, claimed Oak Bay's administration, would supply sufficient water to the municipality for the next fifty years. The issue was being hotly debated by residents in both jurisdictions. The British Columbia Telephone Company, meanwhile, had placed a large advertisement to announce that over two million names were on the waiting list for telephone service in North America and that it would be many months before factory deliveries would enable telephone installations on a "normal" basis. In the meantime, Victoria City Hall reported that it had issued 1,187 bicycle licences, but that thirteen motorists had each been fined $2.50 in city police court on parking violation charges.

The social pages of the *Times* were very full, announcing, among others, that Mr. and Mrs. George Barton, who had spent the war in a Japanese prisoner-of-war camp at Weihsien, China, were staying at the Empress Hotel; that Mrs. Vera Watts Powell would entertain at a cocktail party late that afternoon, and that Mrs. Wilfred Reade of Beach Drive had entertained a party of ten the previous evening; Mrs. L.V. Frazier of 1419 Fort Street reported the promotion of her daughter, Athalie, to the rank of sergeant in the Canadian Women's Army Corps; and there were many compliments to Miss Sheila Strachan, December bride-elect. Dorothy Dix, agony aunt, sternly and rather unhelpfully admonished a Mrs. R.C. that she was evidently "cut out for an old maid and...not wife material," after Mrs. R.C. had written requesting advice on how to manage a difficult husband. At the Capitol Cinema, Judy Garland and Robert Walker were starring in *The Clock*, while Bernie Parker and his all-star orchestra, featuring Lois Moore, were playing at Sirocco Tops Nightclub, "The Northwest's Smartest Nite-Spot." Admission was 75 cents – $1 on Saturdays.

Post-war Victoria was a city of cultural complexity, ethnic blandness, and many social contradictions. Behind its "Tweed Curtain" lived a large number of wealthy British immigrants, who still dominated the character of the city with their English gardens, Tudor houses, and tea and crumpets lifestyle. The descendants of some of the early settlers of the city – the Pembertons (to whom Peggy was, incidentally, no relation), the Gillespies, and the Todds, among others – were still very much the aristocrats of Victoria. On the other hand, it was also a city that seemed to welcome newcomers of all kinds. Many older upper- and middle-class British "China hands" like Rod and Muriel Mackenzie had chosen to retire in Victoria, with its gentle climate and pleasant landscape, rather than return to England. But there were also a number of poorer, less sophisticated European immigrants trickling into the city, escaping from the devastation overseas and setting up small businesses or taking up jobs as teachers and social workers and labourers.

Victoria's once-thriving Japanese community had ceased to exist in 1942, when Japanese Canadians were banished by the Canadian government to internment camps in the interior of British Columbia for the duration of the war. Very few of them returned to the city, and one of the few reminders of their former presence was a thousand flowering cherry trees that had been planted by the Japanese-Canadian residents of Victoria in 1941 as a contribution to its boulevard renewal program. But with the post-war removal of anti-Chinese legislation, the residents of Victoria's small Chinatown, on the north side of the central business district, started to spread out into other areas of the city, especially the more rural northeastern side, and to open market gardens and nurseries in the suburbs.

Few aboriginal faces were seen on the city's leafy boulevards. The native population of the area had long since been pushed back onto Indian Reserves north and west of the city. In 1945, when Peggy came to Victoria, native people had no voice with which to protest the loss of their land or to assert their presence: Peggy, ironically, would receive the right to vote in Canada before they did. First Nations people would not be enfranchised in British Columbia for another two years; and it would be 1960 before they received the right to vote in federal elections, as citizens of Canada. But if Peggy was ever aware of these issues, she made no remark upon it. And in 1945, Victoria's cultural landscape was in fact very well suited to receiving a wealthy British socialite like Peggy Pemberton-Carter into its midst.

With the announcement of the end of the war, many spontaneous celebrations erupted on the downtown city streets. Anglican Reverend Michael Coleman had reportedly dragged a newspaper desk out into the middle of Broad Street to give an impromptu sermon of thanks to a circle of enthusiastic worshippers, one of many given on that long-awaited day. But local concern soon followed global thankfulness. The end of the war also spelled severe economic difficulties for Victoria, whose industry up until then had been almost entirely based on supplying the military effort. As Vancouver's bigger markets started to attract Victoria's businesses away, the city lost a vital tax base and could no longer afford to pay for essential infrastructure. And when veterans started returning home en masse, Victoria also started to suffer a severe housing shortage, which would persist for several years. Construction materials were extremely scarce, and by 1948 fifteen hundred families were still waiting for housing in what was reported to be one of the "most congested municipalities in North America."

Victoria residents Leonard and Daisy Hopkins wrote a letter on September 6, 1946, trying to describe the social conditions in the city to their friend Keith Watson in England, who was thinking of immigrating. Houses, they told him, were at a premium, having gone sky-high in price and out of all proportion to their value: "A new stucco finished modern home of five rooms...sells for $6,000." Rentals, they advised, were also high, and hard to get. As to employment, the Hopkins also commented that Victoria's character was more residential than industrial, with increasingly large numbers of unemployed workers. The unions were demanding a forty-hour week, with increased wages and holidays with pay, and the Hopkins thought that there were, currently, about forty strikes in progress. Salesmen, however, were in demand, and if a position could be found the minimum wage for men was $18 a week; for women, $15.

Little of this would have been obvious to a person in Peggy's position when she first arrived. For her and for the Mackenzies, who were by then living in the affluent eastern suburb of Fairfield, the glowing and superlative descriptions of Victoria contained in the 1946 *Victoria City and Vancouver Island Directory*, reminiscent of the over-the-top cinema travelogues of that era, would have matched their impressions far more closely: "Victoria, owing to its really beautiful setting and mild climate, makes an especial appeal to the man or woman lucky enough to have a fixed income, and who is, therefore, no longer under the necessity of engaging in business or other means of making a livelihood." The directory described Victoria as the "Mecca" of such fortunate souls, claiming that as many as eighty percent of the city's residents owned their own homes. It spoke scornfully of the tendency elsewhere to build small houses "with rooms scarcely affording sufficient space to swing the proverbial cat," and assured the reader that in Victoria, the building of large homes with spacious gardens continued apace. The new home builder could apparently choose from a wide selection of sites: rocky, treed, waterfront, or rural. The directory also waxed lyrical about Victoria's setting in the broader landscape of Vancouver Island, describing it as a "veritable island wonderland," abounding in mountains, forests, lakes, and streams, all awaiting the eager farmer, hunter, or traveller.

In this purportedly superlative setting, Peggy and the Mackenzies celebrated a quiet and thankful Christmas of 1945 together. Muriel's daughters, Elizabeth and Maureen, were thrilled to have their "Dragon Aunt" Peggy staying with them at last — so-called because when they had last known her in Shanghai, she had told Muriel firmly that "these girls need to be taught etiquette!" and was the one who would forcibly drag the little girls to the dentist and such other unpleasant appointments of necessity. Elizabeth and Maureen Mackenzie were no longer intimidated by their Dragon Aunt, though — if anything, she had been the one who was quite terrified of the good-looking, robust teenagers who met her at the wharf when she arrived, and the Dragon Aunt label had been a good defence mechanism. But her fears soon dissipated as they got to know each other all over again, and Peggy quickly settled into the relaxed way of life at the Mackenzie residence at 424 St. Charles Street in Fairfield (many years later, the street numbers were changed, and 424 became the current 524). Rod Mackenzie, now retired, spent his days gardening or going to his club; fishing with friends in his sailboat, "Ho-Ho"; and playing golf, in which he could indulge year-round in Victoria's mild climate. Muriel, who was much younger than her husband, was working hard at bringing up two very different daughters. Both of them were intelligent, attractive, and athletic, but while one was ambitious and confident, the other was difficult and high-strung. Money was certainly not a concern at that time for either the Mackenzies or Peggy, who were among those fortunate souls described in the Victoria directory as being on a healthy "fixed income." Peggy was thus able to spend those early days of 1946 very enjoyably, recovering from her wartime experiences in a gentle routine of shopping for new clothes, eating good food, meeting new acquaintances, and exploring the area that she now found herself living in.

The suburb of Fairfield, despite its melodic name, had once been a swamp. Local area historian Ken Roueche quotes Victoria's famous painter Emily Carr, who died the same year that Peggy arrived in the city, as describing Fairfield as a "streak of skunk cabbage bog running between two dairy farms." Vancouver Island Governor James Douglas, who had given Fairfield its name, apparently had a different view. In early 1946, though, Fairfield was still an area with distinctly rural characteristics and relatively few homes. Across the road from 424 St. Charles Street were large fields of vegetables, tended by Chinese gardeners, who lived in small shacks in the centre of the fields. Kerry Langtry Frazer, Muriel's niece, remembered the strong, fragrant smell of celery growing on warm summer mornings as she and Maureen Mackenzie ran south down St. Charles Street to the sheltered swimming beach at Gonzales Bay, just a few minutes away. Large greenhouses and nurseries also stretched along much of Fairfield Road, the main thoroughfare into the area from the city. James K. Nesbitt wrote in his column "Old Homes and Families" in the *Daily Colonist*: "I recall that in a heavy snowfall some of the greenhouses would cave in, and all the small boys for miles around would gather and walk over the

The Mackenzie home at 424 St. Charles Street (now renumbered as 524), Victoria, 1940s. Maureen and Elizabeth Mackenzie are in front. SUSAN HAMERSLEY/MACKENZIE FAMILY

broken glass, crunching it with their feet." Fortunately, such snowfalls were relatively infrequent.

There were also small clusters of neighbourhood shops and local grocery stores within easy walking distance of the Mackenzie home, like the Hollywood Beauty Shop on Lillian Avenue (Prop. Mrs. F.L. Singleton) and William Baylis's country store at the corner of Lillian and Fairfield, which Nesbitt described as "one of those marvellous grocery stores...it was so far out, and neighbours gathered there, sat on boxes, and passed the time of day, it was such a friendly place." Behind the area where the Fairfield Plaza shopping centre sits today was largely vacant land, ideal for local children to play in and explore. And across the road to the south and along the waterfront was Ross Bay Cemetery, an elegant Victorian graveyard. As much a park as a cemetery, Ross Bay is the final resting place of some of British Columbia's most famous pioneers, leaders, and artists, as well as many ordinary private citizens, many of them from other countries, who ended their days in Victoria. Tourists visiting the city now take walking tours of its shady paths; but in 1945, the cemetery had only been recently planted with pine trees and ornamental cherries, and was more favoured as a destination by small boys with big imaginations than by anyone else.

When Muriel and Peggy went for a walk together, the place they would most often go was an empty lot a couple of streets east and south of 424 St. Charles Street: a rocky outcrop of land, covered in long grass and flowering wild broom and dotted with native Garry oak trees, at the corner of Fairfield Road and Foul Bay Road. From the rocks at the top of the hill, Peggy and

Muriel would sit in the late afternoon warmth and admire the sun slowly setting over Juan de Fuca Strait, bathing the snow-capped Olympic Mountains to the south in glorious shades of gold and pink. There were very few homes nearby – only pharmacist Thomas Shotbolt's glamorous house, "Hollywood," below, and next to that, the Newbury home; across Foul Bay Road, to the west, was Margaret Jenkins's School for Girls and the terminus for the No. 6 streetcar from downtown; and to the east, "Windyhaugh" and "The Leasowes," the two homes that settler Jacob Todd had built for his daughters, May and Nellie, who had respectively married the Gillespie boys, Hebden and Alexander. Sheila Anderson, Nellie and Alexander's daughter, was living at the time in the closer house, Windyhaugh. Sheila was close to Peggy's age and had also lived in China; it was not long before the two met and became friends.

Peggy had a stable income from her overseas investments and was receiving sporadic payments from T.S. Yeh, her Chinese lawyer, as he sold her remaining assets in Shanghai and recovered what was left of her investments in China. Some "optimistic person" had bought her garden there for a fraction of its former value, but it was still a reasonably substantial sum – enough to make a down payment at least on another property. Peggy could have had little sense of what the future might hold for her elsewhere, and Victoria must have seemed a very attractive place, where she felt quite comfortable. So it did not take much persuasion from the Mackenzies, as the spring of 1946 rolled around and the city's gardens burst into bloom, for Peggy to decide that this was quite a different Canada from the one she had previously experienced, and that, at least for the present, she would postpone her plans to go to England.

Peggy gave people the impression that her decision at that time did not mean she intended then to stay in Victoria forever; one thing she had clearly learned was to keep all her options open. But she immediately launched three initiatives that certainly suggested some permanence to her thinking, if only subconsciously at that stage. First, exercising her newfound determination and confidence, she managed to take advantage of a loophole in the heavy-fisted British financial regulations of the time – she had never resided in Britain as an adult – that would allow her to transfer her British bank accounts and investments to Canada, something that would otherwise have been almost impossible to do. Then, having secured the means to solidly establish herself financially in the country, Peggy also set about acquiring Canadian citizenship, taking advantage of both her connections in Ottawa and sponsorship by Rod and Muriel Mackenzie. Finally, she cancelled tentative plans to go on a clothes-shopping spree to Paris, using the money she had received from Shanghai, and decided instead to buy the rocky outcrop of land on Fairfield Road and build a home. If she was going to stay in Victoria in the meantime, she would need somewhere to live, and apart from her liking the property, its purchase also seemed to be an excellent investment. With the shortage of housing in Victoria, property values seemed set to rise dramatically in the near future.

The land was owned by the City of Victoria, which was holding a substantial number of properties that had reverted to it after the First World War for unpaid taxes. Somewhat callously, since most of the properties had been owned by war veterans, the city had simply started selling them for well under market value whenever the opportunity arose. So, when Peggy offered on March 4, 1946, to buy the rocky strip of land on Fairfield Road for the sum of $1,850, the city promptly accepted the offer. Peggy immediately paid the required deposit of $500, and ten days later she was a proud landowner again – and she got to work straight away.

Peggy had not wanted to buy the entire piece of property, but only the long, rectangular lot right next to the nearest Gillespie house, because of all the Garry oak trees on it – at her age, she pointed out, she couldn't afford to wait for oak trees to grow. It was about an acre in total, accessed from Fairfield Road. The property still had to be subdivided by the city and registered in her name, but Peggy approached architect John Wade of Birley, Wade & Stockdill to get started on house plans, to be ready for her to look at as soon as possible. In the meantime, she also arranged for the

The property at 1964 Fairfield Road, Victoria, when Peggy Pemberton-Carter purchased it in March 1946.
University of Victoria Archives

The property Peggy purchased was covered with scrubby weeds and long grass. UNIVERSITY OF VICTORIA ARCHIVES

BELOW: *Peggy Abkhazi once commented that high fences make good neighbours. A sturdy fence was one of the first things she had built when she purchased her property in March 1946.* UNIVERSITY OF VICTORIA ARCHIVES

property to be fenced, despite the shortage of construction materials, allowing for a small gate to permit access to the lot from the Gillespie property. Muriel remarked to her subsequently that the fence "has completely and altogether robbed every one of nails, not a nail to be had in all Canada or a ten cent packet of cement." Peggy also had work started immediately on clearing the lot, which was riddled with discarded household items and rubbish. Old photographs show the property covered in gorse and broom, long grass, blackberry bushes and weeds, which Peggy kind-heartedly paid Sheila Anderson's energetic little boys, Malcolm and David, twenty-five cents at a time to help clear

New trees were quickly planted on the Fairfield Road property, although many of them were removed in later years. UNIVERSITY OF VICTORIA ARCHIVES

away. The main work, of course, was done by landscapers, and Peggy hired gardener Frances Barr to start putting in a lawn and get some planting of shrubs under way as quickly as possible, especially around the rainwater pond that had been created out of a depression in the rocks. Fruit trees were put in, and Rod Mackenzie collected some irises from his garden to plant around the pond. Peggy also paid a small construction company, Parfitt Bros., two hundred dollars to build a summer house, designed by John Wade to match his vision of the future house. From the veranda in front of the summer house, located at the northern end of the property, Peggy could sit with the Mackenzies in the long summer evenings and admire the rapid progress being made on her new garden and consider where her new home should be built.

It was a very pleasant way to spend the spring and early summer of 1946, and Peggy appeared to have nothing else on her mind but watching her new property start slowly to gain some semblance of order, shopping for clothes, and spending time with her friends. She bought herself a new piano and seems also to have acquired for herself a new companion: a black Scottie dog named Heather. There seemed little more that the forty-three-year-old needed or wanted in her life.

13

Awake my heart

> *"Falling in love is indescribable and incomprehensible until it occurs to you, and if and when it does, you know and understand."*
>
> — Peggy Abkhazi, letter to Philippa, March 20, 1969

IN JANUARY OF THAT HAPPY, CAREFREE YEAR OF 1946, A LETTER FROM Paris that had wound its way around the world to Victoria, via Shanghai, was delivered to Peggy at 424 St. Charles Street. It was from Prince Nicolas Abkhazi, of whom she had not heard anything for nearly six years. Until then, she had not known whether he was dead or alive.

As his mother had previously written to Peggy, Nicolas had enlisted with the French army. He had been captured near Bourges in 1940 and was imprisoned in a labour camp near Hanover, in northwest Germany. After little more than a year, however, he had been released and sent back to German-occupied Paris, along with other French prisoners of war who were over forty years of age. Younger and stronger men were sent to the labour camps, and older prisoners were by then no longer considered a threat by the Germans. Going home had enabled Nicolas to take care of his sick mother until her death from cancer sometime during 1942. But life in Paris had also been extremely difficult for men like Nicolas, who refused to register with the German-controlled government in order to get the only available jobs. He had been forced instead to make a living by his wits, engaging in black market trading in order to survive. It was not the way of life, as Peggy would say later, that men of his honour or standing – or, indeed, anyone at all – would have wished for. Even the end of the war brought little relief. What few assets that Nicolas had owned before the war were completely gone. Paris was devastated; employment was difficult to find in the city, and the available jobs had been taken by younger men than Nicolas, who was by then forty-seven years old.

With no remaining close family and few friends left alive in Paris, Nicolas had little desire to remain there. But his choices were even more limited than Peggy's had been, with his less mobile French citizenship and his complete lack of resources. He did have cousins living in Connecticut, with whom he seemed to have kept in contact. There is also some suggestion that the Kellys, the wealthy American couple whose affairs Nicolas had managed in France a few years previously and who had returned to the United States, may have offered to sponsor his immigration to America. Whether or not this was the case, the funds that Peggy had left in trust with the Red Cross in New York in 1940 could finally be sent to Nicolas, allowing him to leave Paris. He wrote to Peggy at her last address in Shanghai, not knowing whether or not she still lived there – or if she was even still alive – to thank her for her attempts to help him and his mother.

Although he had not seen her in more than thirteen years, Peggy Pemberton-Carter, as Nicolas would have remembered her, must have represented some very important things to him in that desolate time. They had last met in 1933. In his mind's eye, Peggy would have been a beautiful, elegant reminder of the honourable and dignified life that he had led when he was younger; and she was a beacon of hope for him now, saving him from his dreadful existence in post-war Paris with the Red Cross funds. Most important of all, through twenty-four years of their lives they had enjoyed an enduring intellectual and affectionate friendship, despite infrequent meetings and large gaps of silence in their correspondence. With nobody and nothing left for him in Paris, Nicolas would have had every reason to try to track down one of his oldest friends – and perhaps, this time, to pursue more than just friendship. In his letter to Peggy, Nicolas indicated that he intended to travel to New York, and he suggested that she might meet him there sometime.

To what specific end he was suggesting a meeting we cannot know for sure, for the letter that Prince Nicolas Abkhazi wrote to Peggy is long gone – as is any reply that Peggy may have sent – but its contents were certainly the catalyst for the next most significant decision she would make in her life. In all likelihood, several exchanges of letters occurred between them over the next few months. But resolving whether or not to meet Nicolas in New York was not something she took lightly; she examined her own thoughts and feelings and discussed them at length with her dearest friend at the time, Muriel Mackenzie. Even if a romantic relationship had never developed previously between Nicolas and Peggy, the likelihood of it was clearly occurring to Peggy now – and it seemed that it might be a desirable option, despite the risks. At her age, and after her experiences, the gregarious life she had been living in China in 1938 and 1939 no longer held the same appeal for Peggy, nor would it have been really possible to replicate that life in staid Victoria anyway. With much of the frivolity of her younger days stripped away from her life, Peggy's romantic feelings for Nicolas may suddenly have become clear to her in a way that they could not have been previously, during her strange, naïve existence with Florence Pemberton or as she was finding her feet as an independent adult in pre-war Shanghai.

There certainly were risks in the decision for Peggy. Among her possible reasons for anxiety and doubt were the length of time since the two friends had last met and the desire not to repeat the terrible mistake she had made in entering into her first marriage. When Peggy received the letter from Nicolas, she was as contented as she had ever been since she was a child. During that spring and summer of 1946 her life in Victoria was coming along nicely, with her new property and the house plans under way, and the potential for all of it to be disrupted could have been overwhelming. Peggy may also not have been certain of Nicolas's intentions in writing to her and suggesting a meeting, especially if he had not been clear in his letter. From her perspective, for all she knew, perhaps he simply wanted to look up an old friend. On the other hand, what could she lose in going to New York? If nothing else, she would renew a long-lost friendship. But at best, she might find that her feelings were returned, and even greater happiness might finally be hers.

The old, passive Peggy, waiting for life to happen to her, was long gone, replaced by a new, decisive Peggy, who had very clear ideas about the kind of things that she wanted out of the rest of her life. Muriel encouraged her to go to New York by swearing that Nicolas and Peggy were meant for each other. So, having examined the issue for long enough, Peggy decided to throw caution to the winds. She made arrangements for the work to continue on her land while she was away and planned a trip to New York at the beginning of September 1946. Ostensibly, the purpose of the trip was to see friends in Connecticut and attend some concerts in the city, stopping in Seattle on the way for a little clothes-shopping with her two "nieces," Elizabeth and Maureen Mackenzie. Writing to Muriel from Seattle about the shopping trip, Peggy told her that in preparation for her meeting with Nicolas, she had bought "a perfectly swooning little black hat, with a white, brown-tipped ostrich feather dripping down the back [and] a very lacy blouse, you always say I need softening!" From Seattle, on September 4, Peggy also called Nicolas for the first time and arranged to meet him three days later in New York. The telephone call, she wrote in a letter to Muriel that night, caused her "far greater emotion than I would have thought possible. But I suppose it is rather a moment, two people hearing each other's voices after so many years." Back in Victoria, Muriel Mackenzie was on tenterhooks, waiting to hear news of the meeting. She had still not heard any news when she wrote to Peggy on September 11: "I travelled with you to New York and I have been thinking about you so very much for your first spell there...I do hope that you are very happy that your meeting with Nico has been all that you could wish for yourself, you deserve all the happiness you can get, and I somehow feel sure you are happy."

There appears to be only one document that records the immediate outcome of the meeting between Peggy and Nicolas: a photograph of the two of them, taken on top of the Empire State Building. Nicolas, lean and handsome and wearing dark sunglasses, looks shy and a little uncertain, squinting into the sun. But Peggy, wearing an elegant dress and a little black hat – possibly the one she had bought in Seattle – has a radiant grin from ear to ear. At the bottom of the photograph, in turquoise-blue ink, is written:

"The Triumphant Female. The Prisoner will be shot at Dawn." Along the side are scribbled the words "Ha Ha." It is a glorious, happy record of Nicolas and Peggy's reunion, which was, as Muriel had hoped, everything that Peggy could have wished for. Their meeting, she wrote decades later, was "for both of us as easy and natural as coming home after a long and arduous journey." In 1922, when they first met, Nicolas and Peggy embarked upon the journey; but on September 7, 1946, their love affair began — and it became the anniversary date that Peggy faithfully marked every year in her diary. Next to that date in every entry, along with the number of the anniversary, she wrote the single word "Kalzo." What it signified will remain forever a secret between Peggy and Nicolas.

On September 23 Muriel received a letter in Victoria from Peggy announcing her engagement to Nicolas. Jubilant, Muriel replied immediately: "I am more than thrilled as I think you deserve every bit of happiness, love and affection in the world and I am so delighted that it is to be Nico who is to bestow all this on you. I know he will be happy with you and so long as you are radiantly happy and contented with him, then that is all that matters. I knew of course that it would all come out like this fairy tale...I am sure that you are made for each other and you are dearer to my heart than ever." Throughout the rest of September and October another flurry of letters were exchanged between Muriel and Peggy, as Peggy worked on immigration permits for Nicolas and Muriel investigated accommodation for Nicolas and Peggy in Victoria, as well as wedding options for them.

It was a golden autumn on Vancouver Island. "Never have I seen a more glorious Indian Summer," wrote Muriel; "the warmth in the sun, the peace and quietness over the whole land, the autumn colourings, the Olympics a magnificent stretch of purple and mauve, the sunsets beyond description, each day more perfect than the last." Muriel's glowing descriptions may have been aimed at ensuring that Peggy would return to Victoria; she was a little afraid that her friend might feel inclined to stay in New York: "you will now feel more satisfied with B.C. than ever, and I do think it is quite a nice place to have as your HOME, it is always a nice place to return to from your travels." She need not have been concerned, however: by early November, all of the arrangements had been made to come back to Victoria for the wedding. Nicolas was looking forward to seeing this city of gardens that he had been told was

Peggy and Nicolas, happily reunited in New York City in September 1946. SUSAN
HAMERSLEY/MACKENZIE FAMILY

on the Strait of Georgia, commenting tongue-in-cheek to Peggy that he should
feel right at home, since it sounded just like Abkhazia. Although he had visited
Canada at least once before, in the late 1920s, he had not come as far as
Vancouver Island and was looking forward to seeing it. Peggy and Nicolas
arrived in Vancouver in time to meet briefly her old friend, John Green, who
was on his way back to settle in England, and the couple landed in Victoria
the next day to yet another riotous welcome from the Mackenzies.

Nicolas was a member of the Greek Orthodox Church, and Peggy was
Anglican, but in the 1940s a divorced woman could not be married in the
Anglican Church. So, on November 18, 1946, Peggy and Nicolas were married
in a civil service at the provincial Parliament Buildings. But they also had a
church service: the couple were married by the Rev. Donald L. Gordon in the
Unitarian Church of Our Lord five days later, and the date of this ceremony
was the one that Peggy would always treat as her wedding anniversary. It was
a small ceremony, attended only by the Mackenzie family and four other friends,
with a quiet reception dinner held at the Empress Hotel afterward.

Newly-wed Peggy and Nicolas on Douglas Street in Victoria, 1946. The handwriting seems to be Muriel MacKenzie's. SUSAN HAMERSLEY/MACKENZIE FAMILY

The bridegroom is listed on the civil marriage certificate, without reference to his title, as plain Nicolas Abkhazi; his occupation, "Perfume Merchant, Perfume of Matchabelle Inc., Paris, France." The bride's occupation is simply described as "At Home." The church wedding certificate is very similar, and Peggy and Nicolas signed it simply as "Peggy" and "Nico." To each other, and to their closest friends, that is what they would be for the rest of their lives. In the wedding notice placed in the newspaper, however, the groom is described as Prince Nicolas Abkhazi. And to the rest of the world, particularly Victoria, it was certainly not Peggy and Nico, but Prince — and Princess — Nicolas Abkhazi who were now in residence in their newly rented home at 930 Pemberton Avenue, Victoria.

OPPOSITE: *Nicolas and Peggy Abkhazi's marriage certificate, with wedding notice inset, Victoria, 1946.* UNIVERSITY OF VICTORIA ARCHIVES

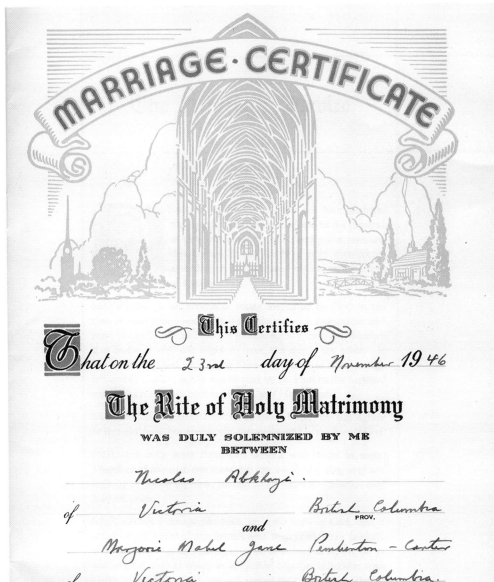

MARRIAGE · CERTIFICATE

~ This Certifies ~

That on the *23rd* day of *November* 19 *46*

The Rite of Holy Matrimony

**WAS DULY SOLEMNIZED BY ME
BETWEEN**

Nicolas Abkhazi

of *Victoria* *British Columbia*
PROV.

and

Marjorie Mabel Jane Pemberton – Carter

of *Victoria* *British Columbia*
PROV.

AND DOMINION OF CANADA

Witness my hand this *23rd* day of *November* 19 *46*

Witnesses

Donald L. Gordon
Officiating Minister

License Number

14

The principality of abkhazia

"Nico and I. . .have lived at such close quarters
with. . .violence, torture, rape, hunger, imprisonment
— and the probability of non-survival. . .and periods
of total poverty. . .I daresay they contributed to a
romantic requirement, or love, for symbols. . .as an
external expression of an internal reality."

— PEGGY ABKHAZI, LETTER TO PHILIPPA, MARCH 15, 1972

IT WAS NO GREAT SURPRISE THAT VICTORIA, THAT MOST BRITISH OF
Canada's cities, embraced this new royal couple in their midst so wholeheartedly.
It is hard to imagine any other city in Canada being such a perfect place for a
European prince and princess to choose to be living: Victoria would provide
an excellent background for the Abkhazis' new life together. Their newly
adopted city also provided plain Peggy Pemberton-Carter with the opportunity
to meticulously reinvent herself as Princess Peggy Abkhazi. And Peggy, who
was quickly becoming a powerful character, set the agenda for her new image
right from the beginning. She must have realized very soon that being a princess
had created a sense of magic about her in Victoria and that it was opening up

Prince Nicolas Abkhazi on Peggy's undeveloped property at 1964 Fairfield Road, 1947. UNIVERSITY OF VICTORIA ARCHIVES

avenues that would not have existed for her as plain Peggy Pemberton-Carter; she had no compunction in taking advantage of that. There also is little doubt that the ugly duckling had at last, without question, become a swan – and that the swan was determined that she be seen as such, at least by the world at large. She "somehow persuaded everyone that she really was a princess," commented one of her neighbours, admiringly.

Peggy may also have been overcompensating for her status as an immigrant to Victoria. Although she hid her feelings of inadequacy at the time, many years later she confessed to her hairdresser's assistant, Michelle Brus, also an immigrant from Europe, that she had found those first few years "very difficult – it wasn't easy to start a whole new way of life that she wasn't used to." This certainly wasn't obvious at the time. "She played her part very well," commented her old friend Roger Napier, whose mother Mary had been in the internment camp at Lunghua with Peggy. "She was an institution, all right." Another factor in the mix was that it must have been very attractive for a woman who had spent most of her life in the social shadows as an unsophisticated "hanger-on" to suddenly become someone whom everyone wanted to know and befriend. From this perspective Peggy clearly relished her newly acquired role, and cultivated an aura of royalty with many people. Finally, Peggy also liked to meet other people's expectations of her – and if they were expecting her to behave like a princess, than that is what she would do. Like a sponge, she had absorbed the elegant manners and protocols of Georgian nobility from Nicolas and his mother in her early days in Paris, and now she brought them out into the light. So she behaved like a princess; but she also demanded that she be treated like one.

Peggy was, however, a contradictory character. Despite the new role that she was playing, she claimed not to have a great deal of time for Victoria "society," and she was highly amused by the excessive deference shown by certain members of the public. She could also be quite scathing about people who tried to curry favour with her simply because she was a princess. With intimate friends like the Mackenzies, she was still the same old Peggy, and she could be very amusing, relating biting anecdotes about the fawning sycophants trying to befriend her. But at the same time, regardless of the pride with which she described her enforced cohabitation during the war with "people from all walks of life," her upbringing and classical education had also left

Work was started on clearing Peggy's property in Victoria by spring of 1946. One year later, the land was already starting to show the promise of the garden it was to become. UNIVERSITY OF VICTORIA ARCHIVES

Peggy with an indelible sense of her innate upper-class superiority. While Peggy could be exquisitely charming and gracious, endearing herself to strangers because of her apparent lack of pretentiousness, at the same time her formal manners and autocratic personality, even without her title, also often made her seem demanding and rigid — especially to the people who worked for her. In her later life, this attitude was more often regarded with tolerant amusement by her friends and helpers. But when she was younger, friendship with Peggy had its price, and liberties could not be taken. "She had very definite views of what a person should be. It turned a lot of people off," commented a good friend who had known Peggy since the early 1960s. "She liked humble people — she liked to be in charge. If people didn't match up, she could tear them apart," said another couple who knew Peggy socially as well as professionally after 1971.

As a result of such contradictory behaviour, some very different recollections exist about the person who turned herself, starting in 1946, into Princess Peggy Abkhazi. There are, for instance, a small handful of people who knew Peggy intimately, especially later in her life, and who have a real sense of the engaging, vulnerable, earthy, and contradictory human being that she was underneath the formal behaviour and the dictatorial style — a real human being who could not only be loved but also liked for who she was, princess or not, faults and all. Many other people seemed to regard her with a deferential state of awe. These were mostly strangers and brief acquaintances, or people with whom she had some common interest, such as gardening, but whom she kept at arm's length. To them, she was and always will be Princess Abkhazi. In many instances she would insist upon it: demanding, for instance, that they address her by her title. In other circumstances, she was simply so successful in inventing her own image as a princess that people automatically responded to that image without any prompting. "I would never call her Peggy — I always called her Princess — you just felt that way about her," said one elderly neighbour reverently after more than ten years' acquaintance with Peggy. "One never put a foot wrong with her, or presumed." To such people she was unfailingly gracious, charming, and regal — unless they were pushy or out of bounds. "Then she would get very regal!" laughed another former neighbour and founding member of the Victoria Rhododendron Society, Diane McLaren, who witnessed a number of people back off rapidly after taking one too many liberties with Peggy. And even then, provided due deference was produced in evidence, the charm and graciousness would soon return.

More than one of her friends described Peggy as a chameleon, capable of being quite a different person to different people. Some of them thought of her as a princess, some as just a friend. Even to those people within her inner circle, Peggy could, and did, show different faces, changing what she said and how she behaved to suit what she thought people wanted to see and to hear. As a result, some people insist that Peggy did not actually care at all about being a princess, and that she had no time for all that nonsense – that is what she told them and what they genuinely believe. There are even people who in the past insisted, quite wrongly, that Peggy was born in Victoria and had made up the whole story about her background. And then there are others, who knew Peggy very well, who are adamant that she was very conscious of her title and demanded to be treated accordingly. Given how contradictory Peggy could be, the conflicting stories, except for the one about her being born in Victoria, are probably equally true. What is certain is this: that Peggy frequently did insist, throughout her life after her marriage to Nicolas, on being addressed as Princess Abkhazi; that, as one friend remarked, "A lot of people thought that they knew Peggy, but they didn't know her as well as they thought they did"; and that the terms on which one got to know Peggy, as a princess or a friend, were quite definitely hers.

A more kindly but certainly less common view shared by a few of her friends is that, having married for love, Peggy would do nothing to shame Nicolas, and that she simply behaved according to what she thought was required by her new status. "She made herself a princess for love," states one of her admirers, adamantly. Perhaps that was part of the equation, but if so, it seems not to have been at any insistence on the part of Peggy's new husband. Nicolas, having found himself a tranquil haven in Victoria with his new wife, seemed quite content to leave his past behind. He had last seen his original homeland of Georgia as a twenty-year-old in 1919. If he did remember much of Tiflis, then Victoria must have felt much like home to Nicolas, at least in its topography and climate. Abkhazia, in the western part of Georgia and on the edge of the Black Sea, had humid coastal valleys "fantastically rich and vigorous" in vegetation, wrote Alexander Nazaroff in 1944 in *The Land and People of Russia*. "Batumi's white houses, descending from hills towards the sea, drown in cascades of roses, camellias, mimosas, magnolias and various exotic flowers, which seem to sprout out of every square foot of ground." The narrow coastal strip along the Black Sea swept quickly upward to the snow-capped Caucasus mountain range, through – in those days, at any rate – thick oak, beech, hornbeam, and pine forests. In the lowlands, around the garden city of Sukhumi, fruit orchards and agriculture predominated; the whole region had always been a popular holiday destination. Language and culture aside, to Nicolas, Victoria must have seemed a twin city to Sukhumi, and Vancouver Island in general almost a carbon copy of Abkhazia.

Nicolas, however, had no apparent desire to transform Victoria into his new kingdom. Unlike Peggy, he seemed to place no great importance on a recognition of his royal title, perhaps because he had no need to. Although they had many experiences in common, Peggy and Nicolas were in a number of ways very different characters; but the combination seemed to work perfectly for both of them. After the hardship of his war years, Nicolas was content to spend his days peacefully in building a new home, in reading and listening to music, and in letting his determined, excited, and energetic wife set the agenda for their life together. "Oh yes, she definitely wore the pants in the relationship," laughed Anita Galitzine, whose Russian husband, Nicholas, was also a refugee prince living in Victoria. "She was the boss," confirmed Peggy's former housekeeper, Maria Serafina Camara. "But," she hastened to add, "she loved him, so she always tried to please him."

Nicolas was a gentle and kindly soul, but he was also a statesman by birth, and very reserved. He rarely spoke of his former life, or of the destiny to rule Abkhazia that had been stolen from him in his youth. That reserve broke only once, when he assured Rosita and Freeman Tovell in Victoria that he was indeed a real prince, not one of those "fake princes" of which there had been so many in Paris. Occasionally Nicolas would also tell anecdotes that bespoke a childhood that was far from ordinary – an electric toy train set that he had had as a child, set up to run through the Abkhazi Palace hallways; or Joseph Stalin coming to the palace as a small boy with his mother, who was one of the palace laundrywomen when Nicolas's father was a child. But, for the most part, he could not have appeared to care less about being a nobleman – although he certainly had no objection to his wife's enjoyment of the role and seemed happy to indulge her in it.

Ironically, then, it was for Nicolas that most people reserved their unqualified homage. "Oh yes, he was a real prince of a fellow — a real gentleman in every sense," recalled Roger Napier. "I was very fond of him." Nicolas was a charming, romantic figure. He was courtly to women, in the old-world style, stately and dignified, but a warm and inviting host. He was highly intelligent and interested in literature, law, and world politics, but his shyness prevented him from engaging in anything more than polite small talk with strangers. Nevertheless people who only met him briefly liked Nicolas greatly, even if they had not managed to learn much, if anything, about him. "Nobody can really look into the soul of a person like Nicolas," commented Anita Galitzine, "and really understand him." But if anyone did understand Nicolas, it was Peggy, who wrote that it was not possible to quickly penetrate beneath "Nico's protective armour of half-teasing reticence, to the unique and enchanting human being underneath" and that "his shyness protects itself with a coating of half-laughing parrying of a direct question — but just give him time...all who know him love and admire him. He is a unique mixture of wisdom, simplicity and kindness — with a well-trained and well-furnished brain and mind and very subtle sense of humour. As Lloyd [McKenzie, a close friend] puts it, 'One savours Nico slowly.'" And as much as they may have loved and respected Peggy, Nicolas was the royal one, stated almost every one of their friends and acquaintances of later years. Peggy, in contrast to Nicolas's statesmanlike qualities and personal charisma, may simply have been too sharp and demanding, too aware of her acquired stature, to attract the unqualified admiration that her husband did.

What is beyond debate or qualification is the expression of love on Nicolas's and Peggy's faces in old photographs, as they look at each other. Despite their differences, Nicolas was the perfect mate for Peggy, the thoughtful and gentle moderator who tempered her more forthright and demanding personality. They were not only devoted to each other, they also served each other's needs completely. As 1947 dawned, Princess Peggy Abkhazi could not have been happier in her choice of a husband. The next step was to create her new realm: the house and garden in Victoria that neighbours and friends would affectionately come to call the "Principality of Abkhazia."

15

The glory of the garden

"I have always found tranquillity in the annual rhythm of gardening."

— Peggy Abkhazi, letter to Philippa, October 22, 1968

What a marvellous situation to be in! Still only in their forties, relatively young and healthy, and with Peggy's solid income from a substantial portfolio of investments, there was no need for the newlyweds to be concerned about money or for either of them to seek employment. They were, effectively, already retired; and the Abkhazis could choose from a range of lifestyles, from ensconcing themselves in some hidden rural retreat to travelling around the world. Despite the attractions that Victoria held for both Peggy and Nicolas, it was by no means certain that they would remain in the city forever. It would have been hard to give up the notion that life still held some other, more sophisticated destination for them. Peggy found Victoria to be quite provincial and Canadians to be less formal and cultured than she would have preferred. She later wrote scathingly (and rather unfairly) in a letter to New Zealand that, in her view, no one in Victoria besides university professors had ever heard of author James Joyce and that "Canadians [are] dedicated to an easygoing enjoyment of untidiness and unnecessary sloppiness."

But alternative places to live were still not readily available to the Abkhazis – Paris had already been ruled out by both of them, and so now had England, which unlike Canada was making it extraordinarily difficult for British citizens to marry French nationals at that time. Peggy had no desire to return to China, which in any event was in the midst of its tumultuous days of civil war leading up to the ultimate declaration of the People's Republic in 1949. New York remained an attractive possibility for both of the Abkhazis, because of friends and family, but it was very expensive to live there, possibly beyond even Peggy's income, and they did not have any connection to the bigger, more sophisticated cities of Canada, or to its French region. The Abkhazis never appear to have considered, for example, living in French-speaking Quebec City or in Montreal, with their European culture and lifestyle, which might have seemed more familiar to them.

Victoria must have been a haven of tranquillity after everything that Peggy and Nicolas had been through. Whether they committed themselves to settling down there for the rest of their lives or not, in the meantime they could devote themselves to whatever kind of lifestyle they chose. And their choice, for now, was to stay. By the beginning of 1947 the subdivision and registration in Peggy's name of the lot that she had bought had been completed, and Peggy's property now even had its own street number: 1964 Fairfield Road. The Abkhazis decided to go ahead with building a

1964 Fairfield Road in January 1947. UNIVERSITY OF VICTORIA ARCHIVES

Peggy Abkhazi on the property, early 1947 – contemplating the work to be done to create a garden. SUSAN HAMERSLEY / MACKENZIE FAMILY

Nicolas Abkhazi in front of Peggy's summer house, January 1947. SUSAN HAMERSLEY / MACKENZIE FAMILY

house on it; and, now that there were the two of them to do it, they also decided to take back direct control of developing the property themselves and to create a garden of their own. Although the Abkhazis may not have been certain how long they would stay in Victoria, their decision seems to have reflected their subconscious frame of mind. A garden, after all, especially one begun from bare rock, takes years – if not decades – to mature. Thus, whether they knew it or not, in making their decision Peggy and Nicolas appear to have committed to stay in Victoria for a very long time.

Both Peggy and Nicolas seem to have enjoyed gardens and flowers all of their lives. Victoria was already becoming famous for its gardening character, and the Abkhazis knew there would be plenty of experts near at hand to help if they needed it. This was fortunate, as neither of them knew a great deal then about the science of plants or the art of gardening. Peggy did have some gardening books that Florence had given to her in England. She had always taken an interest in the design of the various gardens that she had had over the years, even though they were cared for by paid gardeners, and she had especially

Summerhouse and lawn at 1964 Fairfield Road, Victoria, 1947. SUSAN HAMERSLEY/MACKENZIE FAMILY

Peggy on her property in early 1947, holding a box said to be the talcum powder box in which she managed to hide a small sum of traveller's cheques during her internment. SUSAN HAMERSLEY/MACKENZIE FAMILY

enjoyed the last one that she had, in Shanghai. Peggy had also had plenty of practice with cultivation as a result of growing her little prison wildflower garden in Lunghua, despite its limitations. Nicolas, for his part, had a methodical engineering mind and was keen to apply it, and his experience in managing the Kellys' estate in Paris, to the landscaping of the challenging, rocky plot.

Peggy and Nicolas set to work immediately, not wasting any time on a honeymoon: there seemed little need for one after their romantic reunion in New York. They were also both eager to look at Peggy's house plans together and to decide where to build. The plans had been completed by Birley, Wade & Stockdill in August 1946, before Peggy went to New York. Now, with Nicolas's input, John Wade produced revised plans by the beginning of January 1947, and as soon as the weather was suitable, house construction began under the supervision of builder Edwin J. Hunter — the chronic shortage of construction materials plaguing Victoria appeared to be no obstacle where the Abkhazis were concerned. For a site, the couple had chosen the rocky outcrop at the top of the hill that Peggy and Muriel had used as a seat for their sunset viewing the year before.

It was to be an unusual house for Victoria, even in a city that already boasted an eclectic mix of classic Edwardian, Tudor, arts and crafts, and art deco building styles. Several things set it apart, all of them apparently driven by Peggy's determination to have a house entirely dedicated to her lifestyle and preferences. The garden, first and foremost, would be the most important influencing factor in the house's design. As a result of limitations on the size of the house's footprint, owing both to city building regulations and to the small area of level foundation for construction, the Abkhazis had to make careful choices about the use of space. At the back of the house there was to be a huge "garden room," full of tubs, hooks for hanging coats, and mats for rubber boots. "Oh, it was nice," remembered neighbour Joan Fraser wistfully. "It was always full of pails of flowers picked from the garden. It was wonderfully elegant." There was no garage or storage area. The summerhouse held all the gardening implements, and the Abkhazis had no interest in owning a car or driving themselves, so a garage was unnecessary. (A brand new taxicab company, Bluebird Cabs, had just started up business in Victoria, and Peggy promptly signed up for the company's very first account, in the name "Prince and Princess Abkhazi.")

The rest of the house was also planned carefully. A huge living room with vaulted ceilings and a wall-to-wall window, which would permit an excellent view of Juan de Fuca Strait and the Olympic Mountains, would take up about half of the remaining space. The ceilings would provide excellent acoustics for the playing of music, and there would be ample room for a piano. Along the walls on either side of the red brick fireplace would be built-in bookshelves, designed to house the Abkhazis' treasured books. The furnishings would be elegant, but plain — a few Turkish rugs, some Chinese ornaments that Peggy had managed to bring with her to Canada, shelves for vases to hold flowers from the garden-to-be; but no paintings would be hung on the walls. A small kitchen would bridge the living space and the garden room, but although Peggy had no objection to cooking and even enjoyed making some favourite dishes, a dining room was deliberately not included in the plans. If they wished to entertain for dinner, Peggy reasoned, they would take their guests to a restaurant. A master bedroom was to be located to the

Clearing begins for construction of the house, spring 1947. Peggy stands proudly on the foundations.
UNIVERSITY OF VICTORIA ARCHIVES

left of the living room, and separated by a bathroom, a hallway, and the front door; and a small spare room at the back, which would be a den and spare bedroom, completed the plans.

The exterior of the house was to be horizontal wood siding, painted a warm reddish-brown, like the summerhouse. The interior was to be all wood, as a salute, Nicolas said, to the fact that the house was being built in a "country covered in woods." The walls were to be plywood, of a warm, mellow gold. "Walking inside used to be like walking into a big golden jewel box," recalled Joan Fraser. Building materials were still, however, in very short supply, and even Peggy's newfound influence had its limits. For the floors, therefore, the Abkhazis had to be content with used oak parquet flooring, from an old house in Oak Bay that was being demolished. They would have preferred the more traditional Canadian pine boards, but both Peggy and Nicolas had grown up with parquet floors — at least they felt familiar. It was under the floors that the most important feature was installed, at least from Peggy's perspective — the first radiant heating system in Victoria. Peggy was quite determined never to be cold again.

Peggy standing in the house as the walls start to rise, 1947. UNIVERSITY OF VICTORIA ARCHIVES

Construction and landscaping continued throughout 1947 and much of 1948. UNIVERSITY OF VICTORIA ARCHIVES

Housebuilder Edwin J. Hunter undertook the construction of the house, which was ready to be moved into by the summer of 1948, although plumbing and wiring would not be completed for at least another year. The landscape was still quite bare when the Abkhazis moved in. UNIVERSITY OF VICTORIA ARCHIVES

Peggy and Nicolas Abkhazi enjoying their very young garden, 1947. PHILIPPA PROUDFOOT (NÉE DAVYS)

BELOW: *Interior of the house, February 1948. Although Peggy purchased a piano almost as soon as she decided to stay in Victoria, no one can remember ever hearing her play.* UNIVERSITY OF VICTORIA ARCHIVES

BELOW: *Exterior of the new house, 1948.* UNIVERSITY OF VICTORIA ARCHIVES

All of this was still a two-dimensional blueprint dream in early 1947 as work was commenced on the foundations, and Peggy and Nicolas got started on landscaping the property. The summerhouse was far too small to live in, so Peggy and Nicolas stayed for the meantime in the room they had rented for fifty dollars a month in a large house on Pemberton Avenue. The owner had been rather reluctant to let out the room to a pair of immigrants but was swayed by Nicolas's charming manners; not sufficiently, however, to be persuaded to allow Peggy and Nicolas kitchen privileges, except at dinnertime. Peggy solved the problem of daytime nourishment by taking breakfast with them to the garden and cooking lunch on a hot plate in the summerhouse, which had had electricity connected to it. In the evenings the tired pair would trudge back uphill in their dirt-covered overalls the half mile to their rented quarters; Peggy would usually cook steak for dinner – it was easy, she said, and affordable – and Nicolas would do the washing up. Then, as Peggy said, they "went to bed and slept like labourers!" The Abkhazis also hired help, including contractor Peris Atkinson and Rockholme Gardens, to undertake the heavy work of moving rocks and planting large trees and shrubs. Surprisingly, given Peggy's strong tendencies to want to be in charge, it was Nicolas who usually took responsibility for the hiring and management of gardeners and handymen – it was, perhaps, a natural role, given his property management experience in France. Leaving these responsibilities in his hands also allowed Peggy to concentrate on planning the garden.

How does one tackle an acre of steeply sloping, rocky land, with a scattering of mature oak trees and very little else on it, and turn it into a garden of dreamed-of glorious dimensions? The property was rectangular at that stage, thin and long. It sloped upward from Fairfield Road at a twisted angle, so that its northeast corner was the highest, its southwest corner the lowest, and both other corners roughly level, somewhere in height about halfway between the other two – like a blanket held at opposite corners by one tall person and one short person, and held at the other corners by two people of average height. The house was being built on the apex of the property – about halfway along the length of the rectangle, on its upper slope and looking down at a 270-degree angle over the whole garden. The rainwater pond that had already been created was below, and to the right, of the house site, near the summerhouse. But if the house was to have a patio, where would it go? How were steps or paths to the garden from the house, and from the front gate on Fairfield Road, to be created? Most important of all, what kind of plants would grow on such a rocky, sloping site? At first Peggy had no idea at all, but both she and Nicolas thought that, like a child, the garden should simply be allowed to grow. And like any new parents, they learned as they went. As ideas were born, they were implemented – and if those ideas didn't work, then Peggy and Nicolas tried something else. If the tulips that they planted to accent the lily-of-the-valley died out, so be it. The snowy white lilies looked elegant all by themselves.

While beginning such an ambitious garden was a brand-new experience for Peggy, she was quite undaunted. Her most recent experience of design had been her property in Shanghai, which had of course been cared for by her Chinese gardeners. That garden – like all gardens in Shanghai, a city located on a delta – had been completely flat, requiring a very different planning concept; but what Peggy remembered best about it was the effect of a river. It was this memory that gave her the idea of creating a garden in Victoria based on similar Chinese concepts. Although she later claimed never to have had any grand design or master plan for the garden, in Nicole Eaton and Hilary Weston's 1989 collection of essays on gardens in Canada, *In a Canadian Garden*, Peggy spoke of two things that were important to her, and this Chinese concept was one of them. "When planning the garden I had a picture in my mind of the Yangtze River. There would be no sharp angles; it should curve on and on, flowing peacefully, everything circular. The Chinese way of gardening doesn't show or tell everything at once. It involves an arrangement of small 'rooms' with the idea that one is continually going around curves to yet another garden." The second important thing was the rock that she had first sat on to watch the sunsets: "I loved that rock; it seemed to have been there for ever, and, after years of personal upheavals, it gave me a sense of security and permanence."

The notion of small rooms fitted the property at 1964 Fairfield Road perfectly, and Peggy and Nicolas started to implement the idea. Flowing down the lower part of the property from north to south, between the Garry oak trees and bordered by flowering heather bushes, was to be a curved strip of thick, closely cut Japanese bent-grass, to create the central idea of a river. The summerhouse was at the top end of this lawn: one could sit on the veranda and admire the "downstream" effect. The moss-covered rocks above the pathway that bordered the lawn were scraped clean – Peggy apparently preferred the silvery-grey contrast they offered, free of their damp covering. Nicolas, meanwhile, applied his scientific mind to the pond. He could see, by the careful damming of the lower end, that a series of pools could be created in the depressions in the rock, looking as if they naturally cascaded into each other. Peggy was enthralled – she loved the idea of having several ponds and of the wild birds they might attract. The natural basins were carefully scraped out by hand of any debris and filled by a combination of rainwater and handwatering. Later, when the house was built, an artfully placed gutter would help direct rainwater runoff into the lowest pond. Nicolas oversaw technical matters: he looked after soil and insect management; he designed and built planter boxes that could be opened from the sides, allowing the roots of the plants in them to be handled without traumatizing them; and he worked on ideas to stabilize the terraces rising above the bent-grass lawn with careful planting. A keen photographer, Nicolas is also said to have taken hundreds of slides of the developing garden and copious notes on the work being done, to be reviewed over the winter months for new ideas and further planning. It was a practice that he would apparently maintain, and every winter the couple would huddle over the photographs, making plans for the next season. Nicolas also influenced the garden in a more direct, if still subtle way: many of the trees and shrubs in the garden are very similar to, if not the same as, those found in his native Georgia.

In that first couple of years Peggy and Nicolas learned from their books, and by experimenting – and not surprisingly they made plenty of mistakes at the beginning. They had never gardened in a climate like Victoria's and hadn't yet acquired the local inside knowledge of its idiosyncrasies, such as the fact that roses in Victoria suffered badly from blight. When to their dismay they discovered this, their idea of having a formal rose garden was quickly abandoned – but not before a major investment in rose bushes had been made. The same thing happened when Peggy enthusiastically planted hundreds of dollars' worth of tulip bulbs, with fond memories of the tulip gardens from her youth in England. Within two years, her disease-prone tulips were all gone. But her enthusiasm was unlimited, and Peggy and Nicolas started taking advice from some of the experts; and in garden-loving Victoria, there were plenty of those. From one source or another, the practical idea of planting a combination of rhododendrons and alpine evergreens, much more suited to the local environment, was eventually adopted. Peggy set about acquiring as many mature plants as she could, reasoning that at their age, she and Nicolas did not want to wait for seedlings to mature.

They were fortunate to be living in Victoria in the late 1940s, because several nurserymen had wonderful collections of mature plants: Layritz, Lohbrunner, Christianson, Goddard, and Albert de Mezey, among others. Ed Lohbrunner, in particular, was a world authority on alpine plants and conifers, even in his early forties. From his nursery at Union Avenue, which he moved one year later to Lakeview Gardens in the Blenkinsop Valley, Lohbrunner over the years is said to have supplied plants to the King of Sweden, the Emperor of Japan, and English royalty. Now he had another royal customer, in the shape of the determined Princess Peggy Abkhazi. Lohbrunner, according to his daughter Joan Alston-Stewart, did not particularly like dogs; but he was so enamoured of both Princess Abkhazi and her little shelties that when she showed up at his nursery in a taxi with her dogs in tow, not a murmur of objection was ever raised. From the charmed Lohbrunner and from others, Peggy managed from time to time to acquire mature rhododendron plants, grown from seed, some of which had never flowered despite being up to fifty years old. Nor would they, she was told, until they were at least another twenty years older. Whether she purchased or was given the plants is uncertain – Peggy told both versions to enough people that the truth is difficult to gauge – but Ed Lohbrunner in particular was very generous with his special plants and was known for giving them away. Either way, it was surprising that it was so easy for a newcomer to Victoria to acquire the plants, when there must have been many other well-known and experienced rhododendron growers on the island who would have coveted them. But then, after all, Peggy was not only a princess, but a very charming and determined one – she had decided that she wanted the unusual plants, so she got them. Her faith was later rewarded when the plants did flower, on schedule, at about seventy years of age.

The Abkhazis also invested heavily in evergreens at the beginning. The fences that had been erected around the property were fairly high, based on Peggy's premise that "high fences make good neighbours." Along the Fairfield Road side, they planted a cypress hedge for additional privacy. This they later replaced with spruce, then with hornbeams, a native of Abkhazia, when the

Peggy working in her developing garden, late 1940s.
UNIVERSITY OF VICTORIA ARCHIVES

spruce overgrew — something else that Peggy hadn't anticipated. But if she did not have much practical knowledge about plants, she certainly had an artistic flair, and she combined it with learning fast about what would work and what did not. Along much of the sloping rock faces, close to the ponds, she employed weeping spruce in a traditional Chinese fashion, positioning it to grow downward, draping itself against the grey rocks. On the banks, conifers were trained to grow down along the steps toward the ponds. They would eventually cascade down the rocks, like a waterfall, with dark green weeping yew providing a contrast against the blue of the spruce. "These are slow-growing plants," remarked contemporary Victorian conifer expert Gordon Mackay, "but they are really well-situated. The Abkhazis were obviously prepared to wait twenty-five years to see them mature."

As it turned out, they were indeed prepared to wait. The Abkhazis moved into their new house during the summer of 1948, even though it was far from complete and would not be fully finished for another two years. And on January 31, 1949, the City of Victoria accepted another offer from Peggy — this time to purchase a 20,000-square-foot parcel of land about halfway along the western edge of the property, which would turn the property into a sideways "T" shape and connect it with Foul Bay Road on its western side. The purchase price was $832.50, and the title, like that of the rest of the property, was registered only in Peggy's name. The extra space — nearly a third again the size of the existing property — would allow for the accumulation of much-needed compost, without spoiling the look of the garden; and although houses could be, and were, built on either side of it, it would also ensure that no one could build directly in front of their view.

With the growing investment in their garden, both financial and emotional, it was starting to look very much like the Abkhazis had, indeed, decided to stay put in Victoria.

Ponds were created in the natural depressions in the rocks on the property by scraping out the hollows and using a combination of handwatering and rainwater. UNIVERSITY OF VICTORIA ARCHIVES

Peggy with Muriel and Rod Mackenzie in the still-developing plot at 1964 Fairfield Road, late 1940s. SUSAN HAMERSLEY/MACKENZIE FAMILY

Peggy relaxing in her garden, which is starting to show signs of its future promise - late 1940s.
UNIVERSITY OF VICTORIA ARCHIVES

Christmas Day, 1948, in front of the Abkhazis' new home at 1964 Fairfield Road. From left to right: Norman Barr, Elizabeth Mackenzie, Muriel Mackenzie, Rod Mackenzie, Oriane Bell; in front, Peggy and Maureen Mackenzie. SUSAN HAMERSLEY/ MACKENZIE FAMILY

16

Halcyon days

"My life began in my forties."

— Peggy Abkhazi, letter to Philippa, August 31, 1986

THE INSULATED AND IDYLLIC LIFESTYLE THAT PEGGY CREATED FOR NICOLAS and herself in the Victoria of the 1950s and 1960s is hard for most people to imagine today, amid the rush and bustle of the twenty-first century. There was no need for either of them to work in order to pay the bills, and they were surrounded by hired help, especially in the garden, despite Muriel Mackenzie's earlier warnings that they would have to "do for themselves." Life was a constant round of gardening, playing with their dogs – Peggy had quickly acquired two shelties, in addition to her little black Scottie, Heather – and socializing with a select group of friends and acquaintances. The Abkhazis were invited to the annual balls at the Lieutenant Governor's residence and other such elite functions; and they frequently travelled to San Francisco, New York, and Paris, to see concerts and go shopping. Peggy held deprecative views about North American materialism – she once wrote: "I was reminded once again of the difference in the sense of values of this new American continent where material comfort and possessions and status symbols are considered as being of the greatest importance – as compared to the older European aristocratic tradition, where hospitality, generosity in sharing, warmth, courage, gaiety and wit – and above all, ideas, are considered to be of infinitely more value." Nevertheless, she loved buying elegant clothes for herself, now that there was no one to stop her wearing them – and she seemed to shock her friend Muriel Mackenzie more than once with the extravagant number of dresses that she seemed to own.

It was like living in an old-fashioned movie, and Peggy was not only writing the script but acting as its meticulous and demanding director. After the long years of being deprived of any self-indulgence, Princess Peggy was uncompromisingly determined to do exactly as she pleased and to ensure that everything in her life should be as perfect as possible. The Abkhazis' daily life while they resided at 1964 Fairfield Road was therefore also pleasant and orderly, and the emphasis was always more on enjoyment and ease than on domestic toil. They took taxis everywhere, for shopping, socializing, and travelling. Peggy once took a Bluebird taxi to Portland, Oregon, to catch a flight to Honolulu; it was simply, to her, more convenient than any other form of transportation. She did her banking – where else? – with the Royal Bank of Canada. Although this may have been done with her tongue held firmly in her cheek, Peggy was not immune to symbolism. Laundry was sent out to be done, and someone came in to clean the house regularly; and if any serious entertaining was required, the Abkhazis, as Peggy had planned, would take their guests out to a restaurant.

Peggy would cook meals only for herself and Nicolas. Although the Abkhazis held cocktail parties for small groups of friends in their living room, dinner parties were a different matter entirely. By the 1960s, the Union Club of Victoria had become the preferred venue for their soirées; Nicolas had joined in 1962, at the persuasion of some friends and with Peggy's encouragement. The Union Club was a venerable Victoria institution, founded in 1879, according to its own literature, to be "an oasis of calm in the turbulent early days of Confederation" — a refuge for Victorian gentlemen from the Wild West atmosphere of post–gold rush B.C. politics. It provided lounges and dining, game rooms and accommodation — but, until the 1980s, while a gentleman could take his dog to the Union Club, his wife could not be a member. Women were confined, if they insisted on coming, to the Ladies' Dining Room. Once a year, as a gesture to the feminine element, the club would hold a ball for couples to attend. The Union Club was a somewhat staid and leather-clad institution, where "the elite went to eat" (and still essentially is, despite its protestations that "like all great traditions, the way of the Gentleman's Club is not without flexibility, and the Union Club has adapted to modern needs"). A full meal with drinks cost about two dollars in the 1960s — a cocktail, all of forty cents. Peggy described the club in 1967, with her typical forthrightness, as having a "slightly frowsty elegance" and as being from a vanished era. But regardless of such affectionate scorn, the club was still apparently a suitable venue for her to entertain according to the style that she preferred — a style that was itself rapidly vanishing — and the Abkhazis held court there quite regularly. "It was their second home," remarked one frequent guest. A former Union Club president, Judge Lloyd McKenzie, recalled that Peggy would carefully select the menu in advance and held the chef and the manager, Paul Bissley, in constant terror of failing to meet her exacting standards. Judge McKenzie recollected that Bissley made a habit of informing the current president of the club whenever "the royal family" were to be dining; and their guests certainly noticed that Peggy and Nicolas always received the very best of service.

Peggy tended to keep the different parts of her life quite separate in those early days. She did not mix her friends, if they were from different social circles, nor her gardening acquaintances with members of the dog training group to which she belonged. Until she was much older, and had mellowed to a certain extent, even her direct neighbours were kept politely but firmly behind the fences, as of course neighbours should be. That way, when neighbourly disputes arose — as they did, for example, when Peggy and Nicolas burned garden waste and the smoke blew over the houses downwind of them, or when a television aerial was erected at the back of the property, without consultation, right in the middle of one neighbour's view of the mountains — the dispute could be resolved without the complication of friendship being involved. Peggy's strategy, which seemed to be effective, was to stand firmly on her royal dignity. The one exception Peggy made was in the case of the Anderson family, with whom she was friends already, and who in any event moved away from Fairfield Road before very long.

And as much as Peggy loved to see visitors, they were never invited to stay at the Abkhazi home. The pretext was that the second bedroom was needed for Nicolas, in case of an asthma attack – he suffered chronically from allergies, especially when the broom in the garden was in flower – but the more likely reason was a complete aversion to having to share her private space with anyone but Nicolas. When she went on vacations, it was either just with Nicolas or with one or two companions that she had carefully selected. Nicolas was less inclined to travel than Peggy was. He had seen enough upheaval by then to be quite content with staying at home. His last long excursion with Peggy was to Paris, in 1963 – and he flatly refused to go to Hawaii with her at all. Lying on a hot tropical beach was definitely not his style, and Peggy always had to find someone else to go with her, for she was equally determined not to be deprived of her winter escape to Waikiki.

But one of their favourite destinations together for a vacation, from as early as 1947, was, all the same, a beach: Long Beach, on the west coast of Vancouver Island. One of the most westerly parts of British Columbia, the area generally known as Long Beach is really a collection of dozens of surf beaches and rocky bays. The actual Long Beach stretches along the six-mile length of Wickaninnish Bay, sandwiched between Florencia Bay with its gold-bearing sands at one end and a collection of small golden bays at the other. All of these beaches and bays run alongside a strip of thick cedar and spruce forest between the fishing villages of Tofino to the northwest and Ucluelet, at the head of Barkley Sound, twenty-six miles to the southeast. Barkley Sound itself narrows quickly to a saltwater inlet that runs another twenty-five miles inland, north and east again, to the industrial town of Port Alberni, several hours by road north from Victoria. It is now a relatively short drive from Victoria directly to Tofino on a good road: but in 1945, twenty-five years before a decision was made to turn most of this strip into a world-famous national park reserve, Long Beach was an isolated and wild community, inaccessible by road from the east coast and with fewer than one thousand inhabitants.

Until that time, the only access to the area from the outside world for decades had been the twice-monthly visit of the steamship MV *Maquinna*, out of Victoria. The *Maquinna* had to take the long coastal route through the rough waters of Juan de Fuca Strait and across the rolling swells of the open Pacific Ocean. As a result it was never popular with its seasick passengers, of whom there were relatively few. On a research trip along the coast in 1946, Californian marine biologist Edward Ricketts wrote this about the area in a letter to his good friend, American novelist John Steinbeck: "It's amazing how few people even in Victoria have been on the west coast; it's far more a terra incognita to them than here it was to us." Ricketts went on to depict a colourful and raucous, laid-back way of life for the rugged coastal people, despite their isolation from the rest of the world. While the arrival of the *Maquinna* with its load of mail and supplies was always eagerly awaited, these people must also have greatly enjoyed their freedom from the bustle and woes of the modern world.

By 1946, however, those days of blissful isolation were numbered for the west coast of Vancouver Island. During the Second World War an airfield had been built on part of the land beside Long Beach to service a small military base and a rough road had been constructed to connect Tofino and Ucluelet. This meant much easier access to Long Beach from Victoria – instead of having to take the long, wallowing trip on the *Maquinna* from Victoria, it was now much simpler to drive a few hours north to Port Alberni, catch a small boat west up Barkley Sound to Ucluelet, and complete the journey to Long Beach by the new road. And as early as 1952, tourism promoters were strongly advocating pushing through yet another road: this time, to join the west coast at Tofino all the way to the east at Port Alberni. While that road would not be open for another twelve years, in the meantime the regular boat service from Port Alberni up Barkley Sound was bringing an increasing number of visitors to the coast each year. There were also scheduled and charter flights into the airfield at Long Beach, serviced by no less than four different companies, including the charmingly named Ginger Coote Airways.

George Nicholson, a former Tofino resident who had a regular column in the *Daily Colonist* newspaper in Victoria, wrote glowingly of the possibilities for tourism at Long Beach and was one of the strongest advocates of opening up the new road. "Long Beach is the coming seaside resort," he trumpeted in the newspaper on May 24, 1952. Nicholson waxed lyrical about the many recreational activities that could be undertaken. At low tide, he urged, the sand was firm enough to drive on – pilings that had been sunk into the beach to prevent enemy aircraft landing had already nearly all disappeared and now presented little hazard. One could beachcomb for Japanese glass fishing floats, still plentiful at the time – taking care of course not to pick up a floating Japanese mine, some of which were still washing up on the tide. For culinary pleasure, Nicholson recommending trying whale meat; whaling was still a viable industry on the coast. It was, he assured his readers, very palatable, "especially when eaten cold...the mistake most housewives make is serving it hot, and a slightly oily odour is noticeable."

Apart from the beauty and the wildness of Long Beach, the area had several attractions as a holiday destination for both Peggy and Nicolas when they first started going there in 1947. For Peggy, it was the nearest thing to one of the tropical swimming beaches of her youth that Nicolas also would go to; and she could take her beloved dogs to roam on the beach with her for hours on end. For Nicolas, Long Beach was a place to get some welcome respite from his seasonal asthma and allergies, and after their first visit, if Peggy was busy with the garden he would often go to Long Beach on his own. But at least once every year until the late 1950s Peggy and Nicolas went there together. The couple would bundle their bags and the dogs into a Bluebird taxi to drive up the coast on the narrow two-lane road from Victoria to Nanaimo, south of Port Alberni, and then charter a private flight over to Long Beach. There they would stay at the south end of Long Beach at the Wickaninnish Cabins, owned by Joseph and Nellie Webb.

The accommodation was a far cry from the latter-day luxury of the modern Wickaninnish Inn at Chesterman Beach, a little farther north along the coast toward Tofino. In 1947 the Wickaninnish Cabins did boast a main lodge building, but most of the guest accommodation was in half a dozen self-contained buildings cobbled together from salvaged Quonset huts from the defunct military base and materials gathered from the beach. The cabins were serviced with spring water and heated by open fireplaces; insulation was provided by old newspapers and magazines stuffed into the walls and offering little resistance to leaks in a rainstorm. But Peggy and Nicolas adored their rustic and primitive retreat. They would spend long hours walking along the beach with the dogs and relaxing in the sunshine, or reading in front of the

Nicolas Abkhazi at Long Beach, on the west coast of Vancouver Island, 1950s.
UNIVERSITY OF VICTORIA ARCHIVES

Peggy Abkhazi and two of her shelties at Long Beach, 1950. SUSAN HAMERSLEY/MACKENZIE FAMILY

fire. Nicolas, ever the engineer, is said to have helped build the original pathway from the Wickaninnish Cabins over to South Beach, now a tourist trail from the National Park office located at the same site. Whether this claim is accurate or not, Long Beach was about as far removed from Nicolas's unhappy experiences in Europe as it was possible to be, and it seems to have been one of his favourite places on earth. It was less so for Peggy, who unlike Nicolas had already spent plenty of her life in such reclusive retreats. She very much enjoyed going there for vacations, but Peggy recounted much later, with absolutely no regrets, that when she was given the opportunity in the early 1950s to buy something like a thousand acres of land on Wickaninnish Bay for a dollar an acre, she had opted instead to spend the money on a trip to San Francisco to see friends and go to the opera — and that she had "had a ball!"

Almost every year, Nicolas and Peggy had the same neighbour in one of the nearby cabins — a satirical and cultivated fellow who appeared to spend most of his time sketching on a notepad. He hit it off particularly with Nicolas, who shared his sense of humour, and the two would greet each other with delight each year when they saw that the other had returned. In jest, the neighbour would sketch caricatures of Nicolas, depicting him as Don Quixote, off to do battle on the beach. Now most of these sketches are in the safekeeping of the Art Gallery of Greater Victoria. The artist was Arthur Lismer, one of

Peggy walking at Long Beach, a favourite holiday destination for the Abkhazis.
UNIVERSITY OF VICTORIA ARCHIVES

Peggy and shelties on the dock at Tofino, near Long Beach, 1955. UNIVERSITY OF VICTORIA ARCHIVES

Canada's most important landscape painters and a member of the famous Group of Seven. Long Beach was a favourite vacation spot for Lismer and his wife, Esther, throughout the 1950s, and the cove at the south end of Wickaninnish Beach, where he used to draw his sketches of Nicolas, is now named Lismer Cove.

Sometime in the late 1950s Peggy stopped going to Long Beach altogether; Nicolas may have kept visiting longer than she did. Even without the road, more and more people were coming into the area, and it was losing its aura of exclusivity. By the mid-1960s the rustic Wickaninnish Cabins were gone completely, replaced by a more sophisticated lodge built by Robin Fells, and the south end of Long Beach was becoming populated with squatters' cabins and a burgeoning hippie crowd. "It was quite the party spot," admits local historian Ken Gibson. "There were hippies, dogs, kids, everywhere. It was pretty wild." By then there was a general store and a gas station, as well as several campgrounds on the beach. Peggy would have been horrified. In the early 1970s, when the area was turned into a National Park reserve, the resident population was turned out and all the private land in the area was expropriated

Peggy was always an avid outdoorsperson. Long Beach offered the Abkhazis a rustic retreat that they thoroughly enjoyed. UNIVERSITY OF VICTORIA ARCHIVES

Old Wickaninnish Cabins, Long Beach, 1955. UNIVERSITY OF VICTORIA ARCHIVES

by the federal government for the park. Even if Peggy had bought land in the area, it too presumably would have been acquired by the government. By that time, however, there was little trace of the idyll that Peggy and Nicolas had once enjoyed.

Muriel and Rod Mackenzie remained close friends with the Abkhazis, but Rod, much older than the others, died in 1957 and was followed by Muriel in 1964. As both Muriel and Peggy had anticipated, their lives had grown further apart after Peggy's marriage, and the old intimacy was replaced with a less intense, but more comfortable, companionship. Peggy was absorbed with her new husband and her garden, while Muriel, who was six years older than Peggy, was dealing with an aging and difficult husband as well as two maturing daughters. During the 1950s both of Muriel's daughters, Elizabeth and Maureen, were married. Elizabeth moved away with her new husband, Jack Breen, eventually settling in Port Alberni, and Maureen, after marrying Mike Hamersley, stayed in Victoria.

Peggy retained a strong bond to both of Muriel's daughters, even after

Maureen Mackenzie and her cousin Kerry Langtry Frazer in the Abkhazis' garden, 1950s.
SUSAN HAMERSLEY / MACKENZIE FAMILY

The Mackenzie family at 424 St. Charles Street, Victoria: Elizabeth is about to depart for Vancouver - early 1950s. SUSAN HAMERSLEY / MACKENZIE FAMILY

Peggy and Maureen in the garden at the house at 1964 Fairfield Road, 1950. Peggy is holding the first of many dogs that she acquired in Victoria, her little black Scottie, Heather.
SUSAN HAMERSLEY / MACKENZIE FAMILY

their mother's death, and took an interest in their children as well — especially Elizabeth's son, Rod Breen, who had suffered health problems as a child. She also carried on teaching etiquette to Maureen's daughter, Susan Hamersley, who remembered knowing how to properly uncork wine and champagne at dinner, courtesy of "Auntie Peggy," before she was ten years old. But, although Peggy was clearly very fond of them and dedicated her draft memoir *A Dragon Aunt Remembers* to them, she never treated Elizabeth and Maureen like daughters. She was

Peggy and Elizabeth Mackenzie at 424 St. Charles Street, on the day of Elizabeth's wedding to Jack Breen, August 1955. SUSAN HAMERSLEY/MACKENZIE FAMILY

The Langtry farm in Duncan, British Columbia, 1954. From left to right: Peggy, Muriel Mackenzie, Winnifred Langtry (Muriel's brother), Frances Langtry, Rod Mackenzie. SUSAN HAMERSLEY/MACKENZIE FAMILY

generous to them, but she was not their mother, and she never attempted to assume a role of that nature with them even when their mother was gone. The person for whom that role was reserved, if only for a few years, was Philippa Davys, Stanley's daughter and Peggy's goddaughter.

In 1960 Stanley Davys and Peggy had met, for the first time since 1941, in San Francisco. But by then each of them had been married for nearly fifteen years, and they had both changed greatly — and the shipboard magic that Peggy had once shared with the rugged New Zealander was long gone. Their spouses were with them, and they had little in common. The meeting was amiable but awkward for all four of them. But although Peggy and Stanley were never as close again as they had been in 1941, the relationship between Peggy and Stanley's daughter, Philippa, when they finally met, was another matter entirely.

Peggy and Nicolas were already in their forties when they got married, and the idea of having a child never seems to have entered into the equation.

Peggy had never been comfortable with young children — her self-imposed title of "Dragon Aunt" with Elizabeth and Maureen Mackenzie may have been as much for her own protection as anything else. She had not even attended her New Zealand goddaughter's christening in 1947, although the huge distance to travel was a reasonable enough excuse to have given. But in July 1966, when Peggy did meet nineteen-year-old Philippa Davys for the first time, she completely lost her heart to her. Perhaps it was because Philippa reminded Peggy of her father Stanley and brought back the fond memories of their relationship before the war; or maybe Peggy simply decided to throw herself wholeheartedly into the godmotherly role. It may well have been a combination of the two, together with the fact that Philippa, even at that age, seemed to thoroughly enjoy Peggy's companionship for its own sake, and Peggy responded accordingly.

Peggy in San Francisco, 1957: Peggy and Nicolas would frequently go to San Francisco to shop, visit friends, and especially go to the opera. PHILIPPA PROUDFOOT (NÉE DAVYS)

Peggy with her goddaughter, New Zealander Philippa Davys, in Victoria, 1968-69. PHILIPPA PROUDFOOT (NÉE DAVYS)

Nicolas and Peggy with Philippa Davys, at their home in Victoria, 1968-69. PHILIPPA PROUDFOOT (NÉE DAVYS)

Peggy and Philippa, in the garden, 1968-69. PHILIPPA PROUDFOOT (NÉE DAVYS)

Peggy on holiday in Waikiki, Hawaii, late 1960s. PHILIPPA PROUDFOOT (NÉE DAVYS)

The young New Zealander had just spent a year going to school in New York state on an American Field Scholarship and was passing through San Francisco on her way home to New Zealand. Peggy, who until then had only exchanged sporadic and formal correspondence with her goddaughter, decided to fly down and spend a few days with Philippa to get to know her. On their meeting, Peggy fell instantly in love. She had not even returned home before she wrote fervently to Philippa from the Seattle airport: "The past three days have been amongst the happiest in my life – for which I thank you – it is a joy to know that we speak the same language. You have taken a piece of my heart with you and it will remain yours for so long as I live." Saying goodbye had been very difficult: "You so disoriented me, that I, who thought I had forgotten how to cry, was extremely glad of my sunglasses as a defence."

It was the first letter in a series that would see long missives exchanged regularly between the two women for the next several years and beyond, discussing literature, politics, the state of Philippa's love life, and her difficult relationship with her stubborn father. The pair spent two vacations together in Hawaii, where Peggy could indulge her love of the sunshine and have her goddaughter to herself for several weeks. In her letters, Peggy lovingly and blithely dispensed advice on all manner of issues, much of which the equally strongly opinionated Philippa would reject, in strong terms – very much as a mother and daughter would. But Peggy could be far more daring with Philippa than she had been with her own mother. "Opera without sex," she declared boldly to Philippa in one letter, "is a contradiction in terms!"

Peggy diligently copied out literary reviews and excerpts of articles that she thought Philippa might be interested in, and the two would compare movies they had seen, music, and books. Peggy had loved Peter Ustinov's *Hot Millions*, finding it "a work of genius, funny, witty, satirical, and quite enchanting – Nico and I laughed until tears streamed down our cheeks." On the other hand, she had found *The Sound of Music* to be "treacly glue." She derided political science when Philippa discussed studying it at university: "I cannot imagine [it] being anything other than difficult, especially for the feminine mind." This was surprising, because Peggy frequently discussed international politics in her letters and took an active interest in them in Canada at both a local and national level. On June 25, 1968, she wrote to Philippa: "Today we in Canada are all voting – I hope that...Pierre Trudeau will win...whoever wins will have a fearful array of problems...with strikes – woodworkers, Great Lakes ships, railways, and the hotels connected with them, and the Post Office." She frequently commented on the terrible state of provincial as well as federal politics, and wrote so many letters about the proposed tax reforms of the late 1960s to Prime Minister Trudeau and to her young new local member of Parliament, Sheila Anderson's son David, that she was invited to join a local "think tank" symposium on the issues. But the theory of politics evidently bored her, and she had no hesitation in telling Philippa so. Peggy also raised Philippa's ire when she dismissed the younger woman's summer vacation work with mentally and emotionally disturbed children as being, effectively, a waste of time – and then spent much of her next letter to Philippa apologizing profusely for upsetting her.

It was odd that Peggy did not understand Philippa's desire to help solve social problems, because by then Peggy's letters also reveal a much stronger awareness of the social and political problems in the world than she had ever demonstrated as a young woman. But while Philippa, who had not yet lived close to war or revolution, was very focused on the problems of individuals, Peggy still related everything she saw to her wartime experiences. After watching the moon landing in 1969 on television, she wrote: "There were thrilling moments. Though to my way of thinking, the billions spent on this accomplishment would have been better spent on relieving the tragedies on this earth of ours...One may as well be thankful that the US spent this sum on the moon, or else they might well have embarked on...another Vietnam."

So Peggy and Philippa wrote back and forth to each other over those early years, arguing and analyzing – Peggy maternal and soothing, Philippa rebellious and headstrong. It was an enjoyable relationship for both of them, and Philippa seemed to fill a gap in Peggy's life that she hadn't known existed before. During the late 1960s and early 1970s, Philippa was the most important person in Peggy's life after Nicolas – and therefore could cause her the greatest emotion as well. Eventually their physical distance apart would take its toll: the letters became less frequent and less intimate as they grew older and more occupied with their own problems, but for more than twenty years they continued to meet and to exchange affectionate correspondence with each other.

The other frequent topic covered in Peggy's letters to Philippa and to her other friends was the subject of her beloved dogs. "The dogs were hugely important to Peggy," emphasized her friends. After Heather, the Scottie, Peggy owned a series of shelties that she always gave Scottish names to: Jean and Tessie, Jamie, Morag. In the beginning, she always had two or three at a time. She adored shelties, and their motto, she thought, was fitting: "Born to Please." As Ed Lohbrunner had discovered, the dogs went almost everywhere with Peggy, and if you were going to be friends with her, remarked Sheila Anderson's daughter, Fiona Hyslop, it helped if you liked the dogs. Peggy lavished care and attention on them, and they ruled the household – if she was the Princess of Abkhazia, then the dogs were the kings and queens, and Peggy was very indulgent with them. The dogs also seemed to fill a rare space in Peggy's life where she could have pure, simple, and unqualified fun.

In 1951 Peggy decided to try her hand at dog training and joined the Greater Victoria Dog Obedience Training Club with her shelties Jean and Tessie. She took immense pleasure from the sense of achievement that came with receiving the Utility Degree – the highest obedience standard possible – for both of her dogs. It was a far more meaningful achievement to her than all the music awards she had received in her youth, perhaps because it was something she had chosen to do for herself. "The only lasting thrill I can ever recall," Peggy wrote to Philippa once, "was when I completed all the courses of dog obedience training with my sheltie Tessie." She became a life member of the club in 1962 and remained involved for thirty-five years, donating a trophy in honour of Jean and gold medallions to be awarded to every dog achieving a Utility Degree. Peggy also liked to take her dogs to obedience trials and dog shows, and she was very successful, regularly winning in the categories in which she entered her dogs. In 1966 her sheltie Morag even became Canadian champion, of which Peggy was enormously proud – even though it was the same Morag who, two weeks earlier, had fallen into one of the ponds while chasing dragonflies and had to be rescued "shrieking for her doting Mamma!"

She also met two great friends through having the dogs – Judge Lloyd McKenzie and his wife Betty. In the early 1950s McKenzie was a young lawyer in Victoria, doing a little *pro bono* work on the side for the Victoria Society for the Prevention of Cruelty to Animals. When a milk delivery truck accidentally ran over and killed one of Peggy's beloved shelties in the Abkhazis' driveway, Lloyd McKenzie was engaged by the company to defend the action for damages

that an outraged Peggy had immediately brought against it. McKenzie met the Abkhazis for the first time with their lawyer, Bob Wootton, at the old Victoria Courthouse. Princess Abkhazi, so she informed him, was disconsolate that the SPCA's lawyer could have seen fit to take this case for the milk company. Not so disconsolate, however, that she forgot her manners once honour was satisfied. When the case was promptly settled out of court, Peggy immediately invited both lawyers for cocktails the following Friday. After that, the Abkhazis and the McKenzies became

Peggy enjoying the summer sunshine in her garden with her beloved sheltie dogs.
UNIVERSITY OF VICTORIA ARCHIVES

good friends and would frequently dine together. Both Nicolas and Peggy greatly enjoyed Lloyd's robust and genial sense of humour. Peggy, herself a great storyteller, thoroughly appreciated Lloyd's anecdotes, while Betty McKenzie practised her conversational French with Nicolas. As a result, "her French accent," Judge McKenzie related, "was completely and utterly Russian!"

Prince and Princess Abkhazi, at a Union Club event in Victoria in 1967. FIONA HYSLOP

Princess Peggy Abkhazi at the Lieutenant-Governor's Ball, early 1960s. FIONA HYSLOP

Nicolas outside the Abkhazis' home, with one of Peggy's shelties. UNIVERSITY OF VICTORIA ARCHIVES

With each passing day of those gentle, contented years, Peggy and Nicolas, eccentric but well-regarded, became more and more woven into the fabric of Victoria. There was a never a defined point at which they overtly made a decision to stay or at which the property Peggy had bought as an investment had become a much-loved garden, but as the 1950s and 1960s dawned and faded, and Peggy and Nicolas started to grow old together, it was becoming clear that they were never going to leave Victoria. Nicolas had received his Canadian citizenship by April 1952, and had given up his French citizenship in the process. Each of them had worked hard to become involved in the aspects of Victoria's lifestyle that they enjoyed – the Dog Training Club and the Union Club, as well as the various horticultural societies that they had joined. Both of them took a strong interest in the new University of Victoria, which opened in 1962, especially in the Department of Russian Studies. Peggy and Nicolas were still receiving invitations to "madly elegant parties at Government House" for various ambassadors and would go from time to time to such functions, but Peggy was by then becoming as well known for her developing

Peggy and one of her shelties in her living room, September 1965. By then, the piano behind her had become purely decorative. UNIVERSITY OF VICTORIA ARCHIVES

garden as she was for being a princess. It was, of course, a princess's garden, and this was a great part of the attraction for visitors. As early as 1950 the Abkhazis were opening their garden each spring to tours by members of the Victoria Horticultural Society, as well as to any other group that showed an interest in seeing it — although more than one visitor was somewhat disconcerted by the dead crows hanging from various trees. They were put there, Peggy would tell them earnestly, to scare away "les autres." She had been advised very early on that it was an Oak Bay tradition, and Peggy was nothing if not traditional.

In the meantime, the piano in the living room had fallen silent; it was now a mere decoration. Playing the piano was no longer the "food for the soul" that it had once been during Peggy's loneliest years, and, as she herself said, fingers that had been grubbing in the earth were hardly suitable any more for the delicate keys of the piano. Nor, realistically, would there have been any time to keep in practice. Peggy preferred to spend her spare time with Nicolas and with her shelties. She may have played oc-casionally in the early days of living in Victoria, but no one now can recall ever hearing Peggy play her piano. But if it was a sacrifice, it was one she  apparently was happy to make. She could still listen to her adored music on records, and she continued to attend concerts and the opera.

Princess Peggy Abkhazi had her husband, her dogs, her goddaughter, and her garden, and she was very contented. Her life, at last, was all that she could have wished for. In the Principality of Abkhazia, those were halcyon days indeed.

Prince Nicolas and Princess Peggy Abkhazi,
circa 1960.

OPPOSITE, AND LEFT:
Peggy relaxing with one of her shelties,
Morag, who later became Canadian
champion – May 1965.

17

A garden is always changing

*"Nico has just suggested that I should dash down to
San Francisco to see you — so like his complete
selflessness. Much as I'd love to see you, I don't think
it is the 'right moment,' near as you are. I'd have half
my mind and heart in Victoria with Nico."*

— PEGGY ABKHAZI, LETTER TO PHILIPPA, MARCH 30, 1971

ALTHOUGH PEGGY AND NICOLAS ENJOYED MORE THAN TWENTY-FIVE
idyllic years together, travelling, gardening, and leading a royal lifestyle in
Victoria but without any of the drawbacks of obligation, Peggy remained
conscious of the almost equal number of years of her adult life that she had,
effectively, lost; and of the lateness of her found happiness. As the couple
aged, they grew ever more devoted to each other; and, more and more, simply
stayed put in their peaceful garden, in a state of companionable contentment.
But by the end of the 1960s, with Nicolas nearing his seventieth birthday,
Peggy became troubled by how fast the years seemed to be passing her by.
"Time for me and Nico," she wrote sadly to Philippa, "is so fleeting." Despite

her relative good health, plagued only by the normal ailments of increasing age, she would frequently comment gloomily – and quite inaccurately – that the end was undoubtedly near. But Peggy had described herself more than once as a "creative pessimist," and her pragmatic side was usually irrepressible; while making such sombre predictions, she also seemed able to appreciate and enjoy her life thoroughly. "One of the redeeming features of old age, as I have found it," Peggy commented, "is the instant recognition, at any odd moment, that 'I am happy now' – possibly because one knows that the number of these moments is limited…I savour each passing day with an extraordinary appreciation and thankfulness…perhaps this is the only thing that I have learned in the course of my life."

Although Peggy and Philippa continued to clash on generational issues – they were strong-willed, intelligent women who were determined about how they wished to lead their lives, and had markedly different philosophies – they continued to hold each other in great affection. To Peggy's great joy, Philippa married a young American named Stanley Bissell in early 1971. There was no doubt that Peggy would travel to the wedding, which was held in New Zealand. In honour of Peggy and Nicolas, Philippa wore the "Abkhazi jewel" on her wedding dress – an ornamental jewelled button that Nicolas had inherited from his family and that he had given to Peggy. She had tried in turn to give it to Philippa, telling her that the button was meant to be worn and loved by someone in the family, "rather than lying behind glass [in a museum] to be glanced at vaguely by a public to whom the name Abkhazi means absolutely nothing. It was worn by men [Nicolas] honoured and loved, his great-grandfather, grandfather, and famous father." Peggy placed a high value on such symbols as markers of certainty in the world of violence and change that she had lived in, and she wanted to pass on this symbol to the person she thought of almost as a daughter. But Philippa was a young woman of the 1960s to whom, like others of that generation, such symbols were not meaningful; and she refused to keep the button. It was Peggy, instead, who would always wear the Abkhazi jewel on formal occasions.

By the mid-1970s grand formal occasions started to become fewer and fewer for Peggy and Nicolas. Their friends of a similar age were also less inclined to hectic social activity. "Death, sickness and old age have thinned the ranks," Peggy wrote soberly in 1972 to Philippa, now living with her new husband in Victor, New York. But Peggy's appointment diaries indicate that her social schedule at any rate nevertheless continued to be busy. She was far from ready to let go of the routines, customs, and traditions that she and Nicolas had brought with them from a more elegant and conventional era, and she retained a formality concerning most social occasions, requiring calls or appointments to be made well in advance. She still loved to have cocktail parties with small, select gatherings of friends; and the couple also continued to dine regularly at the Union Club, almost always dressed formally in evening gown and dinner suit. Even at home, once the day's work was done, Peggy would often change into a long dress for drinks and dinner. Some of the more modern aspects of twentieth-century life crept into their routine — watching television, for example (Peggy loved the British class-based series *Upstairs, Downstairs*) — but for the most part the Abkhazis still preferred to entertain, or simply to spend time together, playing with the dogs, listening to music, and reminiscing about a way of life that they had both experienced in a distant and graceful time. By 1976, after thirty years together, the Abkhazis enjoyed a simple contentment and ease of familiar routine that needed few words to be exchanged.

The one place where Peggy did not insist on formality was in her garden. More and more throughout the early years of the 1970s the garden became Peggy's recreation and major occupation; and, in times of pessimism, her solace. "I have always found tranquillity," she commented once, "in the annual rhythm of gardening." Now reluctant to leave the ailing Nicolas alone for any length of time, she travelled less and spent more time working in the garden, dressed in her favoured working garb of baggy men's pants and an oversized checked shirt. "As I sit on my little stool (spectacles firmly latched on and hair tied up in a kerchief) working at my patient-Chinese job of removing the thousands of spent rhododendron-azalea blooms, my mind and imagination ranges freely…" This job of deadheading the rhododendrons could take her several weeks to complete. It was, she said, "such a happy occupation; my mind and memory travel miles and whole lifetimes whilst fingers are occupied mechanically." Nicolas was starting to suffer increasingly from physical ailments, particularly a poor hip and arthritic hands, and was less able to contribute to the garden's maintenance; but he still managed the hiring of gardeners and handymen and oversaw the repair of equipment. In the summers, especially, the couple would keep what Peggy called very "Spanish hours" — taking advantage of the long daylight to get as much as possible done in the garden, eating late, often after 10:30 at night, and retiring after midnight.

Peggy, who had never liked crowds since her enforced internment and who was usually happiest being alone with Nicolas, was pleasantly surprised at how much she enjoyed having visitors to the garden, whether it was a group on a prearranged visit or simply people dropping by to admire the latest blooms. By the end of the 1960s the garden was fairly mature and quite spectacular, with its rocky terraces carefully scraped free of moss, its towering rhododendrons and alpine conifers, and its series of meandering, Chinese-style spaces, filled with various flowering shrubs and perennials. The attraction for visitors to the garden was twofold, however: the garden itself was of course reputed to be spectacular, and Peggy's carefully accumulated knowledge of plants, which she freely shared, was also of great interest. But there are many spectacular gardens in Victoria. The magic of that particular one was, and still is, inextricably linked to Peggy's acquired royal status. There was an understandable public fascination not just with the garden but with the gardener herself: her complex and elegant history, her aura of royalty — her polished conversation, dotted with French expressions, her hair always secured by a diamond pin, even under the battered scarf that she would wear while working — and her gracious and charming character. It was Peggy's apparent generosity in sharing her knowledge and garden with others that became her most enduring legacy — but it is also quite definitely the legacy of not merely any gardener, but of Princess Abkhazi, the royal gardener.

Peggy's image as a princess was by then solidly established, and her garden visitors were usually duly deferential. Peggy enjoyed the deference, but she also seemed to feel secure at last that her title had been accepted by the residents of Victoria and the world at large. In the garden, therefore, she felt little need to stand on ceremony. It had also become a source of great pleasure and pride to her, and was the one area of her life in which she started to keep an "open door" policy. Visits to the garden were arranged by personal invitation or request, rather than through any advertising; but anyone who wanted to look at the garden was welcome, unannounced or not. As the Abkhazi Garden became more and more well known, visiting garden enthusiasts, anticipating meeting an elegant princess, often would instead surprise Peggy in the garden, weeding or deadheading the rhododendrons, and dressed in her comfortable and dirt-smeared gardening attire. To such visitors, she was unfailingly charming and perfectly mannered, regardless of her appearance, thus unintentionally enhancing her reputation as a gracious if eccentric princess even further.

For the little orphan and young woman whom once no one had wanted to know, it must have been gratifying to have so many people eager to spend time with her learning about her garden. Peggy responded to the attention wholeheartedly, talking for hours on end with anyone who was interested. One of the people she later taught about gardening in Victoria was her young mail carrier, Margaret Hantiuk, who had moved to Victoria from the colder climate of Alberta. To deliver the mail Hantiuk would enter the Abkhazis' garden through the little gate that used to be in the fence between the old Gillespie place and 1964 Fairfield. "When she saw me come through the gate, she would invite me to walk around the garden with her," said Hantiuk. "She had this attitude that everyone was worth talking to if they were interested. She was always very kind and patient and generous, never condescending. My garden owes a lot to Princess Abkhazi." It is a description of Peggy echoed by many others. An unassuming middle-aged photographer named Enid Lemon leaned over the gate one day and asked if she could take photographs – and very quickly became a regular for smoked salmon sandwiches and tea with Prince and Princess Abkhazi. Al Smith, an avid gardener then working for the city, met Peggy through business – the city would take her larger rhododendrons for transplanting into various city parks and provide her with much-needed mulch in trade – and Smith became a good friend almost immediately, later inheriting from Peggy the unique planter boxes that Nicolas had designed.

In the shadows of this pleasant routine, however, Nicolas's health was becoming increasingly worrisome. Hip surgery had granted some relief in 1972, but he was becoming more and more frail and less able to spend time in the garden. Visitors, other than good friends, rarely saw Nicolas, who stayed well in the background of Peggy's growing gardening fame. It was a large cloud on Peggy's horizon, and her concern grew as his disabilities seemed to increase. "He bears them with composure and disdain," she wrote to Philippa, "as though they were enemies unworthy of his attention – such a Georgian characteristic!" By March 1976 he needed emergency hip surgery again, possibly because of a fall; and on April 8, 1976, Nicolas suffered a serious stroke.

Characteristically, after she recovered from her initial shock, Peggy demanded the best of care for her husband; and, casting caustic aspersions on hospital food, insisted on bringing him home-cooked meals in the hospital every day to aid his recovery. But Nicolas was seventy-seven years old, and his health was increasingly problematic, partly as a result of his experiences during the war. He returned home, only to dislocate his other hip within weeks, forcing him back into the hospital. For the first time since Peggy had known him, his self-control deserted him and Nicolas broke down completely. She was rocked to the core. She did not have an intimate to whom she could turn for consolation or support – Muriel Mackenzie was long gone, Lloyd and Betty McKenzie had moved to Vancouver – and Philippa was far away in Victor, New York, preoccupied with her own life. The emotional intensity of Peggy and Philippa's relationship had started to dissipate fairly soon after Philippa's marriage. Despite Peggy's great plans for regular visits, only one or two had occurred in the five years since the wedding. Philippa had personal problems of her own to deal with, and as a result could not pay close attention to her godmother's needs or wishes. By the time of Nicolas's stroke, the two had drifted away from each other to some degree, and were not corresponding as frequently as they had in former days, or quite as intimately. Peggy had no one therefore with whom she shared her darkest fears. Nicolas's breakdown was, she wrote in her diary that night, "the worst day ever."

But, again with her characteristic strength and pragmatism, Peggy rallied and brought Nicolas home once more to care for him. With her help he slowly recovered his poise and was able again to join in some quiet socializing and occasional gardening. "It has been an ordeal," Peggy wrote in her diary a year later, "but also an enriching experience. And if, in a sense, Nico and I are living on borrowed time, the tempo is 'andante cantabile,' borne with courage by Nico. If Nico can bear the residual damage with good humour and 'style' – I am learning not to grieve about it." There was little time to spend grieving about the state of his health in any event. Peggy's days were full with the garden and the increasing number of visitors to it, and with taking care of Nicolas. Her mind was also increasingly occupied with the other large cloud that drifted back and forth across her horizon more and more often as the years progressed: her precarious and fluctuating financial position. With Nicolas's poor health, it was not a burden that she could share with him, and she shouldered it alone.

Peggy had always been naïve about managing her money, spending frivolously and as if there was no limit to her means. As a result, she was thought to be very wealthy by many people who did not know her well. Certainly, neither of the Abkhazis ever felt any need to seek work after moving to Canada. And for a time, Peggy was relatively wealthy, especially before post-war inflationary trends started to raise the overall cost of living in Victoria. Unfortunately, she often spent her capital rather than her income from her investments; and as early as the 1960s Peggy had started to outspend her means. She had always employed gardeners and servants. She bought only the best food and kept the pantry well stocked with the ingredients for her favourite cocktails. She entertained lavishly and travelled frequently. And Peggy always wanted comfort and the best service – she did not hesitate to fly herself and Philippa first-class to Hawaii, despite claiming even then that she had to be careful with her money. As a result, by the end of the 1970s her yo-yoing finances were reaching a crisis point.

Whenever it came to needing more money over the years, Peggy had simply sold some of her valuable items. She had even considered selling portions of her treasured garden. In addition to the costly lifestyle that the Abkhazis favoured, the garden itself was a huge financial drain that required expensive maintenance. Disposing of unnecessary parts of it seemed therefore to be a logical solution to the money squeezes that Peggy encountered from time to time. A proposed subdivision plan dated September 19, 1963, shows that Peggy was considering severing the entire top portion of the garden, as well as the side lot that she had purchased in 1949 – almost half of the property. Somehow or other, a windfall came through, possibly from China, and the subdivision plan was apparently dropped. But the troubles continued to surface from time to time, accentuated by fluctuating investment returns and changes to Canadian tax rules. In the spring of 1970 Peggy had again been so concerned that she considered selling 1964 Fairfield Road in its entirety. "Finances," she wrote to Philippa in August that year, "are in a baddish way at the moment." By June of the following year she was able to afford help in the garden for only one and a half days a week, instead of the four days a week she had employed help in previous summers. Things improved for a while in the early 1970s, but they certainly did not do so to the extent that Peggy could afford not to think about money at all. The pages of her appointment diaries through those years are filled with meticulous calculations of returns on investments, the expected amount of Nicolas's pension payments, and bills coming due, even in the smallest amounts; and, with the reduced help in the garden, its condition slowly deteriorated, losing the spectacular bloom it had had in the 1960s.

Astonishingly, despite all of these difficulties and her age – she was in her seventies – Peggy's energy seemed undiminished. She decided to turn the journal that she had kept from the days in the Lunghua internment camp into a book. Peggy had been considering this project since as early as 1973, and now, with the encouragement of Professor Toby Jackman, as well as Nancy Simpson, who had also been in Lunghua and was by then living in Victoria, she embarked on the project. Dick Morriss of Sono Nis Press was enthusiastic and agreed to publish the book. Toby Jackman helped Peggy to edit the journal into a workable draft and added an introduction; and on August 14, 1981, *A Curious Cage* was published. Peggy held book-signings at the Hudson's Bay Company department store in downtown Victoria and at Ivy's Bookstore in Oak Bay, celebrating her advent as an author at the age of seventy-nine.

The reviews, unfortunately, were lukewarm at best, and in one instance at least, quite scathing of what the reviewer described as the "privileged" and "sheltered" Englishwoman whom the book revealed, condemning her as simplistic and naïve. But the reviewer had missed the point: Peggy had merely wanted to record daily events and her reactions in a simple, plain way, not undertake a political and social treatise about conditions in China. If Peggy's letters and diaries are any indication, however, she simply ignored these reviews. She claimed to be absolutely delighted by the attention that the book received; and it also had other enjoyable and interesting consequences. The one that she perhaps treasured most was the receipt of a letter from the widow of her former lawyer in Shanghai, T.S. Yeh, who had overseen Peggy's financial affairs and cared for her well-being all through the years of her internment, and who had worked so hard to recover her assets after the war. Peggy, not at all sure whether he was still alive or even able to receive books like hers under the communist regime in China, had sent a copy to him anyway at his last known address. The book, reported Mrs. Yeh, did indeed reach her husband, and just in time – if it had arrived even a week later, it would have been too late, for T.S. died only a few days afterwards from lung cancer. As it was, he had been able to read the book and to enjoy what

Peggy had written about his kindness and foresight in looking after her.

A Curious Cage, Peggy said, also stimulated new relationships with other authors and people around the world. Three years after her book was published, J.G. Ballard's novel *Empire of the Sun*, a fictional account of the internment experience, was published in England. According to Peggy, Ballard had been a child in the internment camp at Lunghua; but his book painted quite a different picture of the internees, and in her view the novel cast them in an unfairly bad light. She condemned it in letters to correspondents in England as being based on the flawed memories of a child. It was, after all, simply a novel, and therefore a romanticized version of events that she likened to a "Treasure Island" type of story. Peggy must also have been a little resentful that Ballard's book was highly successful financially; it sold more than one hundred thousand copies and was shortlisted for the Booker Prize, and a popular film by Stephen Spielberg was based upon it. But if so, she would never have expressed that sentiment publicly — and she definitely retained a firm belief throughout her life that the English had been models of good behaviour in the internment camp at Lunghua and should not be described as anything less.

Peggy also harboured a strong resentment against the Japanese government for putting her and her friends in Lunghua in the first place. Most eighty-year-olds would have been content to leave the past in peace, but not Peggy. Her memories were fresh in her mind after the publication of her book when she read in the Victoria *Times-Colonist* newspaper of November 26, 1982, that the president of the National Association of Japanese Canadians, Gordon Kadota, was seeking an apology and compensation from the Canadian government for the internment of Japanese Canadians during the war. She immediately took pen to paper. Writing to the Japanese ambassador in Ottawa, she demanded her own apology and compensation. "Mr. Kadota mentions that civilian internment is one of the most serious violations of human rights," she wrote. "I agree with this statement, regardless of which country's government enforces the internment." She was anxious, however, not to be considered a bigot. "Between the years 1908–1930 I have spent many happy months in your beautiful country," she went on, "and I have enjoyed friendship with a number of your fellow countrymen. Furthermore, my first husband was born and brought up in Yokohama. I mention these facts so that you may know that I am not a narrow-minded, ignorant chauvinist."

It was a glorious but of course vain attempt. The prompt and courteous response from the first secretary at the Japanese embassy in Ottawa explained helpfully why Peggy would not be receiving any recompense – the Japanese peace treaty had already dealt with the issue, and Japan had apologized many years previously for its actions. Unfortunately, in a misguided attempt at political correctness, the letter was addressed to "Ms." Abkhazi, and it set the eighty-year-old off again like a rocket. Writing back immediately to ask for more information, she also demanded huffily: "In our future correspondence, would you be good enough to address me either as Princess Nicolas Abkhazi, or if you prefer a more democratic approach, as Mrs. Nicolas Abkhazi? I am sure that you will appreciate that for a woman of my age and position 'Ms.' Abkhazi is inappropriate and unacceptable at any time." But if she failed in her attempt to get any money out of the Japanese government, Peggy did enjoy the financial success, limited as it was, of her book. From time to time she had expressed envy of women who had been able to make their own living independently; and now, for the first time in her life, Peggy was also earning money entirely from her own efforts. In one of her by then increasingly rare letters to Philippa, she remarked: "I am childishly proud to have earned, via royalties, money, at my time of life." The receipt of her small royalty cheque was always a cause for celebration, with champagne and Russian caviar.

It was a reckless way to spend the money, given Peggy's uncertain financial situation, although of course the gesture was typical. In the latter half of the 1970s, it was becoming more and more difficult for Peggy to turn a blind eye to her situation. She became increasingly concerned with her husband's health. With Peggy distracted and worried about Nicolas and about her finances, which were in a downward cycle again as the 1970s drew to a close, it became an insurmountable struggle to maintain her precious garden in its previous spectacular state. By the time Nicolas had his stroke in 1976 the garden had already started to suffer from the lack of Peggy's close attention, and in subsequent years the many visitors became almost impossible to handle. In the back of her busy mind, however, Peggy had already started to formulate a complicated plan to solve her financial crisis – by offering to dispose of the garden to the City of Victoria, but in a way that would allow her and Nicolas to remain living there. By November 1979, when the Abkhazis hired a young gardener named Christopher Ball, Peggy was ready to go about implementing her idea.

18

The time of age

> "*I savour each passing day with an extraordinary appreciation and thankfulness. . .perhaps this is the only thing that I have learned in the course of my life.*"
>
> — PEGGY ABKHAZI, LETTER TO PHILIPPA, NOVEMBER 3, 1968

CHRISTOPHER BALL, TWENTY-FIVE YEARS OLD, WAS WELL ESTABLISHED AS a gardener in Victoria, despite his youth. Although he was really too busy to take on more work, he had been given the Abkhazis' telephone number by one of his clients who knew that they needed help in the garden. Christopher's father, Bill Ball, who had worked for Peris Atkinson in the late 1940s and helped with the original landscaping of the garden, and Logan Mayhew, an acquaintance of the Abkhazis, also urged Christopher to call the Prince and Princess and see the garden. Intrigued by their enthusiasm, the young gardener called Peggy, despite his busy schedule, and arranged to drop by to meet the Abkhazis the following day.

Meeting Peggy was, Christopher recalled, a "magic moment," and the garden was a special place that "sent a charge right through me." It took Peggy nearly three hours to show Christopher the garden, but to him the time passed as if it had been mere seconds. The Abkhazis took an immediate liking to the fresh-faced young man, who seemed to understand what Peggy wanted in the garden. Nicolas's treasured 1951 Atco customized lawnmower, an English machine, had broken down and required urgent attention; and Christopher was familiar with Atcos. Nicolas slyly tested him, asking the young man where the date plate was located on the distinctive machine: to Nicolas's delight, Christopher knew exactly where it was, and thought that he could probably get the Atco going again. "Knowing about the lawnmower," Christopher said, "is what really did it." The relationship was sealed when Peggy showed the young man photographs of the property in its infancy, and Christopher recognized his father working in the garden in 1947. Even Christopher's grandfather, also a gardener, had a small connection to the property: picking Bill Ball up after work, he had sometimes strolled around the property, commenting on the work being done and providing advice to the workers. Peggy was delighted with the connection, and when she hospitably offered him a Campari, Christopher was pretty certain that he had the job, even though he declined the drink. His instincts were correct: Peggy called within a few days and asked if Christopher could start work immediately.

She may have liked the young gardener, but, like Nicolas with the Atco lawnmower, Peggy wasn't beyond testing Christopher out initially. After all, she still demanded the best service, and she was not about to accept anything less. Soon after he had started working for her, Peggy gave Christopher cash to buy a proper wheelbarrow. When he brought her the correct change from the purchase, she smiled to herself in satisfaction — while he had been gone, she had telephoned the hardware store to check the price, and the change matched properly. The young man threw himself enthusiastically into his work in the garden, doing far more than he was being paid to do, and he soon endeared himself to his new employers. His probationary period was, therefore, quickly over. Nicolas Abkhazi, he was given to understand, was doing very poorly; and Peggy, who had asked Christopher to call her Mrs. Abkhazi, needed to spend most of her time caring for Nicolas. Although she had very little time for the garden by then, she wanted it to look attractive again. She was working on her plan, she told him, to have the garden taken over by the City of Victoria, and it needed to be looking good as quickly as possible. Christopher was told to do as he wished, so long as he kept the costs reasonable.

Peggy's plan had evolved out of the realization that she needed to consider once again either disposing of at least part of the property or selling it altogether by as early as 1979. The growing costs of maintaining the garden and the expense of health care for Nicolas were once again outstripping her income. But by now, Peggy had no desire to leave 1964 Fairfield Road, and neither did Nicolas. So, in casting around for other options, Peggy had come up with the idea of getting the City of Victoria to acquire the garden, perhaps as a public park, and take over its maintenance.

Part of her plan was that the condition of acquisition would require the city to permit Peggy and Nicolas to continue to live in the house until they both eventually passed away or had to go into permanent care. As soon as Christopher Ball had the garden spruced up again in the spring of 1980, Peggy started making diligent efforts to persuade staff and members of city council to take the garden, but to no avail. For once, Peggy's persuasive powers could not overcome the hard reality. Without even beginning to discuss what an acquisition price for the property might be, the holding costs were much too high for the city to consider – garden maintenance alone was estimated to be around one thousand dollars a month – and it was not within its municipal mandate to provide the Abkhazis with a life interest in a city park. Peggy also tried church organizations as well as the provincial government, but despite her best efforts, by April 1981 her proposal had been firmly declined by everyone she had approached. In June 1981, closing her mind to any regrets, Peggy made the pragmatic decision to subdivide and sell most of the extra lot that she had purchased in 1949 on the west side of the garden, keeping only a narrow strip as a buffer zone for her privacy. By the summer of 1982 the subdivided lots had been transferred to their new owner, a developer, who promptly put up two new houses on the property.

In the meantime, Nicolas's health became worse. He was now eighty-three years of age, his arthritis was very debilitating, and he was frequently in and out of hospital. On at least one occasion, Christopher Ball had intervened to save Nicolas from falling in the garden – from the terrace patio into one of the pools – when he had turned and lost his precarious balance. The stress was enormous for Peggy, whose emotions rose and fell like a roller coaster as her husband's health went up and down from week to week and she found herself getting increasingly tired. "Why?" she wrote desperately over and over in her diaries, as she watched her beloved Nicolas suffering. By 1984 he was also becoming mentally confused. "Jean á la lune," Peggy called him affectionately and sadly, happy for him that he was escaping his miserable situation in his mind but desolate at the effective loss of her best friend.

There were still moments of great happiness for the two of them, which Peggy always joyfully seized upon and celebrated – especially on anniversaries and other special occasions. On her wedding anniversary in 1984 Peggy wrote in her diary: "38 years. After some discouraging weeks, at 5 pm a happy change in Nico. So it was a good celebration, Veuve Clicquot and memories going back to 1922." But by then, more or less, Nicolas had been permanently in residence in the Gorge Hospital for more than a year. Peggy's housekeeper and cook, Maria Serafina Camara, was shouldering much of the physical burden of caring for Nicolas on her employer's behalf, visiting him frequently in the hospital to look after his personal needs. Sad as it was for Peggy that Nicolas was no longer living with her in the house, this situation was probably much better for her. Alleviated of the heavy load of caring for Nicolas twenty-four hours a day, Peggy's own physical and emotional health rapidly improved, and to her relief Peggy was able to re-engage in some of the activities she most enjoyed, especially in the garden, which helped distract her from her concerns.

On New Year's Eve of 1983, after spending a few hours visiting with Nicolas, Peggy wrote in her diary: "Happiest evening. Champagne, smoked salmon, crème brulée á deux…and remembrance of things past – acceptance of and thankfulness for the present – including…Maria and Chris, garden, home and for me the possibility of the same for…a little longer?" Since the late 1970s three people had become increasingly important in Peggy's life. They were Christopher Ball and his wife Pamela, and Maria, Peggy's faithful and devoted housekeeper. Maria had been a twenty-four-year-old recent immigrant from the Azores when she was hired in 1976 to cook and take care of the couple. The romantic young woman had fallen completely in love with the Prince and Princess and their peaceful garden paradise, and had developed a very special relationship with Nicolas in particular, whom she adored and looked after as if he were her own father. She had quickly become part of the

Abkhazi family, as had Christopher and Pamela Ball.

Pamela had taken an immediate liking to the older couple when she met them, and while Christopher worked, she also spent many hours in the garden with Peggy on weekends, helping her with pruning and other chores, and talking about life; and the two became close friends, despite their age difference. Pamela also shared many of Peggy's interests and views, and Peggy seems eventually to have largely substituted Pamela for her distant goddaughter Philippa in her close affections. And although Christopher and Maria were employed by Peggy, their relationship with her went far beyond the paid work that the housekeeper and gardener did for the Princess. The two of them, and Pamela Ball, quite clearly loved the difficult and complex woman in whose life they had become entwined. The affection was mutual: Peggy lovingly called all three of her young friends the "honorary grandchildren," and Maria her "good angel."

"Peggy changed into a much nicer person as old age caught up with her," Philippa commented. "When I first met her, I thought she was very haughty and snobbish. I think she was humbled by her dependence on Christopher and Pamela and Maria." When Peggy was living in Shanghai, she held an almost feudal attitude toward employees: her faithful and loyal retainers in China had been part of the family, and dependants whose well-being had to be looked after, but they were also chastised for their errors as if they were children. But Peggy's experience in China had also taught her that it was her advisers and the members of her staff and their families who proved to be her best friends, looking after and protecting her – to the extent, in T.S. Yeh's case, of saving her life – and she was now finding herself in a similar situation again.

In October 1986, when Peggy's much-loved sheltie, Jamie, had to be put down, Christopher and Pamela kept Peggy company while it was happening and Christopher buried the little dog under the copper beech tree in the garden. Nicolas was in the hospital, and Maria comforted Peggy. "After the touching loving-kindness of the children I've fallen to pieces," she wrote in her diary that night. And when she decided to replace Jamie shortly afterward with a young sheltie puppy named Shamus, Peggy turned to Pamela and Christopher, asking them if they would take Shamus when she could no longer care for him. The soft-hearted couple, seeing Peggy's need for the company and affection of the little dog, could not refuse. The same loyalty and sense of friendship would lead them to accept Peggy's much more significant proposal to them, when she made it two years later, to purchase the garden from her — a proposal that was to have far more serious implications for the next fifteen years of the Balls' lives than they could possibly have anticipated.

With Nicolas effectively lost to Peggy, at least in spirit, the garden was much more important to her than it had been when she was younger, and she became greatly occupied with it again. By 1985 its fame had spread nationally and abroad. The hard work that Christopher Ball had done since 1979 had restored the garden fully to its former glory, and hundreds of visitors flocked again to see the royal Abkhazi Garden every spring and summer. Peggy and her garden had been featured in numerous magazine articles and television documentaries, and it had been photographed by some of Canada's most famous photographers, including Malak Karsh and Freeman Patterson. Her own interest in the garden had been rejuvenated as a result, and she had also enjoyed the publicity immensely. Ironically, despite making so many new acquaintances Peggy had in many ways become isolated from the outside world. Many of her oldest friends had passed away or moved elsewhere, and those friends that she did have in Victoria all had busy lives of their own to lead. Maria, Christopher, and Pamela, by contrast, were devoting most of their spare time, as well their working hours, to Peggy's care, and were her closest and most constant companions. All Peggy really wanted by then was to be able to keep living at 1964 Fairfield Road for as long as she could, and preferably until the end of her life — and her three friends, she was starting to think, could help her to do it.

When she was a much younger woman Peggy had considered leaving her jewellery and the money from the sale of the house and garden to Philippa and to Maureen and Elizabeth Mackenzie. But Elizabeth had died in 1984; Peggy had by then lost touch with Maureen, who was very ill; and Philippa had never expressed any interest in her godmother's jewellery or other assets. Peggy appears to have changed her mind, therefore, or forgotten her original intentions. Instead, although she hadn't done anything about it at that stage, Peggy had already told one or two of her trusted gardening friends that she wanted Christopher and Pamela to have the garden after she died. Some time before Nicolas had moved permanently into hospital, he had on one occasion insisted to his wife, in Pamela Ball's presence: "They are the ones, Peggy"; but Pamela had not understood his meaning at the time. Peggy and Nicolas had also already decided that Maria, the third "grandchild," was to have the contents of the house.

But Peggy, who was now in her mid-eighties, also realized that she would need home care for herself in the foreseeable future and would need to pay for it; and simply leaving the property to the Balls in her will would not achieve that end on its own. She no longer simply wanted to sell the garden and move into more practical surroundings. It was all that she had left, and she wanted desperately to stay in the home in which she and Nicolas had been so happy together. The house and the garden continued to be expensive to maintain, however, and Peggy had to come up with something to pay the bills while she was still alive and in residence there. In March 1986 she came up with the first stage of her proposal to the Balls, which she described in her diary as her "brilliant idea: the most practical solution for the four of us." Her initial idea was to sell the remaining part of the western lot – the buffer zone that she had kept after the 1982 sale – to Christopher and Pamela, in order to gain the additional income. The Balls had been looking for a home of their own to purchase, not a bare lot, but when Peggy offered it to them they decided to buy it. It would place them under a financial strain of their own; restrictive covenants on the lot would prevent them from building on it until after Peggy's death, thus requiring them to buy a place to live elsewhere and make payments on that home at the same time. But Peggy needed the money from the sale of the lot, and the thought of strangers buying it distressed her terribly. So, in June 1986, the Balls bought it from her at market value. It was a good bargain for both sides – Peggy gave Christopher and Pamela an interest-free loan, payable over a period of ten years, and in the meantime she received an income from the monthly payments sufficient to cover her property taxes and maintenance costs on the remainder of the property.

It was a sufficient step for the time being. But Peggy's mind was already at work on the next step – the second stage of the proposal, the one that would ensure that both she and the garden would be looked after and dealt with as she wished.

19

Stop all the clocks

"Your words showed how well you understood and appreciated the inner essence of that great human being, especially in your summing up: 'A Prince among Men'."

— Peggy Abkhazi, letter to the Rev. Cedric A. Jones,
January 1, 1988

On Christmas Day, 1987, all that Peggy could find to write in her diary were the following simple words: "Nico left me tonight." What else was there to say, regarding the loss of her best friend and soulmate for forty years? In truth, as everyone already knew, Nicolas had left Peggy long before. By 1985 she was asking herself if she must learn to let him go free, since he seemed already to have escaped, at least in his mind, from his miserable cage of pain and immobility in the Gorge Hospital. His passing was a relief and freedom for Peggy, too, from the heavy strain of visits to the hospital to see Nicolas that she felt had been increasingly meaningless to him, and that had simply worn her out. All the same, her sense of joy at any moment of clarity for him, any evidence that he had remembered a shred of their existence together during one of her visits, had been almost painfully intense and was recorded in treasured detail – and when the moment came at last, it was far from easy to bear. The date made it especially hard, not because it should otherwise have been a day of celebration, but because Nicolas had never liked Christmas and had never wished to make a special occasion of it. The holiday was associated in his mind with some sad memory of his past, and he had always been sombre at that time of the year.

Peggy kept her head held high through a quiet and peaceful funeral service conducted a few days later by the Rev. Cedric A. Jones, the chaplain who had spent a great deal of time with Nicolas in his last years at the Gorge Hospital. She continued to keep her emotions firmly under control and did not mention Nicolas's passing to strangers that she met over the next few weeks; she did not even immediately inform some of her friends. Christopher and Pamela and Maria kept a tight circle of much-needed support and affection around her, and to the outside world Peggy appeared to be managing fine.

But even though he had not been able to meaningfully relate to Peggy for a long time, in his dying, Nicolas severed the final link to Peggy's distant and elegant past; a past that no one else in Victoria, no matter how close or how loving, could share with her. He had been the only one left in her life of that long-ago world of pre-war Europe and the aristocratic lifestyle she had inherited from her adoptive parents; the only one who had known her as a striking and engaging young woman, on her way, perhaps, to becoming a concert pianist. Nicolas had known Peggy's flamboyant, difficult, loving mother, Florence; he was the one to whom she had still spoken her beautiful, classic French. Of all the men Peggy had known, Nicolas was the man who had been, in every sense of the word, her prince. Their forty years together, after all, must have seemed far too fleeting a moment in time.

It was not therefore just the man himself, but also the loss of this world, this connection, as well as this love – indeed, all of her vanished past – that Peggy must have mourned that night when she wrote those simple, sad words: "Nico left me tonight."

20

The full current
of human life

"The garden gives me an abiding mental interest and plenty of work within my physical capacity."

— PEGGY ABKHAZI, LETTER TO PHILIPPA, NOVEMBER 6, 1988

AT THE BEGINNING OF 1988 PEGGY WAS EIGHTY-FIVE YEARS OLD, AND her health was not what it used to be. But she was still a robust and commanding woman, completely alert, and as determined as ever to get her own way. The garden, its visitors, and her dog Shamus were now her sole remaining sources of recreation and pleasure. A developer had offered to purchase her property several times by then, but Peggy refused each time. But, even with the sale of part of it to Christopher and Pamela Ball in 1986, she was again becoming afraid that she would not be able to afford to stay there. Her financial situation was a matter of great stress: "I cannot afford so many work hours monthly (almost half my entire income)," Peggy wrote in her diary, "even if the garden is less immaculate. I have had to reduce M. from 4 to 3 days weekly...I must refrain from drawing on the GIC's capital each time they mature." For the second time in two years, Peggy turned to the only two people she thought could help her to achieve what she wanted. This time, she proposed through a letter from her lawyer, Bob McKay, that Christopher and Pamela Ball buy the garden outright from her while she retained the mortgage and a life interest in the property, enabling her to continue living there for as long as she wished.

The Balls were stunned to receive the letter. Peggy had told Christopher once, before Nicolas's death, that she wanted the couple eventually to have the garden, but Pamela's reaction was that the idea was unrealistic, and she had told Peggy so; and Peggy had dropped the subject. Until they received the letter from Bob McKay, the Balls had thought the matter closed. They were living somewhere else and already making mortgage payments on a home, and it would be a huge financial strain on them to agree to Peggy's proposal. But Christopher and Pamela also genuinely loved the garden — keeping it "in the family" was a strong motivation, and they had no desire to see it go to a developer either. And Peggy, whom they also cared about, was appealing to the Balls as if they were family.

Who else could she have asked? She clearly did not want to approach anyone in her social circle for support — for someone like Peggy, it was not done to discuss her finances, and her pride may well have prevented her asking for help from her contemporaries. With her young gardener and his wife, Peggy may have felt at more of an advantage — to them, she had some tangible benefit to offer — the chance to own the garden and, one day, to live there. Peggy knew that the Balls cared a great deal about her as well as about the garden. Apart from the fact that she had already decided by then that she wanted them to own it eventually, they were also certainly her best, if not her only option, to have her cake and eat it too — to sell the property immediately, but to be able to stay there — and she desperately wanted them to accept her proposal.

If Peggy considered anyone else to help her solve her problem in this fashion, she certainly never asked them. Beyond the one or two people that she had told previously about wanting the Balls to have the garden, she appears not to have consulted anyone but her lawyer and her accountant about the proposed transaction. She may have been afraid that people would tell her she was making a mistake, and since coming to Victoria after the war Peggy Abkhazi had never been prepared to accept anyone else telling her what to do. Peggy knew what she wanted, she did not want anyone else to persuade her otherwise, and so, it appears, she did not consult any of her other friends.

Christopher and Pamela, however, were in a dilemma of indecision. Back in that magic moment in 1979 when he had first met the Abkhazis, Christopher Ball had never envisaged that nearly ten years later Peggy would appeal to him in this way – but the magic feeling that he had always had about the garden, and the connection with it that had made him and Pamela put so much effort into caring for it and for its owners, suddenly must have made sense to both of them now. Trying to decide what to do, Christopher asked his employer what she really wanted; his friend provided the response. Peggy told him quietly and simply that she just wanted to live at 1964 Fairfield Road, with her dog Shamus, until she died. "So we did it," said Christopher and Pamela. "It was too hard to say no to her. And we did genuinely feel that it was a good deal for all of us."

The initial proposal that had been made was not financially feasible for the Balls, and Bob McKay and the Balls' lawyer, Bill McElmoyle, spent several months negotiating. In the end, the interest rate settled on was more than reasonable, especially for those days of the late 1980s when commercial interest rates were often well over twenty percent, and the price – $302,300, the assessed value – was a good deal for such a large property in a high-end market, reflecting the fact that it was subject to Peggy's life interest. A small deposit was required, and the couple would have to cover the costs of the transaction; they would also start making payments immediately, with interest, and would take over the payment of property taxes after a period of two years. If Peggy had to move into permanent residential care elsewhere, then the Balls would have the option of moving into the house, and Peggy would arrange for its remaining contents to be given to Maria. But whether or not the Balls took up residence, the monthly mortgage payments on the property would double, and after two years, triple. Upon Peggy's death, payment in full of the balance owing would be due to her estate.

On October 15, 1988, Peggy, Christopher, and Pamela signed the papers, and the Balls became the new owners of the garden and started making yet another set of mortgage payments. What Christopher and Pamela didn't anticipate was that exactly one month later, Peggy would secretly make a new will. In it she renewed the provision that her faithful Maria be given most of her personal possessions. In addition, she included a new provision that on her death any remaining payments owing by the Balls on the property were to be forgiven completely – it was intended to be their eventual reward for solving her difficulty. But Peggy did not tell the Balls about the new will; and to the outside world, things looked little different. It seemed that neither Peggy nor the Balls had told anyone other than their advisers, and their families, and one or two close friends about the change in ownership of the garden. The Balls did not feel it was proper to do so unless Peggy wanted to – and Peggy, contrary as ever in her old age, was enjoying the fact that people didn't know. "Let an old lady have her fun," she would tell Christopher and Pamela. When other people asked her what her plans for the garden were, she simply listened politely to their ideas, smiled enigmatically, and changed the subject.

In the meantime Christopher and Maria continued to look after the garden and the house and to take care of Peggy's needs, with Pamela's help. It was difficult – Pamela was working part time at a bank and managing Christopher's business, spending all her spare time in the garden; and both Christopher and Maria had other contracts as well. The payments on two houses and the lot they had purchased earlier stretched the Balls' finances considerably, and the demands on their time were also a strain. But although Peggy hadn't told the Balls about her will, she assured them repeatedly that everything would eventually be fine.

Convinced that her days were numbered, Peggy told several people that she couldn't possibly live much longer. At the same time, knowing that her future was now secure and that the garden would be in good hands was an immense relief. Her letters and her diary entries reveal a quite different, far more light-hearted attitude than she had displayed for some time. Immediately after the property was transferred to the Balls, Peggy wrote one of her last letters to Philippa. It contained no explanation of the transaction that had just occurred, but spoke of her pleasure in defeating the efforts of the "ruthless developer, who boasts that he will buy this last acre of land on Fairfield, [and] destroy the garden and trees." Peggy also had a schedule that was ambitious for a woman half her age, continued to entertain magazine photographers and journalists and show off "her" garden, and seemed in general to take a great deal of pleasure in life. "The first day of spring???" she wrote excitedly in her diary on a sunny day in late February 1989. "Mum and Come-Come [Shamus] happily weeding and galloping!" The mallard ducks in her ponds

Christopher and Pamela Ball in their garden,
mid-1990s. GLENDA PAYZANT/CHRISTOPHER
AND PAMELA BALL

Maria Camara, Peggy's former housekeeper, in
the Abkhazi Garden, summer 2002.
GRIMOALDA DE AMARAL/MARIA SERAFINA
CAMARA

were also a great source of entertainment to her, and she recorded their movements daily, ascribing affectionate names to them – the "Black Mafia," "Mr. and Mrs.," Pic-Pic and Pépé. She was still writing letters to gardening clubs and newspaper editors, and proudly sending off copies of her book to interested acquaintances. And Peggy still wanted her regular evening cocktail, now prepared by Maria – her favourite by then was a Negroni, but a glass of chilled white wine or a Campari would also do.

Peggy had recently befriended her next-door neighbour, Joan Fraser. Initially Peggy had clung to formality, inviting Joan to address her as "Princess Abkhazi," but the two shared common interests, and what Joan described as a "shipboard friendship" developed quite quickly. Over a glass of wine together one day, Peggy decided that she wanted to preserve herself better for posterity, and with Joan's help she sorted through her remaining papers and photographs from nearly ninety years of living. Over those years Peggy had given away many of her old photographs to Philippa Davys and to Elizabeth and Maureen Mackenzie. Many of her more intimate letters and mementoes, especially those from Nicolas, were, sadly, destroyed – she did not want those read by anyone else. Peggy had already decided that she wanted Christopher and Pamela to have the gardening photographs, books, and tools, and Maria to have all of her other precious books, but everything else – five boxes of photographs, letters, and documents, including Peggy's original diary from Lunghua – was carefully inventoried and sent to the University of Victoria Archives for safekeeping. Peggy was also happy that the name "Abkhazi" was to be preserved in another, very appropriate way. In June 1988 the rhododendron varieties "Prince Abkhazi" and "Princess Abkhazi" were officially registered with the Royal Horticultural Society by H. Vaartnou. In August 1989 her friend Bill Dale would go one step further and register the variety "Peggy Abkhazi." Peggy, even if she really thought she did not have long to live, was secure and relatively happy.

Not even her honorary grandchildren saw it coming when on June 20, 1989, pottering alone in her beloved garden, Peggy suffered a severe stroke. Temporarily incapacitated, she was immediately taken to Royal Jubilee Hospital. Several weeks of recuperation were needed before she was deemed fit enough to return home, but, indomitable to the core, Peggy rebelled against being in the hospital. She was terribly concerned about the well-being of her dog Shamus, and on at least one occasion she managed to get out of bed and work her way as far as the main hospital doors before being caught by the hospital staff. The heavy swinging doors had trapped her, and she was promptly returned to her bed. "If those damned doors hadn't caught me," she muttered that night to Christopher and Pamela, "I would have made it, too." But if her sense of humour was intact, her physical well-being was extremely frail.

Christopher and Pamela and Maria were having their own problems. Peggy had instructed them carefully about what she wanted them to do in the case of what she called an "interregnum" – any period of time that she might be hospitalized, or between leaving the garden and her eventual death. But their intentions in trying to look after the house and garden in Peggy's absence were being misunderstood by people who didn't know about the arrangements that Peggy had made. One person – perhaps believing, in error, that Christopher was taking unfair advantage of the situation – tried to fire him from the garden that he now owned. Diplomatically, Christopher revealed the truth. It was no longer possible for Peggy to keep her little secret – allowing her to have her fun had become too great a burden for the Balls.

In any event, it seemed that the interregnum was about to become permanent. Peggy could no longer go on living in her own beloved home, although she desperately wanted to, and despite the fact that the Balls and Maria between them had offered to do whatever was necessary to help care for her there. She came home in August, and initially seemed to be managing fine: she had a temporary resident caregiver, whom she liked, and Maria, Christopher, or Pamela were at the house almost every day to check on her. A few weeks later, however, when Peggy was medically assessed for her suitability for long-term home care, her regular doctor was away overseas, Peggy was nervous, and for some reason she failed to meet the minimum requirements for being able to stay in her own home. A decision was made that she must go into permanent residential care.

Peggy's close friends were greatly dismayed by the decision, which was out of their hands. The Balls and Maria, in particular, had wanted to see Peggy cared for in her own home for the rest of her life, and were convinced it should have been possible. But there was nothing that Peggy or her friends could do. Although she did not want to leave her home, in her frail condition Peggy was also very anxious again about her financial situation. Despite her income from the Balls and her remaining investments, money had continued to be a problem. The house, according to observers at the time, was suffering from a lack of much-needed and expensive maintenance, and its contents were becoming more and more threadbare. Peggy, once so clothes-conscious, hadn't bought herself anything new to wear in years. Although the cost of long-term residential care was much the same as that of staying in her own home, Peggy was fearful of the possibility that she would not find an alternative to the one immediately available to her — a room in the Douglas Care Manor, a permanent care facility in Victoria. A few precious personal possessions were packed, and the rest were given to Maria, except for Peggy's jewellery, which her prudent lawyer kept in safekeeping in case Peggy ever needed it to be sold. By November 1989 Peggy was in residence in the Douglas Care Manor, and the Balls had made the difficult decision to move into 1964 Fairfield Road.

It would probably have been far easier for Christopher and Pamela simply to sell the garden at that point, pay the money owing on it to Peggy's lawyer, and keep their own home. The mortgage payments increased dramatically after Peggy moved out into care, and the Balls certainly could no longer afford to keep making three sets of mortgage payments, let alone two. But they had already invested a great deal in the garden and were very attached to it. They knew that Peggy wanted them to have it and take care of it for her, at least as long as she remained alive, and they did not want to let her down. If they did not know that she intended to forgive the outstanding mortgage on the house and garden in her will, they may have considered the possibility that she might have done so. Despite the criticism that they had already encountered from some corners, they made the decision to sell their home and move to the garden. Pamela Ball borrowed money from her brother to pay off the first small lot they had bought from Peggy in 1986, and raised a line of credit on it to pay him back and help bridge the first few mortgage payments on the property until they sold their own house. The Balls tried not to think about the future, when they would eventually be required to pay for the whole thing in full. Least of all did they want to think about their beloved friend dying.

Peggy would have been appalled, however, if she had known that she

June 5, 1989. Two weeks before Peggy suffered a stroke, she celebrated a friend's birthday in the garden. She is seated between her friends Professor Toby Jackman and Professor Diana Priestley.
DR. JEAN MCCAW

would live for another five years. She was well cared for in the Douglas Care Manor, appreciated her good fortune in being comfortable and secure, and presented a tranquil and often humorous face to the world at large. But she could not read or write letters, and she hated her confined existence and being forced once again to live by someone else's rules. "This," she confided to one friend, "is far worse than internment ever was." As proud as ever, Peggy did not want to keep company with all the "other old ladies" or have to eat in a dining room or participate in the residence's group "activities," whatever they were. But she was not a self-made princess for nothing – and if the flesh was weak, the spirit was still robust and alert. She defied the rules, enjoyed her daily cocktail, and won the battle to have her meals in her own room by simply wearing down the resistance. "Every time they took me down to the dining room in my wheelchair," she told her friends Roger and Barbara Napier with a twinkle in her eyes, "I somehow seemed to faint!" When another elderly male resident wandered into her room one day without any trousers on, she simply surveyed him calmly and commented, "Well, I've seen worse." Visitors never found Peggy without her hair beautifully done, and they always found her properly dressed, as a social occasion had always demanded. She listened to her beloved music on the compact disc player that Logan Mayhew had given to her and, sitting in the sunshine in her wheelchair, would reach into the Manor's window boxes to pick stray weeds out from among the flowers. Determined as ever to control what people would think of her, she even dictated her own obituary, giving it to the Rev. Cedric Jones to read at her funeral when the time came: Peggy Abkhazi was not about to allow someone else to make up an obituary for her of which she might not approve. On her ninetieth birthday, December 12, 1992, she celebrated in style with her friends, some champagne, and her beloved dog, Shamus, who was being cared for by the Balls.

Peggy had not been let down by her three "honorary grandchildren." Maria was busy in a new job in a delicatessen, but she faithfully visited every Thursday and Sunday for lunch with her former employer and benefactor. The Balls visited even more often, bringing Shamus to see her and arriving with flowers from the garden and photographs. When they couldn't visit they would call, carefully following the treasured ritual of putting Shamus on the end of the line to bark his greeting to Peggy. And as often as they could, they fetched

Peggy Abkhazi in her garden at 1964 Fairfield Road, wearing her favourite gardening attire, 1980s. UNIVERSITY OF VICTORIA ARCHIVES

Peggy to the garden so that she could see it continuing to flourish. It was a bond of affection and dedication on the part of Christopher and Pamela and Maria that far surpassed any sense of obligation — and certainly surpassed what real children or grandchildren often do for their parents. Peggy had once written that she had no concept of what a blood relationship meant; but for more than fifteen years she had enjoyed the love and compassion of three people who almost always put her interests before their own. Even through the romantic haze that more than a decade of time's passing had put over Christopher's and Maria's memories, it is clear that working for the Abkhazis and being the "honorary grandchildren" had been far from easy for them and for Pamela. Peggy was always charming and gracious to strangers, but she could be very hard on those who were closest to her. Such was the magic of the Prince and Princess Abkhazi, and the strength of Peggy's personality, however, that they stood by her to the end. Peggy Abkhazi was a remarkably lucky woman. She was loved and cared for by several people, right up until her death, and at the end of a long and very good life.

Princess Marjorie Mabel Jane Abkhazi died on November 14, 1994, at the age of ninety-one. Her farewell gift to her beloved Maria was the remainder of her estate, some jewellery and a small sum of money. To Christopher and Pamela, she had indeed left the balance of the amount owing on the house and garden, releasing them from the obligation to make any more payments. There were no other beneficiaries. And it was those three friends who gathered alone in the garden, the following spring, to scatter the Abkhazis' ashes together and toast their reunion once more.

"I want you," Peggy had written to Philippa years before, "to have the rich, happy, and fulfilled (not necessarily easy) life that I have had." By the time of her death, Peggy was greatly admired and respected by hundreds, if not thousands, of people who had the chance to get to know her or to visit her garden. "Gardeners," she wrote once in an attempt to describe herself, "are an absurd mix of perpetual hope and perpetual pessimism." Over the years she had gained an extraordinary insight into life and understood well the cruelty and contrariness of human beings and the hard realities of the world, but she also loved her own little corner of it and maintained a sense of perpetual hope almost always. And she had been singularly successful in the creation of her image as a princess, one of her most compelling legacies. There will always be a genuine and special magic reserved for the woman who had become Princess Nicolas Abkhazi. The Rev. Cedric Jones, who officiated at her funeral, recalled a child asking him once if he had really known a princess. Eyes shining, he had replied, "Yes, I did indeed. I really *did* know a princess."

In those last few weeks or months, perhaps even years, when Peggy was a captive within the confines of her body and her room in the Douglas Care Manor and when her mind and spirit were yearning for release, it would be nice to think that that indomitable and unvanquished mind was ranging as freely and as far and wide, even then, as it once had in those far-off summer days, years before; when she would sit on a stool in her garden for hours on end, working on her rhododendrons and azaleas and recalling her elegant youth, her adventures, and friends gone long before. She had waited a long time to rejoin Nicolas, much longer than she had wanted – but a garden, as Peggy once said in 1986 to journalist John Colapinto of *Saturday Night* magazine, is a constant reminder that there are no shortcuts to the important things in life.

"The garden," she had told him then, "is about every passage of life. Youth, adolescence, old age. Even death."

A Letter to Philippa

Victoria, June 17, 1969

Dearest Philippa,

Our letters always seem to cross nowadays — is it a sort of ESP, or just co-incidental with the vagaries of the Canadian Post Office — where chaos has reigned ever since the last postal strike? Whatever the reason, I am always so happy to hear from you.

Whilst you are in deep in Nabokov, I'm sending you a second edition of his autobiography which was given to us some time ago, "Speak Memory" — published in the USA. I prefer the shorter first edition (less padding) published by Gollancz in London in the fifties. I think it gives clues to many of his present day manifestations, as well as being a wonderful picture of the life of the "intellectual" Russian aristocracy (as opposed to the dissolute ones) who were in their heyday in the 1890's. Vladimir was born in 1899 — and granting the essential basic differences between the Russian with his Slavic soul, and the gay, extrovert, wine and song-loving (fanatical only on the subjects of the honour of the family name, clannishness and quite demented courage) of the Georgian — I find much in common between his "zeitgeist" (apologies for the German, but I can't think of an English word that will do as well) and that of Nico's. I still regret that the combination of awful weather, galloping around at parties etc. prevented you, in those few days, from penetrating beneath Nico's protective armour of half-teasing reticence, to the unique and enchanting human being underneath. I speak after knowing him for 49 years! He has just celebrated his 70th birthday.

We are in the midst of the hottest summer ever — at the moment 88 degrees in the shade — May and June have been wonderful — and our garden a green and shady oasis. It only needs the city to forbid garden watering if this goes on. Eric [Stuart-Taylor, a friend] left on the 6th, and writes that England (the countryside) looks too beautiful, and full of the strawberries and cream of our (his and my!) youth.

Much as I disliked "Brand" as a character — Ibsen's ultra-Lutheran, and to me, unchristian, in its literal and non-liturgical sense, attitude to the ethics of living — possibly as a creative writer it was Ibsen's intention to leave the critics divided in their guesses as to what Ibsen really meant by the ultimate cry of "God is love" when the avalanche overwhelmed Brand. To me, Brand in failing to "love his neighbour, and do unto others etc": was a poor miserable wretch, enveloped in spiritual pride and stubbornness, and I imagine that 'God is love' must have been the extreme moment of irony and disillusionment — or perhaps, one instant of enlightenment and self-recognition? — in the whole of his misguided, unloving, obstinately courageous life.

I cannot ascribe to God the human characteristics of mercy and recognition of worthiness, unless I also ascribe to Him the characteristics of cruelty and injustice. So here I am back to my Chinese duality of principle, Yang and Yin, male and female, good and evil, light and darkness, summer and winter, life and death, etc — always the opposites swinging to and fro — and somehow some kind of balance is achieved. (What a muddled paragraph — 2 phone calls, Morag had to be let out and in, and Nico wanted to know if his clean socks were a matching pair!)

Chekhov's short stories I love — all of them. I have never seen any of his plays, and I find a certain unreality in reading <u>any</u> play at all. But even with this private objection, I do think that he conveys marvellously the rather decadent charm, as well as the complete ineffectiveness and unfulfilledness of the characters he depicts. ". . .if only I could get away from this provincial town of Moscow." If only — if only. But from what I have heard, and read, this was all very typical of the 'intelligentsia' living on pensions or in reduced circumstances, in the provinces at that time. Clinging to the old conventions of their parents, and at the same time, to feeling slightly emancipated — especially the women. Probably knowing, even unconsciously, that the Tsarist regime was tottering to its end — full of dreams of an impossibly brave new world, without a suspicion of the oceans of blood that would be spilled to acquire what we have now. I will not attempt to decide whether the world today is brave — or new — it is just different! Back to Heraclites, "Everything is in a state of flux."

I am now reading a book quite beautiful and fascinating to me — "Meeting with Japan", by Fosco Maraini. He is Italian, and was for many years a teacher in Japan, spoke the language and brought up his family there. He is a wonderful photographer — quite comparable with the famous Edward Steichen. He writes delightfully, and the form of his narrative pleases me — he tells of his modern-day return to the "Americanised democracy" which is Japan, of his travels, of the ancient history of the country, of their arts of calligraphy, pottery, painting, and the mystique behind their ethics and their etiquette — and by a cleverly introduced flashback, he introduces you to his two years (with 14 other Italians, including his wife and two children) as a civil internee. Excepting that they were shorter of food than we were and that 15 people cooped up together would be more nerve-wracking than the 2,000 that we were — it is the most vivid and accurate account of civilian internment that I have yet read. Not physical torture or rape — but unending mindless bureaucracy, hunger, thirst, dirt, smells, extreme cold and heat — that's what internment largely consists of — with the cheering promise that the moment the American or British troops arrived, every single internee in every camp would be shot by the Japanese. I still marvel at our escape, and yet I am appalled that Hiroshima had to occur for us to be granted a new lease of life.

And after it all, with the many hardships and my heavy financial losses, I still admire and respect the Japanese — whereas you already know my unreasonable dislike and distrust of Germany and the Germans. I believe that it is their alternation between bullying arrogance and whining self-pity that so revolts me. Anyway it is nice to be quite unreasonable at times — even at my age!

... "Dracula" films are outside my field of acquaintance. But in the 1920s I saw a real Dracula play acted in London — quite gloriously blood-curdling and terrifying — I fear that now I should get the giggles, as I do now when reading Poe — "The Fall of the House of Usher" — & even listening to the delightful vocal fireworks of Donizetti's "Lucia di Lammermoor" I undergo the same spasm of hilarity alternating with boredom that all Scott's novels now induce — and how I _adored_ them when I was a child!

I am intrigued by your street's name [Aro]. Is it a Maori name? Here we have Haro Strait amongst our Gulf Islands, and Haro Road quite near where Sheila and Andy [Anderson] live. You will probably guess, by now, that this letter has been many times interrupted. It is now June 19th, time 12.20 am — writing in bed, as usual — but only on account of the lateness of the hour. So busy with the garden at this season, that daytime letter writing is out of the question. By my bed I have an old Chinese pewter jug filled with the loveliest pink roses (though I says it as shouldn't!) from the garden. Their delicate perfume is quite hypnotic and I am very happy!

Oh, Philippa, it would be wonderful to see you again. Meanwhile, much love, as always,

Affectionately.

Peggy Abkhazi

Postscript

"I do wish that I could be alive 100 years from now, and see whether mankind, in its arrogance and stupidity and greed has perished in its own poisonous filth — or whether the best of humanity through humility and ingenuity will have learned enough to reverse the process?"

— Peggy Abkhazi, letter to Philippa, December 5, 1970

Eight years after Peggy's death, rhododendrons cultivated by the Abkhazis continue to flourish all over Victoria, in municipal parks — notably, Beacon Hill and Stadacona — and on the grounds of the University of Victoria. Every year the Abkhazi Trophy is presented by the Victoria Rhododendron Society to a member who has made an outstanding contribution. The trophy, a silver tray, was donated by Peggy to the society in 1986. It had originally been given as a wedding present to her parents, William and Mabel Carter.

Gold medallions continue to be given to dogs that reach their Utility Degree with the Greater Victoria Dog Obedience Training Club — outstanding candidates have the chance to win the Haven Bonnie Jean Challenge Trophy, which Peggy donated to the club in 1952 in memory of her sheltie, Jean.

A prize said to have been donated by the Abkhazis to the University of Victoria, to recognize achievements in Russian studies, appears no longer to exist.

The Union Club, however, thrives.

After they moved into 1964 Fairfield Road, Christopher and Pamela Ball continued to open the garden annually to visitors, both local and international, and made it available for fund-raising events for local causes. But despite public interest in the garden, the Balls were unsuccessful in obtaining any financial assistance to help with its high maintenance costs, and it became increasingly difficult to manage. When they had bought the garden from Peggy in 1988, they had assumed she would live there until she died. They had not anticipated that she would be put into residential care only a year later and found themselves caught on the back foot, financially unprepared for the increased mortgage payments on top of their existing obligations. As a consequence, by 1996 they were forced to take out another large mortgage on the property to help pay for its maintenance. The combined financial stress and amount of personal time required to care for the garden became too much, and by 1999 the Balls felt that keeping the property was no longer feasible. Mindful that Peggy had told them they should feel no obligation to hold onto the garden for the long term, they decided to cut their losses and sell.

Despite extensive marketing by the Balls' realtor, there were no takers for several months other than a couple of interested developers, who were turned away: the Balls hoped that whoever did buy the property would maintain the garden. However, the eventual purchaser, a chartered accountant, was subsequently successful in an application to the City of Victoria to have the property rezoned for the construction of townhouses. Faced with this scenario, The Land Conservancy of British Columbia (TLC), a non-profit organization, became involved. TLC raised sufficient funds through an interest-free loan to buy the garden, and the new owner agreed to sell.

The Abkhazi Garden and house, now owned by TLC, are being maintained for the benefit and enjoyment of the public, while TLC continues to raise funds to repay the mortgage and to establish an endowment fund for the maintenance of the property.

The Balls, extremely stressed by the events that occurred following the sale of their property but relieved that it was not to be developed, purchased a new home not far from Victoria, where they live with their mementoes — including Nicolas's treasured Atco lawnmower — and their fond memories of their friends Prince and Princess Abkhazi. There they are creating a new garden, influenced in part by the Abkhazi Garden.

Maria Serafina Camara continues to work at her sister's delicatessen six days a week, and to treasure her memorabilia of a couple that were far more to her than just employers. Philippa Proudfoot, née Davys, lives in Rochester, New York, with her two daughters. After Peggy's stroke, Philippa received a letter from an acquaintance of Peggy's telling her that her godmother was no longer capable of corresponding with her. After that, Philippa heard nothing further about Peggy until a friend from New Zealand sent her a newspaper clipping about the writing of this book. To Philippa's pleasure, she discovered that she had kept most of her mementoes of her godmother, despite thinking from time to time over the last few years that there was no longer any reason to hold on to them. Reminded of the affectionate and stimulating relationship she once had with Peggy, she plans to keep them now.

The Web site of The Land Conservancy of British Columbia, www.conservancy.bc.ca, provides more detailed information about the Abkhazi Garden as it exists today.

Bibliography

Listed here are writings that have been useful in researching this book. The list is by no means a complete record of all works and sources consulted. In these days of Internet technology, various Web sites provide interesting and useful resources to use as a starting point. These include the Web sites of the City of Victoria and the Capital Regional District of Victoria, which contain much useful material, and various Web pages with current perspectives on places ranging from Abkhazia to Paris to Shanghai. As a resource, the Internet cannot be overestimated. It is, however, still no replacement for good old-fashioned research through the dusty pages of real books and the well-worn documents held in libraries and archives. In this respect I am grateful to the City of Victoria Archives, the British Columbia Provincial Archives, and the University of Victoria Archives, which hold many of the remaining original documents pertaining to Peggy and Nicolas Abkhazi. I also spent many hours at the Central Library of the Greater Victoria Public Library, scrolling through microfilm copies of old Victoria newspapers. For Victoria history buffs, I highly recommend it as a very entertaining way to pass a rainy afternoon.

Abkhazi, Peggy. *A Curious Cage.* 2nd ed. Edited by S.W. Jackman. Victoria: Sono Nis Press, 2002.

—————. *A Dragon Aunt Remembers.* Personal memoir, unpublished, 1980. University of Victoria Archives.

Bagley, J.J. *Lancashire.* London: B.T. Batsford, 1972.

Barefoot, Kevin, et al. *Victoria: Secrets of the City.* Vancouver: Arsenal Pulp Press, 2000.

Baskerville, Peter. *Beyond the Island: An Illustrated History of Victoria.* Burlington, ON: Windsor, 1986.

Benet, Sula. *Abkhazians: The Long-living People of the Caucasus.* New York: Holt, Rinehart & Winston, 1974.

Bissley, Paul. *The Union Club of British Columbia: 100 years 1879–1979*. Vancouver: Evergreen Press, 1980.

Blanch, Lesley. *The Sabres of Paradise*. New York: Viking, 1960.

Carney, D.S. *Foreign Devils Had Light Eyes: A Memoir of Shanghai 1933–1939*. Toronto: Virgo Press, 1980.

Church, Richard. *Kent*. London: Robert Hale, 1948.

Dong, Stella. *Shanghai: The Rise and Fall of a Decadent City*. New York: HarperCollins, 2000.

Eaton, Nicole, and Hilary Weston. *In a Canadian Garden*. Photography by Freeman Patterson. New York: Viking Studio Books, 1989.

Fairbrother, Nan. *Men & Gardens*. New York: Knopf, 1956.

Gregson, Harry. *A History of Victoria 1842–1970*. Vancouver: J.J. Douglas, 1977.

Guppy, Walter. *Clayoquot Soundings*. Tofino: Grassroots, 1997.

Hansen, Arlen J. *Expatriate Paris: A Cultural and Literary Guide to Paris of the 1920s*. New York: Arcade, 1990.

Hemingway, Ernest. *A Moveable Feast*. New York: Scribner, 1964.

Howe, Bea. *Lady with Green Fingers: The Life of Jane Louden*. London: Country Life, 1961.

Johnston, Hugh J.M. *The Pacific Province*. Vancouver: Douglas & McIntyre, 1996.

MacLean, Fitzroy. *To Caucasus: The End of All the Earth*. London: Little, Brown, 1976.

Modelski, Sylvia. *Port Said Revisited*. Washington, DC: Faros 2000, 2000.

Molyneux, Geoffrey. *British Columbia: An Illustrated History*. Vancouver: Polestar Press, 1992.

Moore, Charles. *Vienna, City of Melodies*. Melksham: Colin Venton, 1977.

Nazaroff, Alexander. *The Land and People of Russia*. New York: J.B. Lippincott, 1966.

Peh-T'i Wei. *Old Shanghai*. London: Oxford University Press, 1993.

Roueche, Ken. Assorted articles, 2000–2002. *Fairfield Observer*.

Seymour, John. *The Companion Guide to the Coast of South-East England*. London: Collins, 1975.

Wiser, William. *The Crazy Years: Paris in the Twenties*. London: Thames and Hudson, 1983.

Woodcock, Ingeborg, and George Woodcock. *Victoria*. Victoria: Morriss Printing, 1971.

About the Author

QUINTON GORDON

KATHERINE GORDON, born in England in 1963, began travelling the world at the age of three months with her English civil-engineer father, her French mother, and the rest of her family, eventually settling for a time in New Zealand. There she worked in commercial law for several years before globe-trotting again, in South America, Costa Rica, and Canada. Since 1989, she has called Canada home. The lure of the ocean drew her to Victoria, B.C., where she lives with her husband, photographer Quinton Gordon. As well as working in aboriginal treaty negotiations, she has pursued an active writing career contributing to such international publications as *Beautiful British Columbia* magazine, *North & South*, and *Action Asia*, among others. *A Curious Life* is her first book.